TENTS

Significant Changes
   Organizational S...1
   Board of Directors..1
   Officers...2
   Rules Committee...2
   Charter Committee...2
General Information
   Purpose of Little League Baseball and Softball................................5
   Federal Charter..5
   Structure...5
   Administration..6
   Charter Committee/Waivers of Rules and Regulations..................6
   Player Eligibility..6
   Amateur Status..6
   Divisions of Play..7
   Role of the Parent...8
   Volunteer Eligibility..8
   Leadership Programs..8
   Initiatives..10
   Frequently-Asked Questions...10
Residency and School Attendance Eligibility Requirements...............13
Proof-of-Age Requirements...16
   Acceptable Forms of Proof of Birth Date......................................16
   How to Obtain Acceptable Documents Proving Date of Birth...16
   How to Obtain a "Statement in Lieu of Acceptable Proof of Birth"........17
Official Regulations
   Regulation I   The League...19
   Regulation II   League Boundaries...............................28
   Regulation III   The Teams..30
   Regulation IV   The Players...33
   Regulation V   Selection of Players..............................38
   Regulation VI   Pitchers...39
   Regulation VII   Schedules..41
   Regulation VIII   Minor Leagues.....................................43
   Regulation IX   Special Games......................................44
   Regulation X   Night Games..45
   Regulation XI   Admission to Games............................46
   Regulation XII   Awards..47
   Regulation XIII   Commercialization...............................48
   Regulation XIV   Field Decorum.....................................49
   Regulation XV   Appearance of Little Leaguers in the Media.....................50
   Regulation XVI   Use of Little League Name and Emblem.........................51
   Regulation XVII   Tournament Play..................................52

i

CONTENTS

Official Playing Rules
- Rule 1.00 Objectives of the Game 53
- Rule 2.00 Definition of Terms 61
- Rule 3.00 Game Preliminaries 69
- Rule 4.00 Starting and Ending the Game 74
- Rule 5.00 Putting the Ball in Play - Live Ball 82
- Rule 6.00 The Batter 85
- Rule 7.00 The Runner 92
- Rule 8.00 The Pitcher 101
- Rule 9.00 The Umpire 105

Tournament Rules and Guidelines 109
- Tournament Organization 111
- Conditions of Tournament Play 118
- Tournament Playing Rules 121
- Guidelines for Conduct of Tournament 127
- Regional Directors 131
- International Tournament Pool Play Format 132
  - Section I – Guidelines 132
  - Section II – Segments of a Pool Play Tournament 133
  - Section III – Tiebreaker Procedures 134
  - Section IV – Runs-Allowed Ratio 135

- Appendix A Lightning Safety Guidelines 137
- Appendix B Safety Code for Little League 139
- Appendix C Communicable Disease Procedures 140
- Appendix D Bat Modifications and Alterations 141
- Appendix E Heat Illness Prevention Protection Policy 142
- Appendix F Privacy Policy 143
- Appendix G 2016 Little League Age Chart 147

Operating Policies 148
- Local League Administration 149
- Role of League President 149
- League Officers 151
- Process to Obtain Waivers of Rules and Regulations 153
- Local League Draft Methods 154
- Options on Sons, Daughters and Siblings 157
- Local League Maintenance of Rosters 159
- Dividing a League 162
- Local League Election Procedures 163
- The Official Shoulder Patch 165
- Little League Policies and Principles 165
- Sexual Harassment Policy 166

CONTENTS

    Conflict of Interest Policy 168
    Little League Child Protection Program... 168
    Child Abuse - A Five-Step Review 174
    Questions and Answers About The Child Protection Program 174
    Standards for Lighting 178
    Communications and League Promotions 179
    Websites 181
    Little League Trademarks 182
    Crowdfunding... 185
Index..187

Your League Receives 125
Free Background Checks Per Year

Each year, Little League® International provides 125 free background checks. Information on how to utilize this benefit, as well as how to conduct background checks, can be found on the Little League website at:

LittleLeague.org/childprotectionprogram

SIGNIFICANT CHANGES FOR 2016

Significant Changes for 2016

(**NOTE:** Unless noted otherwise, these apply to all softball divisions)

Significant changes will be identified by a shaded background.

GENERAL INFORMATION
Amateur Status - Defines amateur status. Page 6.

REGULATIONS
Regulation I(c) 8 and 9 – Modifies regulations to highlight new state laws regarding mandatory state background checks. Additionally, includes restrictions regarding any person who admits to any crime against a minor. Pages 21-22.

Regulation II(f) - Clarifies that a District Administrator may only recommend adjusting boundaries. Page 29.

PLAYING RULES
Rule 4.15(f) and Tournament Chain of Command - Clarifies that an umpire and the Tournament Committee may impose penalties to a coach, manager, or team for making a travesty of a game. Page 79 and 110.

8.01 – Provides additional clarification that a pitcher must come to the pitcher's plate with the hands separated. Page 101.

TOURNAMENT RULES AND GUIDELINES
Replacement of Player, Manager or Coach – Requires a temporary Tournament coach or manager to be entered on the Eligibility Affidavit. Page 116.

Tournament Rule 10(f) - Provide guidance on how to handle an ineligible pitcher in Junior, Senior, and Big League Softball. Page 125.

OPERATING POLICIES
Operating Policies - The Little League Operating Manual content has been condensed and included in the back of this publication and now referenced as the Little League Operating Policies. Page 148.

> A.R.—An Approved Ruling (A.R.) serves to illustrate the application of the regulations and rules. Approved Rulings follow the regulations and rules they amplify and are indicated by a box.

ORGANIZATIONAL STRUCTURE

Organizational Structure

LITTLE LEAGUE® BASEBALL Incorporated
P.O. Box 3485, Williamsport, PA 17701
(570) 326-1921

Board of Directors

Dr. Davie Jane Gilmour, *Chairman*

Hugh E. Tanner, *Chairman-Elect*	Stephen D. Keener
Dr. James Andrews	Dennis Lewin
Dr. Darrell Burnett	Jon D. Litner
Janice Christensen	Jonathan Mariner
Corinne G.L. Chow	Michael Mussina
Dr. Noel E. Corrales	Kristian Palvia
Chris Drury	Joe Patterson
John Edgerle	W. Dwight Raiford
Jolly Gomez	Tony Richardson
Tim Hughes	Bob Toigo
Sally John	Dwayne Tuggle
Steven Johnson	Bud Vanderberg

ORGANIZATIONAL STRUCTURE

Officers

Dr. Davie Jane Gilmour
Chairman

Elizabeth DiLullo Brown
Vice President of Marketing and Communications

Hugh Tanner
Chairman-Elect

Dan Kirby
Vice President of Risk Management

Stephen D. Keener
President and Chief Executive Officer

Melissa L. Singer
Vice President and Treasurer

David Houseknecht
Senior Vice President of Administration and Chief Financial Officer

Lance Van Auken
Vice President and Executive Director of the Little League Museum

Patrick W. Wilson
Senior Vice President of Operations and Program Development

Joseph W. Losch
Corporate Secretary

Rules Committee

Patrick W. Wilson, *Chairman*

Nicholas Caringi	Tony Richardson
Janice Christensen	Sara Thompson
Corinne G.L. Chow	Dwayne Tuggle
John Edgerle	Lance Van Auken
Stephen D. Keener	Bud Vanderberg
Michael Mussina	Daniel Velte

Charter Committee

Patrick W. Wilson, *Chairman and Secretary*

Nicholas L. Caringi	Sam Ranck
Demiko Ervin	Brent Stahlnecker
Jamie Joy	Sara Thompson
Stephen D. Keener	Daniel Velte
Daniel P. Kirby	

ORGANIZATIONAL STRUCTURE
LITTLE LEAGUE® REGIONS

Little League Regional Offices are fully staffed year-round to provide assistance and direction to Little League volunteers. All general questions, written suggestions for improving this Rulebook, tournament inquiries, rule interpretation requests, and supply orders should be directed to the appropriate office in your region as indicated.

WESTERN REGIONAL OFFICE
6707 Little League Drive
San Bernardino, CA 92407
Phone: (909) 887-6444 | Fax: (909) 887-6135
E-mail: Westregion@LittleLeague.org

SOUTHEASTERN REGIONAL OFFICE
PO Box 7557 | Warner Robins, GA 31095
Phone: (478) 987-7227 | Fax: (478) 987-7232
E-mail: Southeastregion@LittleLeague.org

CENTRAL REGIONAL OFFICE
9802 E. Little League Drive | Indianapolis, IN 46235
Phone: (317) 897-6127 | Fax: (317) 897-6158
E-mail: Centralregion@LittleLeague.org

SOUTHWESTERN REGIONAL OFFICE
3700 S. University Parks Drive | Waco, TX 76706
Phone: (254) 756-1816 | Fax: (254) 757-0519
E-mail: Southwestregion@LittleLeague.org

EASTERN REGIONAL OFFICE
PO Box 2926 | Bristol, CT 06011-2926
Phone: (860) 585-4730 | Fax: (860) 585-4734
E-mail: Eastregion@LittleLeague.org

VISIT LITTLE LEAGUE ONLINE AT: LITTLELEAGUE.ORG

ORGANIZATIONAL STRUCTURE
UNITED STATES AND INTERNATIONAL

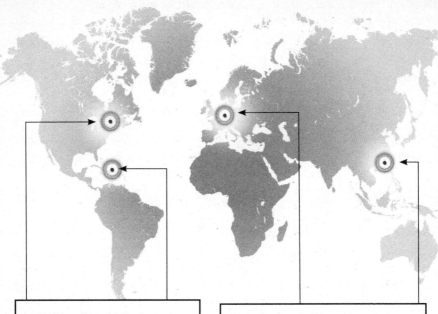

CANADIAN REGIONAL OFFICE

235 Dale Ave | Ottawa, Ontario
Canada K1G 0H6
Phone: (613) 731-3301   Fax: (613) 731-2829
E-mail: Canada@LittleLeague.org

ASIA-PACIFIC REGIONAL OFFICE

c/o Hong Kong Little League | Room 1005
Sports House | 1 Stadium Path
Causeway Bay, Hong Kong
Phone: 011-852-2504-4007 | Fax: 011-852-2504-8629
E-mail: llbapr@hkbaseball.com.hk

LATIN AMERICAN AND CARIBBEAN REGIONAL OFFICE

PO Box 10237 | Caparra Heights
Puerto Rico 00922-0237
Phone: (787) 982-3076
Fax: (787) 728-8164
E-mail: LatinAmerica@LittleLeague.org

EUROPEAN AND AFRICAN REGIONAL OFFICE

Little League Europe | Al. Malej Ligi 1
Kunto, 99-300, Poland
Phone: 011-48-24-254-4569
Fax: 011-48-24-254-4571
E-mail: Europe@LittleLeague.org

GENERAL INFORMATION

General Information
Purpose of Little League Baseball and Softball

Better than any other youth sport activity, baseball and softball have become the thread that has sewn together a patchwork of nations and cultures around the world. Children in diverse nations such as Israel, Jordan, Ukraine, Germany, Japan, Canada, Hong Kong, Poland, Mexico, China, Venezuela, South Africa and the U.S. have discovered baseball and softball — Little League Baseball and Softball - are ways to bring their people a sport that mirrors life itself.

Baseball and softball embody the discipline of teamwork. They challenge players towards perfection of physical skills and bring into play the excitement of tactics and strategy. The very nature of baseball and softball also teach that while every player eventually strikes out, or is on the losing team, there is always another chance for success in the next at-bat or game.

Millions of children on six continents and more than 80 countries can attest that baseball, softball and Little League are synonymous. Little League is a heritage to be carried forward proudly in the future by ever increasing waves of those devoted to teaching children how to play and enjoy these great games.

Little League is a program of service to youth. It is geared to provide an outlet of healthful activity and training under good leadership in the atmosphere of wholesome community participation. The movement is dedicated to helping children become good and decent citizens. It inspires them with a goal and enriches their lives towards the day when they must take their places in the world. It establishes the values of teamwork, sportsmanship and fair play.

Federal Charter

Little League operates under auspices of the highest recognition that may be accorded to any such organization by the government of the United States. By virtue of legislation approved unanimously by both the House of Representatives and the Senate and signed into law by President Lyndon B. Johnson on July 16, 1964, Little League has been granted a Congressional Charter of Federal Incorporation. No other sports organization has been so honored by the Federal government.

Structure

Basically, Little League has three structural components, each dependent upon the other and each vital to the success of the program.

The administrative and service core of the movement is Little League International, a non-profit membership organization that maintains the international program, with international headquarters in Williamsport, Pennsylvania. Part of the headquarters structure includes various Regional Headquarters in the U.S. and throughout the world.

The next component is the district. All the leagues within a district (a geographical area usually encompassing 10-20 leagues) elect a District Administrator (DA). The DA and his/her staff of Assistant District Administrators serve as liaisons between the various Regional Headquarters and the local Little Leagues. They are usually the most experienced Little League volunteers in the area, and are charged with helping to ensure that all the volunteers in their districts are well trained, and all the leagues are operating within the guidelines set

GENERAL INFORMATION

by Little League. The District Administrator does not have the authority to suspend, limit or revoke any rules, regulations or privileges of charter by a local Little League, but may recommend such action to the Charter Committee in Williamsport.

The final, most important component is the local Little League. The league provides its services in the community. It furnishes physical facilities, volunteer services and resources to provide a program for children. Through effective leadership and strong administrative policy at the top level, together with training extensions and adherence to rule and policy at District and local league level, Little League is able to provide liberal benefits to children who participate.

Administration

Little League affairs are administered by the Little League International Board of Directors. Policies, operating procedures and controls of the program are carried out by Little League International staff, under the direction of the President and the Executive Committee.

The local league operates under a charter granted annually by Little League. The league is autonomous in the sense of having freedom to elect its own officers, finance its program and carry on various other related functions, but it must adhere scrupulously to all rules and regulations established by Little League.

The charter privilege extends use of the name "Little League" and its official insignia to the local Little League. It can be suspended or revoked for violation of rules or regulations by action of the Charter Committee.

Charter Committee/Waivers of Rules and Regulations

The Charter Committee is a group of personnel at Little League International in Williamsport, Pennsylvania, in whom is placed (by the Little League International Board of Directors) the responsibility of reviewing, granting, suspending or revoking the privileges and conditions of the local league's charter. When a local league wishes to request a waiver of a specific rule or regulation, it must submit the request in writing to the District Administrator, who will forward it with his/her recommendation to the Regional Director. The Regional Director will present the request to the Charter Committee for a decision. No other person or group has the authority to approve waivers of ANY rules or regulations.

Player Eligibility

The player must qualify under Little League's definition of residence or school attendance as described within this rulebook, must be of the correct "league age" for the division, and must have parental consent. Little League offers baseball and softball programs for players league age 4 through 18. Local Little Leagues are encouraged to provide all programs, thus giving all the children in the area a chance to play Little League Baseball or Softball. League age is defined in Regulation IV(a).

Amateur Status

To be eligible in the Little League Baseball or Softball program, a participant must be an amateur in baseball or softball respectively. This requirement serves to increase interest and competitive balance in Little League Baseball and Softball. An amateur participant is one who engages in the Little League Baseball or Softball program solely for the educational, physical, mental, social, and recreational benefits derived thereof. The amateur status

GENERAL INFORMATION

requirement enhances Little League's goals and values of character development, wholesome community participation, teamwork, sportsmanship and fair play and, also, protects Little League athletes from being disqualified from high school and collegiate athletics.

NOTE: Loss of Amateur Status: A participant loses amateur status and therefore, the right to participate in the Little League program whenever:

- The participant, or the participant's parent(s) or guardian(s), receives compensation, in trust or otherwise, for or related to the participant's athletic ability, participation, or performance in baseball or softball.
- The participant plays on a professional team in baseball or softball
- The participant signs a contract whereby the participant agrees to compete in any baseball or softball competition for compensation. It is not a violation to attend or participate in a professional try-out camp, provided that (1) no compensation or expenses are paid; (2) the try-out lasts no longer than forty-eight hours; and (3) if in the sport of baseball, the participation is otherwise in conformity with the National Federation Major-Minor League Agreement.

Divisions of Play

Most people know Little League through the Major Division for 9- to 12-year-olds. But today Little League provides organized youth sports programs for a wide range of ages. Charter fees are extremely reasonable, with Rulebooks and organizational materials provided free.

Tee Ball Baseball and Tee Ball Softball programs are for players 4-6 years old (with an option for 7-year-olds) who want to learn the fundamentals of hitting and fielding. In Tee Ball, players hit a ball off a batting tee. Rules of the game may be varied to accommodate the need for teaching. The primary goals of Tee Ball are to have fun, to instruct children in the fundamentals of baseball and softball and to allow them to experience the value of teamwork.

Minor League Baseball and Minor League Softball programs may be operated within each division for younger players with less experience. The Minor League may be players ages 7-12. Divisions may be established within the Minor League for "machine pitch," "coach pitch" or "player pitch." The goal of the Minor League is to prepare children for eventual selection to a Major Division team.

Little League Baseball and Little League Softball (also known as the Major Division) are for players 9 to 12 years old. A league may choose to limit its Major Division to 10, 11 and 12-year-olds, or 11- and 12-year-olds. The 9- and 10- and 10- and 11-Year-Old Baseball and Softball Divisions were established as tournament programs to give children the opportunity to experience Tournament Play, up to State level. Leagues may also enter Tournament Play for 11- and 12-year-olds in the Little League Baseball and Little League Softball Divisions, each ending in World Series tournaments.

Little League Intermediate (50-70) Baseball Division is for players 11 to 13 years old. The program is a transitional program for 11- to 13-year-olds using 50-foot pitching distance and 70-foot base paths and offers a full range of tournament play, including a World Series.

Junior League Baseball and Junior League Softball are established as transitional programs for 12- to 14-year-olds. The programs link the Little League and Senior League divisions and offer a full range of tournament play, including World Series tournaments.

GENERAL INFORMATION

Senior League Baseball and Senior League Softball are for players 13 to 16 years old. Both divisions offer a full range of Tournament Play, including a World Series.

Big League Baseball and Big League Softball are programs for players 15 to 18 years old (Big League Softball 14-18) who seek top-level amateur play, each with a full range of Tournament Play including a World Series.

Little League Challenger Division is for players ages 4-18 with physical and/or intellectual disabilities. It incorporates other children in the league as "buddies" for the Challenger players.

Senior League Challenger Division is for players 15 years old and above with physical and/or intellectual disabilities. It incorporates other participants or volunteers in the league as "buddies" for the Challenger players.

Role of the Parent

The parents of millions of Little Leaguers combined with their children, league officials, umpires, managers, coaches and countless volunteer agencies including sponsors, represent an imposing cross section of our world. Parents must take the initiative to make the local program successful. Little League is not a club in which membership implies baby-sitting benefits and entertainment privileges.

Practically speaking, Little League is an adult, volunteer work project constructed, supervised and assisted by parents who want to extend this benefit to their children. The parent who shirks this responsibility cannot, in turn, expect others to assume the burden.

Little League recently developed *The Parent Connection* (LittleLeague.org/Parents), which is a monthly e-newsletter designed to inform and engage Little League parents and families. Topics include the latest rules, registration information, fitness and safety tips, and equipment advice.

Volunteer Eligibility

As a condition of service to the league, all managers, coaches, Board of Directors, members and any other persons, volunteers or hired workers, who provide regular service to the league and/or have repetitive access to, or contact with players or teams, must annually complete and submit a "Little League Official Volunteer Application" (LittleLeague.org/VolApp) to the local league president. Annual background screenings must be completed prior to the applicant assuming his/her duties for the current season. Refusal to annually submit a fully completed "Little League Official Volunteer Application" must result in the immediate dismissal of the individual from the local league. (See Regulation I(b) and I(c) 8 and 9.)

Leadership Programs

In the years ahead there will be millions of children playing Little League Baseball and Softball. Leadership training programs help to widen the scope and improve the standards of leadership at all levels.

Managers and Coaches

It cannot be stated too strongly that qualified adult volunteers must be enlisted as team managers and coaches. It is not enough that candidates for these important roles have previous experience in the game.

GENERAL INFORMATION

Managers and coaches must possess leadership ability and the know-how to work with young children. Training Little Leaguers in the fundamentals of teamwork, good sportsmanship and discipline are attainable goals, and are readily available through publications, videos, seminars and clinics produced for and by Little League.

Little League provides a variety of resources to train your league's managers and coaches, including Little League University (LittleLeagueU.org), the Little League Coaches Toolkit (LittleLeague.org/managersandcoaches/coachestoolkit.htm) and The Coach's Box newsletter (LittleLeague.org/Newsletters). Little League University is a free online resource that provides expert advice on coaching several different age groups of baseball and softball players, as well as drills that will help coaches better prepare their teams for games. The Little League Coaches Toolkit, available at a nominal cost, gives managers and coaches access to instructional manuals, books and training videos. The Coach's Box newsletter provides monthly tips and features on topics related to coaching baseball and softball.

Little League also offers guidance on how your league can effectively screen and qualify managers and coaches through the Little League Child Protection Program. Each local league should have a screening process, including background checks and a volunteer application for those who have contact with children. A sample application is included in the publication, "A Year in the Life of Hometown Little League" found at LittleLeague.org/Hometown. Local leagues should also check their state laws for background check information.

Umpires

Often an overlooked aspect of the Little League program, umpiring is one of the most important. The volunteer umpire is as much a part of Little League as the volunteer manager, coach or concession stand worker.

There is no sound reason for paying umpires, or any other person whose services should be provided on a volunteer basis. Many districts and leagues have found successful ways to operate volunteer umpiring programs, helping to defray the costs that might normally be passed on to the parents.

Little League also offers many training materials, clinics and seminars on umpire education, as well as the Little League Umpire Registry. The registry allows volunteer umpires to receive regular mailings from Little League International on rule interpretations, updates, etc.

Umpire training through Little League University, a free, online tool packed with educational content and video clips on plate and base mechanics and news articles, will provide an opportunity to build, recruit, train and retain a program of volunteers. The resource center will also enable umpires to remain updated on the rules and regulations, exchange ideas and offer suggestions that will continually improve their game. Learn more and register at LittleLeagueU.org.

For more information on how to obtain these materials, how to sign up for the Umpire Registry, or on the clinics and seminars nearest you, contact your Regional Offices or visit LittleLeague.org/umpires.

League Officers

Little League offers free training through Little League University (LittleLeagueU.org) as well as clinics, seminars and materials for league officers in all duties. The booklet "A Year in the Life of Hometown Little League" (LittleLeague.org/Hometown) follows a fictional

GENERAL INFORMATION

league through a year of operation, showing the right way to solve the most common problems that arise. For information on ordering the booklet, or on attending a seminar, contact your Regional Office.

Initiatives

Little League is more than just bats and balls. It is also a part of life for millions of people every year, so it is important to educate children and adults in other aspects of life as well. Information on the following special projects and initiatives is available from your Regional Offices.

ASAP (A Safety Awareness Program) — Designed to share the best safety ideas from around the world.

The Little League Challenger Program — Two divisions of play for intellectually and physically impaired players.

Little League Child Protection Program — A program to educate local Little League officials, parents and children on ways to stay safe, and how to help ensure people with the proper motives are involved at the local level.

Little League Grow the Game Grant Program — A new $1.8 million grant program created to provide local leagues the resources needed for general improvement, to help recover from natural disaster, and to expand or establish Little League Softball, Little League Challenger Division, and Little League Urban Initiative programs and help strengthen the Little League opportunities in communities. For more information, visit LittleLeague.org/GrowtheGame.

Little League Urban Initiative — An initiative to bring baseball and softball to inner-city youths.

Frequently-Asked Questions

Here are some answers to the most common questions we receive at Little League International each year.

Q: Can a local Little League or District set-up an Internet website in which any of the trademarks of Little League are used?

> A: Local leagues and Districts are permitted to host websites that assist with communicating information about their activities in the local community. The local league name, affiliation with Little League, registration, facilities locations, board members, and other information for parents and volunteers should be clearly stated on the website.
>
> Any league or district that wishes to host a website, which includes Little League trademarks in any fashion must submit their league URL (Universal Resource Locator) into the Little League Data Center (LittleLeague.org/DataCenter) annually. The URL should be a combination of a league or district's name in conjunction with the words "Little League" or "LL." An example of how a URL should appear: HometownLittleLeague.org or PA12LittleLeague.org.
>
> Use of the Little League trademarks, logos, and links to LittleLeague.org are permitted on websites operated by local leagues or districts, however, permission must be granted

GENERAL INFORMATION

in advance by contacting marketing@LittleLeague.org. Under no circumstances may a league, district, or person register a website using the words Little League in a website address for any other purpose other than to represent their local league or district. If teams within local leagues also host websites, they are required to follow these guidelines and the guidelines for use of Little League trademarks. Team URLs are not required to be submitted to Little League International. It is strongly encouraged that local league board members visit the websites of their associated teams to ensure appropriate content is being provided.

Leagues are also encouraged to secure model releases as part of the player and volunteer registration process. This allows leagues to host images or video of players participating in league activities.

Little League reserves the right to review any league or district website that uses Little League trademarks and logos. If content is deemed inappropriate, the league will be required to remove the content.

Local leagues or districts are no longer required to maintain an eteamz.com website. Leagues or districts may continue to use at their discretion, if desired.

Additional information on use of websites, online registration and other technology can be found on LittleLeagueToolkit.org.

Q: If a manager, coach or umpire is returning from previous years, do they automatically get the same position in the next year?

A: Volunteers in the local Little League program DO NOT HAVE TENURE, regardless of the years of service. In order to serve, a manager, coach or umpire must be appointed by the league president and approved by the local league Board of Directors annually. Prior service does NOT guarantee re-appointment.

Q: Can a local Little League waive its rights to a player who qualifies within its boundaries, allowing that player to participate in another Little League program?

A: A local Little League does not have the authority to waive such rights. ONLY THE CHARTER COMMITTEE IN WILLIAMSPORT HAS THIS AUTHORITY. (See "CHARTER COMMITTEE/WAIVERS OF RULES AND REGULATIONS" in the previous section). If the Charter Committee votes to grant a waiver, the District Administrator will be informed in writing. Waivers, if granted, are for the current season only.

Q: Can a child who does not qualify within a league's boundaries play in that league for the regular season only, provided he/she is not eligible for Tournament Play (all-stars)?

A: No. However, the local league may request a waiver, listing all circumstances that warrant such a waiver. Only the Charter Committee in Williamsport can make the final decision. (See "CHARTER COMMITTEE/WAIVERS OF RULES AND REGULATIONS" in the previous section). If the Charter Committee votes to grant a waiver, the District Administrator will be informed in writing. Waivers, if granted, are for the current season only.

Q: If a parent signs a notarized statement granting temporary custody of a child to a friend or other family member, can that friend or family member's residence be used for registering a child to play in Little League?

GENERAL INFORMATION

A: The ONLY acceptable documentation regarding a change of custody is COURT-ORDERED CUSTODY, a decree issued by a judge who has jurisdiction in the matter.

Q: Does the District Administrator have the authority to grant a waiver of a rule or regulation? Example: Could the District Administrator give permission for a local league to register players whose residence is outside the league's boundaries? Could a District Administrator waive ANY rule or regulation?

A: NO. ANY waiver of a rule or regulation can only be made by the Charter Committee in Williamsport. No other person or group has this authority. If the Charter Committee votes to grant a waiver, the District Administrator will be informed in writing. Waivers, if granted, are for the current season only.

Q: What is the required method for selecting Tournament (all-star) teams?

A: There is no required method. The local league Board of Directors decides annually on the selection method. However, a suggested method is included in the Tournament Rules and Guidelines section of this book.

Q: How much does it cost to belong to Little League?

A: The Charter Fee paid once per year to Little League Baseball, Incorporated, by the local Little League, is $10 per team. One Rulebook for each team chartered is provided free, although the local league president or designated officer may order additional Rulebooks at $2 each. Each league must also provide adequate accident and liability insurance coverage. If the league purchases the insurance through the Little League group insurance program underwritten by an AIG member company, the cost is between $23 and $60 per team, per season, depending upon the location and division of play. Detailed information on accident and liability insurance offered through Little League's Risk Management department at (570) 326-1921.

Q: What is the difference between Regular Season and Tournament Play (all-stars)?

A: During the Regular Season, every eligible child in the league's boundaries is given the opportunity to try out and participate on a team. Generally, the Regular Season begins in the spring and can last until September, but the start/end dates for the Regular Season vary. In Tournament Play, a league holding charters in the proper divisions may enter teams in up to seven baseball and six softball divisions in the International Tournament. Tournament Play begins around July 1 and ends in late August with World Series tournaments in nine divisions of baseball and softball. Many of the rules and regulations are the same for Regular Season and Tournament Play. However, there are some exceptions, detailed in the Tournament Rules and Guidelines section of this book. Little League also offers a "Second Season" program, sometimes called "Fall Ball" or "Winter League," with details available at your Regional Office.

Q: Can our league or district (or any other level) allow a television station or Internet website to broadcast or web-cast regular season games, Special Games or International Tournament games?

A: No. The only authority that can permit this is Little League International. For more information, click on the "Media" section of the Little League website, LittleLeague.org. Information on radio broadcasting can also be found there.

RESIDENCY AND SCHOOL ATTENDANCE ELIGIBILITY REQUIREMENTS

Residency and School Attendance Eligibility Requirements

Each local Little League determines the actual geographic boundaries of the area from within which it shall select players. These boundaries must be described in detail and shown on a map and dated when making application for a Little League charter. Players will be eligible to play with that league only if they reside or the physical location of the school where they attend classes is within the boundaries provided to and approved by Little League Baseball, Incorporated.

I. A player will be deemed to reside within the league boundaries if:
   A. His/her parents are living together and are residing within such league boundaries, OR;
   B. Either of the player's parents (or his/her court-appointed legal guardian) reside within such boundaries. It is unacceptable if a parent moves into a league's boundaries for the purpose of qualifying for tournament play. As detailed later in these rules, the penalty for violation of this rule may, in Little League Baseball, Incorporated's discretion, result in the disqualification of a player, team, or entire league from regular season and/or tournament play.

"Residence," "reside" and "residing" refers to a place of bona fide continuous habitation. A place of residence once established shall not be considered changed unless the parents, parent or guardian makes a bona fide change of residence.

Residence shall be established and supported by documents, dated or in force between February 1, 2015 (previous year) and February 1, 2016 (current year), from THREE OR MORE of the following categories to determine residency of such parent(s) or guardian:
1. Driver's License
2. Voter's Registration
3. School records
4. Welfare/child care records
5. Federal records
6. State records
7. Local (municipal) records
8. Support payment records
9. Homeowner or tenant records
10. Utility bills (i.e., gas, electric, water/sewer, phone, mobile phone, heating, waste disposal)
11. Financial (loan, credit, investments, etc.) records
12. Insurance documents
13. Medical records
14. Military records
15. Internet, cable or satellite records
16. Vehicle records
17. Employment Records

NOTE: Example – Three utility bills (three items from No. 10 above) constitute only ONE document.

Any documents submitted as proof of residence must show customary usage or consumption to demonstrate bona fide continuous habitation as determined by Little League Baseball, Incorporated in its discretion.

RESIDENCY AND SCHOOL ATTENDANCE ELIGIBILITY REQUIREMENTS

II. A player will be deemed to attend school in the boundaries if:
   A. The physical location of the school where they attend classes is within the boundaries established by the local league. Note: This excludes home schools, cyber schools, sports-related schools, sports academies, or preschools, or after school where a student participates outside of the primary school the player is enrolled.

"School attendance" refers to the (place) physical location the player in question attends school during the traditional academic year. Once established, a location of school attendance shall not be considered changed unless the child is enrolled and attends another school or is no longer enrolled in the previous school.

School attendance shall be established and supported by a document indicating enrollment for the current academic year, dated prior to October 1, 2015, and with the physical location of the school, from ONE of the following categories to determine school attendance by such player:

1. Official/Certified school enrollment record dated prior to October 1, 2015
2. School issued report card or performance record dated prior to October 1, 2015
3. A Little League issued school attendance form completed by the principal, assistant principal, or administrator

It is recommended that the league require some proof of residence or school attendance within the league's boundaries at the time the player registers. Players and their parents/guardians are advised that a false statement of residence or school attendance may lead to ineligibility to play Little League Baseball or Softball. Under NO circumstances does ANY person have the authority to grant a waiver that allows a child to play in a local Little League program IN ANY DIVISION, when that child does not qualify under these eligibility requirements. Any league who accepts any player outside of their boundaries and fails to properly document compliance with the "Residence and/or School Attendance Player Eligibility Requirement" or obtain a waiver through the Charter Committee may result in the disqualification of a player, team, or entire league from regular season and/or tournament play.

If the claim for residency or school attendance is challenged, the above materials must be submitted to Little League Baseball, Incorporated, with an affidavit of residency or school attendance from the parent(s) or guardian. Little League Baseball, Incorporated shall have the right to request additional documentation in support of the claim of residency or school attendance. The parent(s) or legal guardian will be required to provide said documentation to obtain eligibility. Little League Baseball, Incorporated shall decide the issue in its sole discretion, and that decision will be final and binding. Residency or school documents must illustrate that the residence or school attendance (as defined above) was inside the league's boundaries throughout the regular season (as of June 15 of the year in question).

In the case of a Regulation II(d) Waiver Form, or a Regulation IV(h) Waiver Form, the proof of residence for the FORMER residence of the parent(s) or former school that was within the current league's boundaries must be obtained. This proof of residence for the former residence or former school attendance must be supported by the same documentation as noted above.

RESIDENCY AND SCHOOL ATTENDANCE ELIGIBILITY REQUIREMENTS

Tournament Requirement for Non-Citizens: *A participant who is not a citizen of the country in which he/she wishes to play, but meets residency requirements as defined by Little League, may participate in that country if:*

1. his/her visa allows that participant to remain in that country for a period of at least one year, or;
2. the prevailing laws allow that participant to remain in that country for at least one year, or;
3. the participant has an established bona fide residence in that country for at least two years prior to the start of the regular season.

Exceptions can only be made by action of the Charter Committee in Williamsport. Any request for a waiver pertaining to the eligibility of a player must be submitted in writing, by the president of the local Little League through the District Administrator, to their respective Regional Director not later than the date prescribed in Regulation IV(j). Requests submitted after that date will not be considered.

Proof-of-Age Requirements

Acceptable Forms of Proof of Birth Date

1. Original proof of age document, if issued by federal, state, or provincial registrars of vital statistics in the country in which the Little Leaguer is participating.
2. If country of participation differs from the country of proof of age document, original proof-of-age document issued by federal, state, or provincial registrars of vital statistics, or local offices thereof, are acceptable proof of age, provided the document was filed, recorded, registered, or issued within one (1) year of the birth of the child.
3. An original document issued by federal, state, or provincial registrars of vital statistics, or local offices thereof, listing the date of birth, with reference to the location and issue date of the original birth certificate, is acceptable. (The original birth certificate referenced must have been filed, recorded, registered, or issued within one (1) year of the birth of the child.) Also issued by these agencies are photocopies of the certificate of live birth with the certification also photocopied, including the signature, and include the seal impressed thereon. Such documents are acceptable without "live" signatures, provided the original filed, recorded, registered, or issued date of the birth certificate was within one (1) year of the date of birth.
4. For children born abroad of a parent or parents who are U.S. citizens, any official government document issued by a U. S. federal agency or service, is acceptable. For military dependents, Department of Defense identification cards and military hospital certificates are acceptable. These must be originals, not copies, and must refer to a filing, recording, registration, or issue date that is within one (1) year of the birth of the child.
5. A "Statement in Lieu of Acceptable Proof of Birth" issued by a District Administrator is acceptable.

NOT ACCEPTABLE AS SOLE PROOF OF BIRTH: Baptismal Certificate; Certificate of Blessing; Certificate of Dedication; Certificate of Circumcision, etc.; Hospital Certificate; photocopied records; passports.

NOTE: Little League International has authorized the Regional Directors for Latin America and Caribbean, Europe and Africa, and Asia-Pacific, to adopt a policy that excludes No. 1 above. Local Little Leagues and districts in those regions will be informed of the regional policy.

How to Obtain Acceptable Documents Proving Date of Birth

Certified copy-of-birth records may be obtained from the Registrar of Vital Statistics of each state, province, or local office where the child was born. For U.S.-born persons, addresses of these offices or bureaus, fees required and other pertinent information are supplied by the United States Department of Health and Human Services (National Center for Health Statistics). A database listing the method for obtaining birth records from any U.S. state or territory is available at the following Internet address:

cdc.gov/nchs/w2w.htm

PROOF-OF-AGE REQUIREMENTS

Individual states may also have on-line instructions on how to obtain "rush" birth records. To find out a state's latest policies regarding birth records, go to the Internet site listed below and type "birth records" into the search field, designate the appropriate state, then click on "SUBMIT."

usa.gov

Persons in the U.S. who need a copy of a non-U.S. birth record should contact the Embassy or the nearest Consulate of the country in which the birth occurred. Addresses and telephone numbers for these offices are listed in the U.S. Department of State Publication 7846, "Foreign Consular Offices in the United States," which is available in many local libraries. This publication may also be located at the following Internet address: state.gov/s/cpr/rls/fco/. Such proof-of-birth records must meet the criteria for acceptable proof listed above.

How to Obtain a "Statement in Lieu of Acceptable Proof of Birth"

When an "Acceptable Proof of Birth" as described previously is not available, then the appropriate number of items in EACH of these FOUR groups are required so that the participant may obtain a "Statement in Lieu of Acceptable Proof of Birth," which is required for such a participant to be eligible for regular season or tournament play:

Group 1 – Any one (1) of the following, provided the date of birth is listed: a naturalization document issued by the United States Department of Justice; photocopy of birth certificate; original birth certificate or government record of birth if not containing a filing, recording, registration, or issue date within one (1) year of the date of birth; passport; PLUS…

Group 2 – Any two (2) of the following, provided the date of birth is listed: Baptismal Certificate; Certificate of Blessing; Certificate of Dedication; Certificate of Circumcision; or any other religious-related certificate; Hospital Certificate; School Record (must be dated, and date of issue must be at least two years prior to current season); Social Security document; Welfare Department document; adoption record. Any item in this group must be an original document, not a copy; PLUS…

Group 3 – Any two (2) of the following: A written, signed, and notarized statement from…
  … the doctor who delivered the child;
  … a hospital administrator where the child was delivered;
  … the principal or headmaster of the school the child attends;
  … a Social Worker with personal knowledge of the child's date of birth;
  … a Priest, Rabbi, Minister, Mullah, or other titled religious figure with personal knowledge of the child's date of birth;
  … the child's pediatrician or family doctor.

NOTE: In each statement in Group 3, the writer must describe his/her responsibilities or his/her relationship to the child, and must attest to his/her personal knowledge that the child was born on the date claimed; PLUS…

Group 4 – A written, signed, and notarized statement from one or both parents, or the legal guardian (as appointed by a court of jurisdiction), attesting to the date of birth claimed.

The league president will forward the above documentation to the District Administrator (or, if the team is traveling, the Tournament Director). If in the opinion of the District Administrator, such evidence is satisfactory, a "Statement In Lieu of Acceptable

PROOF-OF-AGE REQUIREMENTS

Proof of Birth" will be issued. This statement will be considered to be acceptable proof of age from that point forward, throughout the child's Little League experience, provided all the information submitted is accurate. (**NOTE**: If the District Administrator is unable to review the documents, they may be submitted to the appropriate Regional Headquarters.)

NOTE: Situations where players use the name of an adopting family or the name of the family with whom they live, but whose births are recorded under the surname of the natural father or mother, will be handled as follows: The president of the league will obtain from the parents or guardian a document that qualifies under Proof-of-Age Requirements, as well as a copy of the adoption papers (if the player has been legally adopted). If the player was not adopted, a notarized statement from the mother and/or father or legal guardian (as appointed by a court of jurisdiction), saying that the player living under one or the other of their surnames is the same player for whom the birth certificate was issued) is also required.

These documents will be submitted to the District Administrator. If the documents are found to be acceptable, a "Statement in Lieu of Acceptable Proof of Birth" will be issued and all original documents returned. The information submitted will be kept confidential.

REGULATION I — THE LEAGUE

Official Regulations
LITTLE LEAGUE SOFTBALL® (MAJOR) DIVISION, MINOR LEAGUE SOFTBALL, TEE BALL SOFTBALL, JUNIOR LEAGUE SOFTBALL, SENIOR LEAGUE SOFTBALL, and BIG LEAGUE SOFTBALL

These regulations govern the conduct and operation of chartered Little League Softball programs.

An Approved Ruling (A.R.) serves to illustrate the application of the regulations and rules. Approved Rulings follow the regulations and rules they amplify and are indicated by a box.

Regulation I

The League

(a) The league is the only unit of organization.
  1. The Little League Softball (Major) Division is to accommodate participants league ages 9-12.
  2. The Minor League Division is an extension of the local Little League to accommodate participants league ages 7-12.
  3. The Tee Ball division is an extension of the local league to accommodate participants league ages 4-7 and may utilize the batting tee or the pitched ball (by a coach). The league may opt to deliver a designated number of pitches to all batters and then utilize the tee if necessary.
  NOTE 1: 7 year-olds may play in Minor League or Tee Ball depending on the local structure and ability of the players.
  NOTE 2: Players shall not participate in more than one division.
  NOTE 3: Participants league age 5 and 6 are permitted to advance to Minor League Coach Pitch or Machine Pitch after participation in Tee Ball for one year.

(b) **The league shall be governed by a Board of Directors elected from and by the membership, consisting of volunteer personnel. As a condition of service to the league, all managers, coaches, Board of Directors, members, and any other persons, volunteers or hired workers, who provide regular service to the league and/or have repetitive access to, or contact with players or teams, must complete and submit a "Little League Official Volunteer Application" to the local league president. Annual background screenings must be completed prior to the applicant assuming his/her duties for the current season. Refusal to annually submit a fully completed "Little League Official Volunteer Application" must result in the immediate dismissal of the individual from the local league. (See also Reg. I(c) 8 and 9.)**

Officers shall be elected by the Board (i.e. president, one or more vice presidents, secretary, treasurer, safety officer, coaching coordinator, and player agent or agents). The president may manage, coach, or umpire provided he/she does not serve on the Protest Committee. The president of record or anyone who assumes the position or duties of president, on or after January 1 of the current year, is not eligible to serve as tournament team manager or coach. The president will not serve in the capacity of District Administrator. Player Agents shall not manage, coach, or umpire in the

REGULATION I — THE LEAGUE

respective divisions. Vice presidents may manage, coach, or umpire provided they do not serve on the Protest Committee.

The president, with approval of the Board of Directors, shall appoint managers, coaches, and umpires annually. Manager/coach representation on the Board shall not exceed a minority. **NOTE:** All members of the local league Board of Directors, as well as managers and coaches, whose activities in another youth baseball/softball program are deemed detrimental to the operation of the local league, can be removed by a majority vote of the Board of Directors. **Additionally, the local league's Board of Directors has the right to NOT approve that individual as tournament team manager/coach.**

(c) Each league shall:
1. prepare, adopt, and submit to Little League International, a constitution consistent with all rules, regulations, and policies of Little League Baseball, Incorporated.
2. be considered as a separate and not as a division of the same league.
3. apply for and, if approved, be issued a separate charter certificate.
4. have separate boundaries as provided for in Regulation II.
5. adopt and play a separate schedule of games as provided for in Regulation VII. Interleague play and practice with another league(s) may be permitted during the regular season with the **approval of the District Administrator(s). The District Administrator(s) must verify that all leagues involved in the interleague combination are properly chartered and insured. Interleague play during the regular season between leagues from two districts must be approved by the regional office. Leagues involved in interleague play will field separate tournament teams. Players shall not be transferred from one league to another. Requests to combine for tournament play must be submitted through the district to the regional offices for approval per guidelines established by Little League. Districts will be required to submit interleague play forms with all insurance claims that result from interleague play.**
6. provide all players with conventional uniforms. **Minor League and Tee Ball:** T-shirts and caps/visors are recommended, but hand-me-down type uniforms may be worn if so approved by the local board. (The Little League Official Shoulder Patch must be affixed to the upper left sleeve of the uniform blouse in all divisions of play.);
7. obtain Accident and General Liability insurance.
    A. Accident Insurance coverage is mandatory for all players on all rosters as well as managers, coaches, and umpires. The policy must have a minimum coverage of $100,000 per person per accident.
    B. General Liability insurance is mandatory for the league including its volunteers. The policy must have a minimum coverage of $1,000,000 single limit bodily injury and property damage. **The policy must include coverage for claims involving each of the following: 1. athletic participants, and, 2. sexual abuse and molestation.**

If insurance is purchased locally, a copy of the policy naming Little League Baseball, Incorporated as an additional insured must be submitted to Little League International with your "Charter Application and Insurance Enrollment" form.

REGULATION I — THE LEAGUE

8. require that all of the following persons have annually submitted a fully completed "Little League Official Volunteer Application" to the local league president, prior to the applicant assuming his/her duties for the current season: managers, coaches, Board of Directors, members, and any other persons, volunteers, or hired workers, who provide regular service to the league and/or have repetitive access to, or contact with, players or teams. The "Little League Official Volunteer Application" must be maintained by the president of the local league Board of Directors for all persons named above, for a minimum of at least two years after the volunteer is no longer in the league. When it comes time to dispose of these records, they should be destroyed as they contain sensitive information. Failure to comply with this regulation may result in the suspension or revocation of tournament privileges and/or the local league's charter by action of the Charter or Tournament committees in Williamsport.

9. conduct an annual background check on all persons that are required to complete a "Little League Official Volunteer Application" prior to the applicant assuming his/her duties for the current season. No local league shall permit any person to participate in any manner, whose background check reveals a conviction for, guilty plea, no contest plea, or admission to any crime involving or against a minor or minors. A local league may prohibit any individual from participating as a volunteer or hired worker, if the local league deems the individual unfit to work with minors.

A local league must conduct a nationwide search that contains the applicable government sex offender registry data.

Local leagues shall be required to determine the applicability of, and comply with, all state, local, and municipal laws, administrative rules and regulations, and municipal ordinances regarding background checks including, but not limited to, sex offender registry checks, criminal history records or reports, fingerprinting, certifications, or other requirements associated with volunteers, coaches, participants, and/or employees. Failure to comply with this regulation may result in the suspension or revocation of tournament privileges and/or the local league's charter by action of the Charter or Tournament committees in Williamsport.

Several states have enacted laws that require additional background check requirements that are separate and additional to those mandated by Little League. For more information to assist you regarding state law requirements go to our website at LittleLeague.org/StateLaws.

As of June 1, 2015, those states with additional background check requirements either enacted or pending are: Alabama, California, Florida, Massachusetts, Mississippi, New Hampshire, Oklahoma, Oregon, and Pennsylvania.

NOTE 1: Each year, Little League International provides each league 125 free criminal background checks. Information on how to utilize this benefit,

REGULATION I — THE LEAGUE

as well as how to conduct background checks, can be found on the following Little League website: LittleLeague.org/childprotectionprogram.*

NOTE 2: The National Sex Offender Registry is free and available on the United States Department of Justice Dru Sjodin National Sex Offender Public website at nsopw.gov.*

*Occasionally Sex Offender Registry data may be unavailable for an individual state(s) when you run your background checks. This may occur on the criminal background check tool provided for free by Little League International as outlined in Note 1 and/or on the National Sex Offender Registry as outlined in Note 2. If this occurs, you have the option of going immediately to the individual state(s) SOR website or going back and re-running the Sex Offender Registry data on the National Sex Offender Registry until the data becomes available. Information on accessing individual State Sex Offender Registry data can be found on the Little League Website at LittleLeague.org/childprotectionprogram.

If no sex offender registries exist in a province or country outside the United States, the local league must conduct the more extensive of a country, province, or city-wide criminal background check through the appropriate governmental agency unless prohibited by law.

Failure to comply with this regulation may result in the suspension or revocation of tournament privileges and/or the local league's charter by action of the Charter or Tournament committees in Williamsport. If a local league becomes aware of information, by any means whatsoever, that an individual, including, but not limited to, volunteers, players, or hired workers, has been convicted of, pled guilty, pled no contest, or admitted to any crime involving or against a minor or minors, the local league must contact the applicable government agency to confirm the accuracy of the information. Upon confirmation of a conviction for, guilty plea, no contest plea, or admission to a crime against or involving a minor or minors, the local league shall not permit the individual to participate in any manner.

NOTE: Information regarding background checks is available at LittleLeague.org/background.

(d) The Little League (Major) Division may be composed of not more than ten (10) teams. If more than 10 teams are requested, application for a divisional format must be made to the Charter Committee through the District Administrator. If approved, each division must field a separate tournament team.

(e) Not more than one league will be permitted to operate under the same management without expressed recommendation of the District Administrator to Little League International and subject to final approval by the Charter Committee.

(f) Mergers where there is sufficient enrollment to maintain separate charters, shall require the recommendation of the District Administrator to Little League International and be subject to final approval by the Charter Committee.

REGULATION I — THE LEAGUE

(g) A local Little League is not permitted to sponsor, administer, underwrite, or otherwise support, any team or teams, any individual or group, for the purpose of participating in a non-Little League Softball program or event. Violation may result in revocation of charter and/or suspension of tournament privileges. While Little League does not recommend or endorse participation in more than one softball program, this does not prohibit an individual who plays in a chartered Little League, or a group of such individuals, from participation in a non-Little League program, subject to the provisions of Regulation IV(a) Note 2, and the provisions of the Tournament Rules and Guidelines regarding "player participation in other programs."

(h) A Little League Softball charter can be issued where no Little League Baseball charter exists, providing the softball league boundaries do not overlap those of an existing Little League Baseball charter unless the league requests and obtains approval from the Charter Committee.

Regulation I
The League: Junior/Senior/Big League

(a) Junior League is an extension of the local Little League to accommodate participants league ages 12-14; Senior League is an extension of the local Little League to accommodate participants league ages 13-16; Big League is an extension of the local Little League to accommodate participants league ages 14-18.

NOTE: Junior/Senior/Big League players may participate in other softball programs during the regular season and tournament subject to the provisions of Regulation IV.

Senior/Big League:
Teams from one or more leagues in a district which are currently chartered may join to form a Senior/Big League. Any district which can field four (4) teams, must have its own league. Where one district cannot field four (4) teams, leagues in adjoining districts may combine to form a Senior/Big League not to exceed ten (10) teams, with approval of the Charter Committee.

EXCEPTION: A Senior/Big League may be a district-operated program, supervised by the District Administrator. Such a district-wide program may draw participants from within the boundaries of each chartered league in the district. However, each local league wishing to do so may retain its own team/league structure. **NOTE:** District Administrators, even if they operate a district-wide Senior/Big League program, are not permitted to vote in the election for District Administrator.

(b) The Junior League Division shall be governed by the Board of Directors of the local Little League. The Board of Directors of the local Little League shall elect a player agent and vice president for each division and shall approve the appointment of its managers and coaches annually.

The president may manage, coach, or umpire provided he/she does not serve on the Protest Committee. *The president of record or anyone who assumes the position or duties of president, on or after January 1 of the current year, is not eligible to serve as tournament team manager or coach.* The Player Agent shall not manage, coach, or umpire in his/her respective division. Vice president may manage, coach, or umpire provided they do not serve on the Protest Committee.

REGULATION I — THE LEAGUE

Senior/Big League:
A local Little League organizing a Senior/Big League program of four (4) or more teams shall be governed by the Board of Directors of that league. Where teams of more than one local Little League in a district form a Senior/Big League, such league shall be governed by a Board of Directors of representatives of participating leagues. The local Little League president may manage, coach, or umpire provided he/she does not serve on the Protest Committee. *The president of record or anyone who assumes the position or duties of president, on or after January 1 of the current year, is not eligible to serve as tournament team manager or coach.* The Player Agent shall not manage, coach, or umpire in his/her respective division. Vice president may manage, coach, or umpire provided they do not serve on the Protest Committee. In the latter event, the District Administrator shall serve as Board Chairman and appoint an assistant to administer the league.

As a condition of service to the league, all managers, coaches, Board of Directors, members, and any other persons, volunteers or hired workers, who provide regular service to the league and/or have repetitive access to, or contact with players or teams, must complete and submit a "Little League Official Volunteer Application" to the local league president. Annual background screenings must be completed prior to the applicant assuming his/her duties for the current season. Refusal to annually submit a fully completed "Little League Official Volunteer Application" must result in the immediate dismissal of the individual from the local league.

(c) Each division shall operate under the constitution of the local Little League, which is the only unit of organization. (Senior and Big League exception noted above.)

Senior/Big League:
Each participating local Little League and/or District will:
1. select managers and coaches for its teams;
2. select its players from within the boundaries of the local Little League, or from within the boundaries of chartered leagues participating in the district-wide Senior/Big League program;
3. obtain Accident and General Liability insurance.
   A. Accident Insurance coverage is mandatory for all players on all rosters as well as managers, coaches, and umpires. The policy must have a minimum coverage of $100,000 per person per accident.
   B. General Liability insurance is mandatory for the league including its volunteers. The policy must have a minimum coverage of $1,000,000 single limit bodily injury and property damage. The policy must include coverage for claims arising out of athletic participants.

   If insurance is purchased locally, a copy of the policy naming "Little League Baseball, Incorporated" as an additional insured must be submitted to Little League International with your "Charter Application and Insurance Enrollment" form.
4. supply uniforms, bats, and equipment for its team(s) and contribute proportional costs of softballs, supplies, and operation of program.
5. **require that all of the following persons have annually submitted a fully completed "Little League Official Volunteer Application" to the local league president, prior to the applicant assuming his/her duties for the current**

season: managers, coaches, Board of Directors, members, and any other persons, volunteers or hired workers, who provide regular service to the league and/or have repetitive access to, or contact with, players or teams. The "Little League Official Volunteer Application" must be maintained by the president of the local league Board of Directors for all persons named above, for at least two years after the volunteer is no longer in the league. When it comes time to dispose of these records, they should be destroyed as they contain sensitive information. Failure to comply with this regulation may result in the suspension or revocation of tournament privileges and/or the local league's charter by action of the Charter or Tournament committees in Williamsport.

6. conduct an annual background check on all persons that are required to complete a "Little League Official Volunteer Application" prior to the applicant assuming his/her duties for the current season. No local league shall permit any person to participate in any manner, whose background check reveals a conviction of, guilty plea, no contest plea, admission to any crime involving or against a minor or minors. A local league may prohibit any individual from participating as a volunteer or hired worker, if the local league deems the individual unfit to work with minors.

A local league must conduct a nationwide search that contains the applicable government sex offender registry data.

Local leagues shall be required to determine the applicability of, and comply with, all State, local, and municipal laws, administrative rules and regulations, and municipal ordinances regarding background checks including, but not limited to, sex offender registry checks, criminal history records or reports, fingerprinting, certifications, or other requirements associated with volunteers, coaches, participants, and/or employees. Failure to comply with this regulation may result in the suspension or revocation of tournament privileges and/or the local league's charter by action of the Charter or Tournament committees in Williamsport.

Several states have enacted laws that require additional background check requirements that are separate and additional to those mandated by Little League. For more information to assist you regarding state law requirements go to our website at LittleLeague.org/StateLaws.

As of June 1, 2015, those states with additional background check requirements either enacted or pending are: Alabama, California, Florida, Massachusetts, Mississippi, New Hampshire, Oklahoma, Oregon, and Pennsylvania.

NOTE 1: Each year, Little League International provides each league 125 free criminal background checks. Information on how to utilize this benefit, as well as how to conduct background checks, can be found on the following Little League website: LittleLeague.org/childprotectionprogram.*

REGULATION I — THE LEAGUE

> NOTE 2: The National Sex Offender Registry is free and available on the United States Department of Justice Dru Sjodin National Sex Offender Public website at nsopw.gov.*
>
> *Occasionally Sex Offender Registry data may be unavailable for an individual state(s) when you run your background checks. This may occur on the criminal background check tool provided for free by Little League International as outlined in Note 1 and/or on the National Sex Offender Registry as outlined in Note 2. If this occurs, you have the option of going immediately to the individual state(s) SOR website or going back and re-running the Sex Offender Registry data on the National Sex Offender Registry until the data becomes available. Information on accessing individual State Sex Offender Registry data can be found on the Little League website at LittleLeague.org/childprotectionprogram.
>
> If no sex offender registries exist in a province or country outside the United States, the local league must conduct the more extensive of a country, province, or city-wide criminal background check through the appropriate governmental agency unless prohibited by law.
>
> Failure to comply with this regulation may result in the suspension or revocation of tournament privileges and/or the local league's charter by action of the Charter or Tournament committees in Williamsport. If a local league becomes aware of information, by any means whatsoever, that an individual, including, but not limited to, volunteers, players, or hired workers, has been convicted of, pled guilty, pled no contest, or admitted to any crime involving or against a minor or minors, the local league must contact the applicable government agency to confirm the accuracy of the information. Upon confirmation of a conviction for, guilty plea, no contest plea, or admission to a crime against or involving a minor or minors, the local league shall not permit the individual to participate in any manner.
> NOTE: Information regarding background checks is available at LittleLeague.org/background.

(d) Each division shall be composed of no more than 10 teams.

(e) On or before April 15, the chartered Little League shall apply for and, if approved, be granted permission to operate a Junior League, Senior League, and/or Big League program for the year. On or before April 15, the District shall apply for and, if approved, be granted permission to operate a Senior and/or Big League program for the year.

(f) Boundaries for selection of players shall conform to those of the local Little League. Senior and Big League exceptions noted in Regulation I(a).

(g) Each division shall adopt and play a separate schedule of games as provided for in Regulation VII. Interlocking schedules, interleague play, or practice shall not be permitted, nor shall players be transferred from one league to another except as provided for in Regulation VII.

REGULATION I — THE LEAGUE

(h) Not more than one Junior League will be permitted to operate under the same local Little League. However, where a lack of enough player personnel exists and with the recommendation of the District Administrator and approval of the Charter Committee, two or more adjacent chartered Little Leagues comprising not more than 40,000 population of the same district may combine to form one Junior League. Where two or more leagues have combined to form one Junior League, a tournament team must be selected from each league, unless an exception is approved by the Charter Committee.

(i) Where two or more Junior Leagues combine, each will make application for charter indicating thereon the number of teams each will field and the need for joint operation. Players from more than one league may be pooled for the purpose of organizing Junior League teams, with Charter Committee approval.

(j) Where two or more Junior Leagues combine, the operation shall be governed jointly by the Board of Directors of the local leagues. They shall each elect a vice president and player agent to be in charge of the league(s).

(k) The vice presidents will administer the joint Junior League program subject to the agreement of their Board of Directors.

(l) Each Junior League will select managers and coaches for its teams.

(m) Each Junior League will supply a proportionate number of adult personnel including volunteer umpires.

(n) Each Junior League will supply uniforms, bats, and playing equipment for its teams and contribute proportionate costs for softballs, supplies, and maintenance of playing field(s). When each league has a field, each will maintain its own.

(o) Each Junior League will pay its proportionate share for player accident, liability, and volunteer insurance.

(p) A Junior League, Senior League, or Big League Softball charter can be issued where no Little League Baseball charter exists, providing the softball league boundaries do not overlap those of an existing Little League Baseball charter unless the league requests and obtains approval from the Charter Committee.

Regulation II

League Boundaries

(a) Each league shall determine actual boundaries of the area from WITHIN which it shall select players. Only those participants whose residence or the physical location of the school where they attend classes is within the boundaries of the league shall be eligible to participate. Residence, for the purposes of this regulation, is defined in "Residence and School Attendance Player Eligibility Requirements." **NOTE: Any player who does not reside in or the school where they attend classes is not WITHIN the league's boundaries must have an approved waiver issued by the Charter Committee at Little League International. All waiver requests to the Charter Committee must be submitted and approved in writing by the league president before the start of the league's regular season or June 1, whichever occurs first. Requests must be submitted to the regional office through the District Administrator. Failure to properly document compliance with the "Residence and School Attendance Player Eligibility Requirement" or obtain a waiver through the Charter Committee may result in the disqualification of a player, team, or entire league from regular season and/or tournament play.** These boundaries MUST be described in detail AND shown on a map when making application for the charter. The local Little League boundaries shall be the boundaries of the Junior/Senior/Big League. Exception noted for Senior/Big League district operating in Regulation I.

(b) When there are two (2) or more leagues within a locale, each must have separate boundaries, detailed by a map. No exception to this provision will be made without written approval of Little League International.

(c) Team boundaries may be permitted where communities making up a league are widely separated, upon application to and approval by Little League International.

(d) **The Board of Directors of the local league, with the approval of the player involved, reserves the right to continue as a player, any individual (1) whose residence or school enrollment/attendance changes from within the boundary to outside the league's boundary or (2) who lives or school enrollment/attendance outside the league's boundaries because of a revision of such boundaries even if the child then resides in the territory of another league. Current players, or any sibling of a current player whose brother or sister met the criteria under II(d) at one time may be retained. Any player meeting (1) or (2) above may be retained for the remainder of his/her career, including Little League, Junior League, Senior League, and Big League competition.** NOTE: A player who qualifies under this regulation and elects not to participate for a playing season is not eligible to be retained for the subsequent season.

Regulations II(d) - Processing Procedure

The league president will process a II(d) form. Once the president completes the form, he/she must compile "residency or school enrollment/attendance requirement" verification that each player meets the conditions of II(d) as outlined above. The league president will present this information to the District Administrator for review. Once the District Administrator reviews the documentation in an effort to determine if it meets the regulations, the District Administrator will sign the II(d)

REGULATION II — LEAGUE BOUNDARIES

form. *The league and the district will maintain the form and documentation in their files. This review process is only required once during a participant's career. The league must maintain this form and documentation for this player for the duration of his/her career until the player graduates from the program or breaks service with the league. Tournament team players will be required to carry a copy of this form and documentation with them throughout the tournament. If contested during tournament play, the league will be required to produce the documentation. Additionally, if it is determined at a later date that the player does not meet the conditions of II(d), the player is ineligible for further participation. Situations in which documentation is not available must be referred to the Charter Committee through the regional office for a decision. The decision of the Charter Committee is final and binding.*

(f) Boundaries approved by Little League International for a chartered league shall be protected. No other league will be chartered to accept player candidates from all or any part of the same territory for that calendar year. When necessary the District Administrator shall have the authority to recommend adjusting the league boundaries and be subject to review and approval of the Charter Committee.

(g) **Upon approval of the Little League International Board of Directors, each local Little League's boundary was "frozen" at the status as of April 23, 2007.** "Frozen" means, each league will continue to operate under that boundary. The league shall limit its boundary to and draw its players from an area approved by the District Administrator and Regional Director. Boundary maps for leagues (and any changes made after April 23, 2007, to the approved map on file at the Regional Office) must be signed and dated by the league president and District Administrator with a copy to be sent to the Regional Office. The approved map on file at the Regional Office is the "official" map, provided it does not encroach on any other chartered Little League's boundary. The Charter Committee reserves the right to grant waivers and adjust boundaries where needed. All requests for mergers and to expand league boundaries by adding additional territory must be provided to the Charter Committee through the District Administrator and Regional Director. The decision of the Charter Committee on these requests is final and binding.

Note 1: Each league will be required to have a current boundary map, approved by the District Administrator, in the regional office files. This will be required for tournament privileges for the current season.

Note 2: All leagues currently operating under a divisional format must continue to operate under this method. *Exceptions to the divisional format can only be granted by the Charter Committee in Williamsport.*

Note 3: Any request for newly chartered leagues will be reviewed by the Charter Committee under this regulation before a charter is granted. The decision of the Charter Committee is final and binding.

Regulation III

The Teams

(a) The league shall, at least 10 days prior to the first regular game, establish the number of players on each team. **Little League (Majors)/Junior/Senior:** No team may have more than 15 players (18 for Big League) nor less than 12. **Minor League and Tee Ball:** There will be no minimum or maximum established at the Minor League and Tee Ball levels. Roster size of 8-10 players is recommended. **NOTE:** If a local league elects to roster less than nine (9) players at the Tee Ball and/or Minor League levels, rules 3.03 Note 2, 4.16 and 4.17 do not apply.

The manager of a team must, at least five days prior to the first regularly scheduled game, register the Regular Season team roster. All teams in a particular division must carry the same number of players on their roster.

(b) No more than the number of players established by the league under Regulation III(a) may be in uniform during any game. Batboys and/or batgirls are not permitted.

(c) **Little League (Major) Division:** Local league must establish the age structure for the Little League (Major) Division. At no time shall a team have on its roster more than eight players whose league age is 12. Balance of the team roster shall be comprised of players whose league age is 9, 10, or 11. For **Junior/Senior/Big League**, it is recommended that the local Little League (or district, if the Senior/Big League is administered as a district operation) set a maximum and/or minimum number of participants of a particular league age. (**Example:** If the league has all 15 and 16 year olds in its Senior League Division, it may have a local rule that states that each team must carry between four and eight players of league age 16.)

Minor League: Local league must establish the age structure for the Minor League Division. The Minor League may be sub-divided into Minor League Coach Pitch, Minor League Machine Pitch, and/or Minor League Player Pitch divisions, with the method for division determined by the local Little League Board of Directors. A player listed on a Little League (Major) Division roster shall not be permitted to play with a Minor League team.

Tee Ball: Local league must establish the age structure for the Tee Ball Division. Players league age 4 are eligible ONLY for Tee Ball, unless otherwise approved by the Charter Committee. **EXCEPTION**: Participants league age 5 and 6 are permitted to advance to Minor League Coach Pitch or Machine Pitch after participation in Tee Ball for one year. A player listed on a Tee Ball roster shall not be permitted to play with a Minor League team.

(d) If a team loses any player(s) on the roster during the current season through illness, injury, change of address, or other justifiable reasons (subject to Board approval), another player shall be obtained through the player agent, to replace the one lost. The playing ability of the participant shall not be considered a justifiable reason for replacement. Such replacement must be of such league age as to comply with Regulation III(c), and must be eligible under all sections of Regulation IV. The local league (or district, if the Senior/Big League is administered as a district operation) should specify in its local rules the number of days allowed for a manager to comply with selection of a replacement. When changes are desired, the following procedures

REGULATION III — THE TEAMS

must be followed:
1. Manager shall acquaint the Board of Directors of the local league (or district, if the Senior/Big League is administered as a district operation) with the conditions which necessitate the request for a replacement.
2. If the majority of the Board of Directors (or district, if the Senior/Big League is administered as a district operation) agrees that the reasons are justifiable, the manager may call up a replacement who is eligible under Regulation III(c) and all sections of Regulation IV.

   NOTE 1: A league may adopt a local rule prohibiting replacements from the Minor League program onto a Little League (Major) Division team during the last two weeks of the regular season schedule.

   NOTE 2: When a player misses more than seven (7) continuous days of participation for an illness or injury, a physician or other accredited medical provider must give written permission for a return to full softball activity.

   NOTE 3: If a medical professional, Umpire-in-Chief, the player's coach, the player's manager, or the player's parent has determined a player sustains a possible concussion, the player must be, at a minimum, removed from the game and/or practice for the remainder of that day. The league must also be aware of its respective state/provincial/municipal laws with regards to concussions and impose any additional requirements as necessary. His/her return to full participation is subject to 1.) the league's adherence to its respective state/provincial/municipal laws, 2.) an evaluation and a written clearance from a physician or other accredited medical provider and 3.) written acknowledgment of the parents.

   Little League International strongly encourages all leagues and teams to not only comply with any applicable state/provincial/municipal laws, but also, to review the information and training materials on concussions that are available free of charge on the Centers For Disease Control website, accessible at LittleLeague.org/concussions. This link also provides concussion information from all 50 states.

(e) Managers may request to release players for any justifiable reason {as in (d) above, subject to Board approval} between the conclusion of one season and seven (7) days prior to the tryout session, but not later than the players selection or draft meeting of the subsequent season. In the event, that a player is released, the president of the league (or District Administrator, if the Senior/Big League is administered as a district operation) shall notify the player agent, and the player in writing. Such written notice of release shall be given in sufficient time for the player to qualify for tryouts and selection to another team.

   Minor League and Tee Ball: If a team manager loses any players on the roster during the current season through illness, injury, change of address, or other justifiable reasons (subject to Board approval), another player could be transferred within that Division, through the player agent, to replace the one lost, or a player may be obtained, through the player agent, from a list of participants who registered after the teams were formed.

   NOTE 1: Minor League and Tee Ball players may be reassigned at the discretion of the local league Board of Directors and player agent in order to provide a balanced training program.

   NOTE 2: Minor League and Tee Ball teams must be dissolved at the end of the current season, with all players being returned to a player pool.

REGULATION III — THE TEAMS

(f) *Regular Season, special games, and tournament teams in all divisions of softball must be composed of either: 1. all females, or 2. all males. (Managers and coaches may be of either gender.)*

Regulation IV

The Players

(a) **Little League (Major) Division:** Any candidate with amateur status who will attain the age of 9 years before January 1 and who will not attain the age of 13 before January 1 of the year in question shall be eligible to compete in Little League Softball (subject to the local league Board of Directors alignment of this division). This means that a participant who will be 13 years old on January 1 or later, is eligible to play that year; a participant who will be 13 years old on the previous December 31 or earlier will not be eligible for either local league play or tournament play at any time during the calendar year in question.

NOTE: League age 12-year-olds may participate in Minors Division under certain circumstances.

Minor League Division: Any candidate with amateur status who will attain the age of 7 years before January 1 and who will not attain the age of 13 before January 1 of the year in question shall be eligible to compete in the Minor League Division Softball (subject to the local league Board of Directors alignment of this division). This means that a participant who will be 13 years old on January 1 or later, is eligible to play that year; a participant who will be 13 years old on the previous December 31 or earlier will not be eligible for either local league play or tournament play at any time during the calendar year in question.

Tee Ball Division: Any candidate with amateur status who will attain the age of 4 years before January 1 and who will not attain the age of 8 before January 1 of the year in question shall be eligible to compete in the Tee Ball Division Softball (subject to the local league Board of Directors alignment of this division). This means that a participant who will be 8 years old on January 1 or later, is eligible to play that year; a participant who will be 8 years old on the previous December 31 or earlier will not be eligible at any time during the calendar year in question.

NOTE: If a league elects to operate Tee Ball Softball program only; it must use the determination date noted above.

Junior League: Any candidate with amateur status who will attain the age of 13 years before January 1 and who will not attain the age of 15 years before January 1 of the year in question shall be eligible to compete. This means that a participant who will be 15 years old on January 1 or later is eligible to play that year; a participant who will be 15 years old on the previous December 31 or earlier will not be eligible for either local league or tournament play in the Junior League at any time during the calendar year in question.

Exception:

A 12-year-old player who is otherwise eligible under all conditions would be eligible for selection to either the Major League or Junior League Division tournament team. However, a local Little League's Board of Directors could decide that players league age 12 in the league will not try out for the Junior League Division, and will be eligible for only the Little League ("Major") Division/Minor League Division.

A player may be selected to participate in one or more regular season games on a Major League team and/or a Junior League team. If a player participates in sixty (60) percent of the Regular Season games in each division as of June 15, he/she

REGULATION IV — THE PLAYERS

will be eligible to participate in either the Major Division or Junior Division for tournament play.

If a player only participates in sixty (60) percent of the Regular Season games in one division (Majors or Junior League) as of June 15, he/she is only eligible to participate with that particular division in tournament play.

A player may only be selected to and participate on one (1) tournament team.

Any player who is league age 12 must be permitted to play in the Major Division. The local league cannot force any player who is league age 12 to play in the Junior League Division.

Senior League: Any candidate with amateur status who will attain the age of 13 years before January 1 and who will not attain the age of 17 years before January 1 of the year in question shall be eligible to compete. This means that a participant who will be 17 years old on January 1 or later is eligible to play that year; a participant who will be 17 years old on the previous December 31 or earlier will not be eligible for either local league or tournament play in the Senior League at any time during the calendar year in question.

Big League: Any candidate with amateur status who will attain the age of 14 years before January 1 and who will not attain the age of 19 years before January 1 of the year in question shall be eligible to compete. This means that a participant who will be 19 years old on January 1 or later is eligible to play that year; a participant who will be 19 years old on the previous December 31 or earlier will not be eligible for either local league or tournament play in the Big League at any time during the calendar year in question.

NOTE: All Divisions - The Little League group accident insurance program underwritten by an AIG member company covers only those activities approved or sanctioned by Little League Baseball, Incorporated.

A unit Little League (Majors), Minor League, Tee Ball, Junior, Senior or Big League team shall not participate as a Little League (Majors), Minor League, Tee Ball, Junior, Senior, or Big League team in games with other teams of other programs or in tournaments except those authorized by Little League International.

Little League (Majors), Minor League, Tee Ball, Junior, Senior, and Big League participants may participate in other programs during the Little League (Majors), Minor League, Tee Ball, Junior, Senior, and Big League regular season, provided such participation does not disrupt the Little League (Majors), Minor League, Tee Ball, Junior, Senior, or Big League season.

NOTE 1: See Tournament Rules, ("Player Participation in Other Programs"), regarding participation in non-Little League programs during the International Tournament ("All-Stars").

NOTE 2: Consistent with a manager's ability to conduct the affairs of his or her team, a manager may remove a player from the team, subject to Board of Directors approval, for the current season if the player repeatedly misses practice or games. If a player is repeatedly missing practices or games, the manager must make the local league Board of Directors aware of the situation immediately.

(b) Each candidate must present acceptable proof of age to the league president (or District Administrator, if the Senior/Big League is administered as a district operation) at least 48 hours before the player selection plan is put into operation. When and if such formal proof of age is not available, the league president (or District Administrator, if the Senior/Big League is administered as a district operation) shall

REGULATION IV — THE PLAYERS

gather as much documentary evidence as possible and promptly forward it to the District Administrator. If, in the opinion of the District Administrator, such evidence is satisfactory, a statement to that effect will be sent to the league president which shall be acceptable in lieu of a birth certificate. Such statement will be held in the local Little League files (or district files, if the Senior/Big League is administered as a district operation) as acceptable proof-of-age.

(c) The president of the local league (or District Administrator, if the Senior/Big League is administered as a district operation) MUST certify and be responsible for the eligibility of each candidate previous to player selection. **NOTE 1:** At the time of registration, a player must designate whether he or she will try out for baseball or softball. No player may be on the roster of more than one team or league in the Little League program. **NOTE 2:** Except as noted in Regulation IV(a).

(d) The "League Age" of each candidate shall be recorded and announced at the player selection to guide the managers in making their selections.

(e) "League Age" is that age attained prior to January 1 in any given season. Thus, a participant whose 12th birthday is on the previous December 31 or earlier has a League Age of 12; a participant whose 12th birthday is on January 1 or later has a League Age of 11. This principle applies regardless of age.

(f) **Little League (Major) Division/Junior/Senior/Big League:** Any candidate failing to attend at least 50 percent of the spring tryout sessions, shall forfeit league eligibility unless an excuse is presented which is accepted by a majority of the Board of Directors. **Minor League and Tee Ball:** Any eligible player who qualifies and becomes available after player assignment should be assigned to a team or placed on a waiting list created by the local league.
NOTE: A local league should accept registrations until the time of player selections. Thereafter, registration may be closed.

(g) Player, manager, and coach data must be supplied to Little League International annually. Leagues may submit information from registration by April 1, 2016. Players claimed under Regulation II(d) and/or IV(h) must be declared on appropriate forms available from Little League International annually. It is highly recommended that data be supplied electronically in approved formats to Little League International via the Little League Data Center. Look for related information online at LittleLeague.org/DataCenter.

(h) **If a person had previously resided within the league boundaries for two or more years while serving that league as a dedicated manager, coach, or member of the local league Board of Directors for two or more years, his or her sons and/or daughters are eligible to try out and be selected by teams in that league (1) provided such service to the league from which the person has moved has continued, (2) subject to written agreement from the league within whose boundaries they currently reside and (3) approved by the District Administrator.**

Regulation IV(h) – Processing Procedure
The league president will process a IV(h) form. Once the president completes the form, he/she must compile "residency requirement" verification that each participant meets the conditions of IV(h) as outlined above. The league president will present this information to the District Administrator for review. Once the

REGULATION IV — THE PLAYERS

District Administrator reviews the documentation in an effort to determine if it meets the regulations, the District Administrator will sign the IV(h) form. The league and the district will maintain the form and documentation in their files. This review process is only required once during a participant's career. The league must maintain this form and documentation for this player for the duration of his/her career until the player graduates from the program or breaks service with the league. Tournament team players will be required to carry a copy of this form and documentation with them throughout the tournament. If contested during tournament play, the league will be required to produce the documentation. Additionally, if it is determined at a later date that the player does not meet the conditions of IV(h), the player is ineligible for further participation. Situations in which documentation is not available must be referred to the Charter Committee through the regional office for a decision. The decision of the Charter Committee is final and binding.

(i) Mandatory Play: Every rostered player present at the start of a game will participate in each game for a minimum of six (6) defensive outs and bat at least one (1) time. For the purposes of this rule, "six (6) defensive outs" is defined as: A player enters the field in one of the nine defensive positions when his/her team is on defense and occupies such position while six outs are made; "bat at least one (1) time" is defined as: A player enters the batter's box with no count and completes that time at bat by being retired or by reaching base safely.

PENALTY: The player(s) involved shall start the next scheduled game, play any previous requirement not completed for Section (i), and the requirement for this game before being removed.

The manager shall for the:

    A.   First Offense - receive a written warning.
    B.   Second Offense - a suspension for the next scheduled game.
    C.   Third Offense - a suspension for remainder of the season.

NOTE 1: If the violation is determined to have been intentional, a more severe penalty may be assessed by the Board of Directors. However, forfeiture of a game may not be invoked.

NOTE 2: There is no exception to this rule unless the game is shortened for any reason, at which time the local league may elect not to impose a penalty on the manager/coach. However, the penalty in this regulation regarding the player who did not meet mandatory play cannot be reduced or waived in a shortened game.

NOTE 3: In Minor League, if a half-inning ends because of the imposition of the five-run limit in "Rule 2.00 - Inning," and a player on the defense has played for the entire half-inning, that player will be considered to have participated for three consecutive outs for the purposes of this rule. However, if the player has not played on defense for the entire inning, that player will be credited only as having played for the number of outs that occurred while the player was used defensively.

Big League: Mandatory play does not apply. **NOTE:** Players must meet requirements as outlined in "Tournament Player Eligibility" to be eligible for selection to a Big League tournament (all-star) team.

Minor League and Tee Ball: If a league uses 15 to 20 player rosters they may reduce the Mandatory Play Rule to three (3) defensive outs and one (1) at bat per game.

> A.R.— If a player/batter is called out by an umpire for using an illegal bat or for Rule 6.07 violation, this will qualify as an at bat for the purpose of this rule.

(j) Any request for a waiver pertaining to the eligibility of a player, team, manager, or coach must be submitted in writing, by the president of the local Little League through the District Administrator, to their respective Regional Director not later than June 1 of the current year. Requests submitted after that date will not be considered.

AGE ALIGNMENT FOR JUNIOR LEAGUE, SENIOR LEAGUE AND BIG LEAGUE

The Junior League, Senior League, and Big League Softball age structure allows greater flexibility in these divisions and is intended to increase participation.

The objectives are: 1. to allow leagues with enough personnel to have a two-year age structure, while smaller leagues could retain a three-year structure for Senior League and/or Big League, and; 2. to aid in the retention of players in all age groups, particularly 13 and 16 year olds.

Under the new structure, Big League Softball will be available to 14, 15, 16, 17, and 18 year olds. However, with the 14- to 16-year-olds being the "swing" ages, a league COULD structure its program several ways.

The table below gives each of the possible combinations allowable under the new regulations.

	Junior League	Senior League	Big League
League A	13, 14	15, 16	17, 18
League B	13, 14	14, 15, 16	17, 18
League C	13, 14	14, 15, 16	16, 17, 18
League D	13, 14	14, 15	16, 17, 18
League E	13, 14	15, 16	16, 17, 18
League F	13	14, 15, 16	16, 17, 18
League G	13	14, 15, 16	17, 18
League H	13	14, 15	16, 17, 18
League I	13	13, 14, 15, 16	15, 16, 17, 18
League J	13		14, 15, 16, 17, 18

NOTE 1: Players league age 12 are eligible for the Junior League division at the option of the local league Board of Directors. Regulation IV(a).

The structure for Tournament Play is: 9- and 10-Year-Old Division (9 and 10); 10- and 11-Year-Old Division (10 and 11); Little League Division (11 and 12); Junior League Division (12, 13, and14); Senior League Division (13, 14, 15, and 16); Big League Division (14, 15, 16, 17, and 18).

NOTE 2: Little League International requires each local league to assess and evaluate the participants in its player pool prior to structuring their Junior, Senior, and Big League programs.

Regulation V
Selection of Players

(a) The selection of players for the various teams within a league shall be in compliance with the Little League Draft Selection System as detailed in the Operating Policies section in the back of this book. **NOTE:** All candidates who are league age twelve (12) must be drafted to a Major Division team and/or to a Junior League team. Exceptions can only be made with written approval from the ***District Administrator***, and only if approved at the local league level by the Board of Directors and the parent of the candidate.

(b) When a league decides to substitute a selection system for the ones outlined in the Little League Operating Policies section, a complete description of such substituted system MUST BE PRESENTED in writing FOR APPROVAL when applying for a charter.

(c) **Alternate method of operation**
To aid leagues that are having a difficult time getting enough players for their regular season teams the following option is available: A pool of players from existing regular season teams can be created with players that are willing to participate in extra games during the regular season when teams face a shortage of rostered players for a regular season game within their respective division.
NOTE: Players may not be "borrowed" from an opponent. They must be assigned by the Player Agent.
Guidelines:
1. The league's Player Agent will create and run the pool. The league's Player Agent will use the pool to assign players within their respective division to teams that are short of players on a rotating basis.
2. Managers and/or coaches will not have the right to randomly pick and choose players from the pool within their respective division.
3. Under this option, when a player participates in a game on a team other than his/her own team, such player will not be permitted to pitch in that game.
4. Pool players that are called and show up at the game site must play at least nine consecutive defensive outs and bat once.

(d) Teams are not permitted to enter the Little League program intact, or nearly intact, from non-Little League programs. Under no circumstances will any team or group of players, which did not play on the same team for the previous regular season in the same division of a chartered local Little League, be placed together onto a regular season team in that local Little League. Such players must be processed through the Little League Draft Selection System as noted in this regulation.

Regulation VI

Pitchers

(a) Any player on the team roster may pitch. **EXCEPTION**: A player who has attained a league age of twelve (12) is not eligible to pitch in the Minor League.

(b) **Minors/Little League (Majors):** A player may pitch in a maximum of twelve (12) innings in a day. If a player pitches in seven (7) or more innings in a day, one calendar day of rest is mandatory. Delivery of a single pitch constitutes having pitched in an inning.

LITTLE LEAGUE (MAJORS) AND MINOR LEAGUE EXAMPLE

If a player pitched in seven (7) or more innings on (Column A), that player can pitch again on (Column B):

Column A	Column B
Sunday	Tuesday
Monday	Wednesday
Tuesday	Thursday
Wednesday	Friday
Thursday	Saturday
Friday	Sunday
Saturday	Monday

Junior/Senior/Big League: No pitching restrictions apply.
NOTE: The local league Board of Directors or District may impose additional pitching limitations during the Regular Season and interleague.

Pitching Restrictions for 12 year olds participating in Majors and Junior League

For a 12-year-old participating in the Major and Junior League Divisions as permitted under Regulation IV(a), the pitching rules and regulations regarding days of rest that are pertinent to the division in which the pitcher is used will apply to that game. Innings pitched previously in both divisions are taken into account when determining the eligibility of the pitcher for a particular game, with respect to days of rest and number of innings available.

Example 1 – A player pitches seven innings in a Junior Division game on Sunday. On Monday, she has a scheduled game in the Major Division. She would not be eligible to pitch in that game because the Major Division regulations require her to have one calendar day of rest, as a result of pitching in more than six innings on the previous day.

Example 2 – A player pitches nine innings in a Major Division game on Sunday. On Monday, she has a scheduled game in the Junior Division, and she would be eligible to pitch in that game because the Junior Division has no pitching restrictions.

Example 3 – A player pitches in seven innings in a Junior Division game played on Sunday and has a Major Division game later that same day. The player would be limited to five more innings for the Major Division game (for a total of 12 innings in a day in the Major Division).

REGULATION VI — PITCHERS

(c) A pitcher remaining in the game, but moving to a different position, can return as a pitcher anytime in the remainder of the game but only once in the same inning as he/she was removed. A pitcher, withdrawn from the game offensively or defensively for a substitute, may not re-enter the game as a pitcher. Exception: See Rule 3.03(c).

(d) **Little League (Major) Division/Junior/Senior/Big League:** Not more than five (5) pitchers per team shall be used in one game.
EXCEPTION: In case of illness or injury to a fifth pitcher, an additional pitcher may be used.

(e) Violation of any section of this regulation can result in protest of the game in which it occurs. Protest shall be made in accordance with Playing Rule 4.19.

NOTES:
1. The withdrawal of an ineligible pitcher after that pitcher is announced, or after a warm-up pitch is delivered, but before that player has pitched a ball to a batter, shall not be considered a violation. Little League officials are urged to take precautions to prevent protests. When a protest situation is imminent, the potential offender should be notified immediately.
2. Innings pitched in games declared "Regulation Tie Games" or "Suspended Games" shall be charged against pitcher's eligibility. **NOTE 1:** In suspended games resumed on a subsequent day, the pitchers of record at the time the game was halted may continue to pitch to the extent of their remaining eligibility for that day.
3. **Minors/Little League (Majors):** If doubleheaders are played, the limitation of twelve (12) innings in a calendar day would apply to each pitcher. A pitcher who pitches in the first game may pitch in the second game provided that pitcher has eligibility remaining.
4. There is no limit to the number of pitchers of a particular league age group on a team that can be used.
EXCEPTION: A player who has attained a league age of twelve (12) is not eligible to pitch in the Minor League.

REGULATION VII — SCHEDULES

Regulation VII

Schedules

(a) The schedule of games for the regular season shall be prepared by the Board of Directors of the league (or district, if the Senior/Big League is administered as a district operation) and must provide for not less than twelve (12) games per team per regular season against other Little League teams within their respective division, exclusive of playoff and tournament games. **Tee Ball:** It is recommended that no more than twelve (12) games be scheduled per team per season.

(b) The schedule should provide for not less than two (2) games per week per team. Any facility used for practices and/or games must be approved by the local league Board of Directors. **Junior League**: Interleague play is permitted provided the proper form is submitted to the District Administrator for approval. **Senior/Big League**: Interleague play is permitted within the district.

(c) Where there are two (2) or more leagues in one locality, teams of one league shall not play teams of another league, without approval of the District Administrator, and Regional Director, when necessary as noted in Regulation I(c)(5).

(d) **Minors/Little League (Majors)**: A team may play two (2) doubleheaders in a seven (7)-day period. No team shall play three games in a day. (Exception under condition of Rule 4.12.)
Tee Ball: No team shall be scheduled to play two games in one day. (See Rule 4.12.)
Junior/Senior/Big League: A team may play three (3) games in a day.
If two games involving four teams are played on the same day and on the same field, the first game must be completed before the second game starts. (Exception under condition of Rule 4.12.)

(e) When league size and limited field availability require leagues to schedule more than one game on the same night and on the same field, the league may be permitted to impose time limits on the games. However, the game must meet the requirements of Rule 4.10 or 4.11 to be official.

(f) The schedule shall be arranged so that at least one-half of the games are scheduled prior to June 15.

(g) **Little League (Major)/Junior/Senior/Big League Division:** It is recommended that a split season schedule be arranged with a playoff between the winners of the first and second halves to determine the league champion.

(h) All play must be terminated by the opening date of school for the fall term but no later than September 1st unless participating in the Training and Development Program.

(i) **Little League (Major) Division:** There should be no time limits on games unless necessary, based on field limitations. [See Regulation X(c)].

(j) **Minor League and Tee Ball:** A local league may impose a time limit on games regardless of the number of innings played. It is recommended that no league standings be kept, and no championship games be played.

(k) When approval is granted for two or more leagues - comprising not more than 40,000 population - to form one Junior League, as provided for in Regulation I(h), one regular

REGULATION VII — SCHEDULES

season schedule will be prepared by a joint committee from the two or more leagues.

(l) *Girls softball teams shall not play in games against boys softball teams.*

Regulation VIII

Minor Leagues

(Does not apply to Junior/Senior/Big League.)

(a) The purpose of the Minor League program is to provide training and instruction for those candidates who by reason of age and other factors do not qualify for selection in the regular Little League.
NOTE: League age 12-year-olds may participate under certain circumstances.

(b) The Minor League program is the responsibility and is an integral part of the chartered Little League. It is not and may not be operated as a separate entity. It must be restricted to the boundaries of the local league and its players are subject to selection by draft by any Little League (Majors) Team of the local league. Refusal of a player to comply shall result in forfeiture of further eligibility in the Little League (Major) Division for the current season.
NOTE: The local league should establish a policy, approved by the Board of Directors, regarding players who decline to move up to a Major League team. Such policy should be distributed at the time of registration and/or tryouts.

(c) No player or team may be deemed to be the property of, or under the jurisdiction or control of, a particular team in the local league.

(d) A local league may elect to utilize adult pitch ("Minor League Coach Pitch") or Machine Pitch ("Minor League Machine Pitch") in Minor League games involving players league ages 7-12. Pitching machines, if used, must be in good working order and must be operated by adult managers, coaches, umpires, or any adult approved by the local league.
NOTE: Participants league age 5 and 6 are permitted to advance to Minor League Coach Pitch or Machine Pitch after participation in Tee Ball for one year.

Regulation IX
Special Games

(a) Special Games are defined as games that:
1. are non-regular season games, and,
2. are not Little League International Tournament games, and,
3. involve only teams from chartered Little League programs, and,
4. have been approved in writing by the regional office.

Exception: Junior League: Up to six (6) games played under Special Games against Little League teams may count towards players' Regular Season schedule. **Senior/Big League:** Up to twelve (12) games played under Special Games against Little League teams may count towards players' Regular Season schedule.

(b) Unless expressly authorized under conditions of this Regulation, games played for any purpose other than to establish a league champion (or district champion, if the Senior/Big League is administered as a district operation) or as part of the International Tournament are prohibited. Violation may result in revocation of charter and/or suspension of tournament privileges.

(c) With the approval of the Charter Committee of Little League International, and on recommendation of the Regional Director and District Administrator, chartered leagues may engage in Special Games during and after the regular season but prior to the opening of the school term or September 1st, whichever comes sooner.

(d) Special Games may be played between:
1. Regular season teams or;
2. Tournament teams using either regular season or tournament rules, but not in combination.

(e) Teams participating in Special Games during the regular season shall be regular season teams only. Tournament teams, regular season teams, and Minor League teams involving players below league age 11 may use 9- and 10-Year-Old Division Tournament rules.

(f) **Tournament teams may participate in Special Games after June 15 or two weeks prior to the start of tournament within their respective division, whichever is earlier.**

(g) The league president will be charged with responsibility for conducting special games under all rules, regulations, and policies of Little League Softball.

(h) This rule does not prohibit pre-season practice games between teams in the same division in the same league or the practicing of the league's tournament team against other players in the same division in the same league, provided such practice is done out of uniform.

(i) **Tee Ball:** Special Games are permissible only with regular season teams. However, they are not recommended by Little League International. "All Stars" are not authorized.

Regulation X
Night Games

(a) **Little League (Major) Division, Minor League, Tee Ball, Junior, Senior, and Big League** games may be played after sundown under artificial lights. This responsibility shall rest with the local leagues. In any event, no inning shall start after 10:00 p.m. prevailing time (9:00 p.m. for **Tee Ball**). **Junior League and Senior League:** No inning shall start after 10:30 p.m. prevailing time. **Big League:** No inning shall start after 11:00 p.m. prevailing time. It will be held that an inning starts the moment that the third out is made, completing the preceding inning.

(b) Artificial lights for Little League games must meet the minimum standards approved by Little League International. (See LittleLeague.org/LightingStandards for more information and standards.)

(c) When league size and limited field availability require leagues to schedule more than one game on the same day or night and on the same field, the league may be permitted to impose time limits on the games. However, the game must meet requirements of Rule 4.10 or 4.11 to be official.

Regulation XI

Admission to Games

No admission shall be charged to any Little League (Major) Division, Minor League, or Tee Ball game. Voluntary contributions are permitted.

Junior/Senior/Big League: Admission charge is permitted.

Regulation XII

Awards

(a) Value of awards and material gifts to individual players must be in accordance with the prevailing rules of the High School Athletic Association of the state in which the player participates.

(b) No awards shall be made to players on the basis of comparable skills or accomplishments.
NOTE: Honor certificates, team pictures, inexpensive medals, or pins give adequate recognition and provide lasting mementos from Little League.

REGULATION XIII — COMMERCIALIZATION

Regulation XIII

Commercialization

(a) Exploitation of Little League in any form or for any purpose is prohibited.

(b) Solicitation for fundraising by Little League (Major) Division, Minor League, Tee Ball, Junior, Senior, or Big League players in or out of uniform is prohibited, except for one fund raising project annually under adult supervision. **NOTE:** Reference fundraising guidelines in the Operating Policies section.

(c) A reasonable Little League participation fee may be assessed as a parent's obligation to assure the operational continuity of the local Little League. ***AT NO TIME SHOULD PAYMENT OF ANY FEE BE A PREREQUISITE FOR PARTICIPATION IN THE LITTLE LEAGUE PROGRAM.*** It is recommended that no fee be collected. It is recommended that parents who are unable to pay a participation fee be encouraged to contribute volunteer time to the league.

(d) No Little League volunteer, employee, or participant, while acting in such capacity, shall execute a contract for or otherwise agree to, accept compensation, personal or otherwise, or remuneration for the use of, or for promoting the use of, any product or service.

(e) A local Little League or District shall not require any player to use any specific brand/manufacturer of equipment, for the purpose of the league receiving compensation (including deferred compensation) for such a requirement. **NOTE:** Little League's policy on amateurism can be found on page 6.

(f) A local Little League may permit a Regular Season Team and/or Tournament Team to include the name of a team sponsor on the uniform, and the local league may receive a fee for such sponsorships, provided the sponsorship does not conflict with any Little League Rule, Regulation, and/or Policy. Such sponsor shall have no authority with regard to the composition or operation of the league, the team, or its manager and/or coaches. No district, league, or team may authorize use of any of the Little League trademarks to any local league sponsor without express written permission of Little League International. In other words, no district, league, or team may permit a local sponsor to use the Marks of Little League International. Please refer to the Little League Operating Policies for detailed guidelines. **NOTE:** Once a Tournament Team plays its first game in the International Tournament, a reference to a company, product, or service (including, but not limited to, a slogan or logo) shall not be added to, included on, or appear on any Tournament Team uniform, apparel, or equipment.

(g) Violation of any part of this regulation shall result in penalties up to and including removal from the Little League program and/or revocation of the league's charter and/or forfeiture of International Tournament game(s).

Regulation XIV
Field Decorum

(a) The actions of players, managers, coaches, umpires, and league officials must be above reproach. Any player, manager, coach, umpire, or league representative who is involved in a verbal or physical altercation, or an incident of unsportsmanlike conduct, at the game site or any other Little League activity, is subject to disciplinary action by the local league Board of Directors (or by the district, if the Senior/Big League is administered as a district operation).

(b) Uniformed players, news photographers, managers, coaches, and umpires only shall be permitted within the confines of the playing field just prior to and during games. Batboys and/or batgirls are not permitted at any level of play. Except for the batter, base-runners, and base coaches at first and third bases, all players shall be on their benches in their dugouts or in the bullpen when the team is at bat. When the team is on defense, all reserve players shall be on their benches or in the bullpen. **EXCEPTION:** The on-deck position is permitted in **Junior, Senior, and Big League**.

(c) Two (2) adult base coaches are allowed.

(d) A manager or coach shall not leave the bench or dugout except to confer with a player or an umpire and only after receiving permission from an umpire. (**EXCEPTION**: In Minor League and Tee Ball, managers and coaches may be on the field for instructional purposes, but shall not assist runners or touch a live ball. At least one adult manager or coach must be in the dugout at all times.)

(e) The possession of firearms and/or use of tobacco, cigarettes (including e-cigarettes and vapors), and alcoholic beverages in any form is prohibited on the playing field, benches, or dugouts. Alcohol is prohibited at the game site.

(f) Managers and coaches shall not warm up pitchers.

Regulation XV
Appearance of Little Leaguers in the Media

(a) The appearance of Little League players in uniform in advertisements of any kind, or on commercial television programs, or in motion pictures, without the written approval of Little League International, is forbidden.

(b) Brief, televised reports of games and activities on news programs are permitted.

(c) The televising of regular season games, special games, or International Tournament games on a local or regional basis is permitted, provided a contract (available at LittleLeague.org/GameContracts) is in place, and provided written permission from Little League Baseball, Incorporated has been received to televise the specific game(s) or tournament(s).

(d) Radio broadcasts of regular season games and special games are permitted, provided a "Little League Regular Season Radio Contract" (available at LittleLeague.org/GameContracts) for the specific game(s) is properly completed and on file with the local league.

(e) Radio broadcasts of International Tournament games are permitted, provided a "Little League International Tournament Radio Contract" (available at LittleLeague.org/GameContracts) for the specific game(s) or tournament is properly completed and on file with the district.

(f) Internet web-casts of regular season games and special games are permitted, provided a "Little League Regular Season Internet Web-Cast Contract" (available at LittleLeague.org/GameContracts) for the specific game(s) is properly completed and on file with the local league.

(g) Internet web-casts of International Tournament games are permitted, provided a "Little League International Tournament Internet Web-Cast Contract" (available at LittleLeague.org/GameContracts) for the specific game(s) or tournament is properly completed and on file with the district.

Regulation XVI
Use of Little League Name and Emblem

Use of the Official Emblem "LL," "LLB" and/or words "Little League," "Little League Baseball," "Little Leaguer," "Senior League Little League," "Big League Little League," "Little League Softball," "Little League Challenger Division," etc., (registered under Federal Certificate in U.S. Patent Office), is granted to chartered leagues and cannot be extended by local leagues to any other organization for any purpose whatsoever. These marks are protected both by a special Act of Congress and registrations with the United States Patent and Trademark Office. All rights in and to any and all marks of Little League Baseball, Incorporated are reserved.

Regulation XVII
Tournament Play

This regulation applies to the International Tournament, which includes the 9- and 10-Year-Old Division, the 10- and 11-Year-Old Division, the Little League (Major) Division, Junior League, Senior League, and Big League tournaments.

(a) Tournament team practice or tryouts shall be specified by the Tournament Committee.

(b) The practicing of the league's tournament team against other players in the same division in the same league is permitted providing such practice is done out of uniform.

(c) Tournament rules are published herein.

(d) Unless officially notified to the contrary, each league shall assume full responsibility for expenses incurred in tournament competition.

(e) The structure for tournament play in softball will be: 9- and 10-Year-Old Division; 10- and 11-Year-Old Division; Major Division (11 and 12); Junior Division (12, 13, and 14); Senior Division (13, 14, 15, and 16); and Big League Division (14, 15, 16, 17, and 18).

RULE 1.00 — OBJECTIVES OF THE GAME

Official Playing Rules
LITTLE LEAGUE SOFTBALL® (MAJOR) DIVISION, MINOR LEAGUE SOFTBALL, TEE BALL SOFTBALL, JUNIOR LEAGUE SOFTBALL, SENIOR LEAGUE SOFTBALL, AND BIG LEAGUE SOFTBALL

An Approved Ruling (A.R.) serves to illustrate the application of the regulations and rules. Approved Rulings follow the regulations and rules they amplify and are indicated by a box.

Rule 1.00

Objectives of the Game

1.01 - Little League Softball (Major) Division, Junior League Softball, Senior League Softball, and Big League Softball is a game between two teams of 9 players each under direction of a manager and not more than two rostered coaches, played on a regulation Little League field in accordance with these rules, under the jurisdiction of one or more umpires. **Tee Ball/Minor League Instructional Division is a game between two teams, under the direction of a manager and not more than two coaches, played on a regulation Little League field in accordance with these rules, under the jurisdiction of one or more umpires. NOTE: Competitive Minor Leagues and above may only use nine players on defense. See Rules 4.16 and 4.17.**

1.02 - The objective of each team is to win by scoring more runs than the opponent. (**Tee Ball:** It is recommended that no score be kept.)

1.03 - The winner of the game shall be that team which shall have scored, in accordance with these rules, the greater number of runs at the conclusion of a regulation game.

1.04 - THE PLAYING FIELD. The field shall be laid out according to the instructions, supplemented by Diagrams No. 1 and No. 2.

The infield shall be a 60-foot square. (**Tee Ball option:** The infield may be a 50-foot square.)

The outfield shall be the area between two foul lines formed by extending two sides of the square, as in Diagram 1. The distance from home base to the nearest fence, stand or other obstruction in fair territory should be 200 feet or more. A distance of 200 feet or more along the foul lines, and to center field is recommended. ==The outfield fence must be a minimum of 180 feet and a maximum of 225 feet from homeplate.== The infield shall be graded so that the base lines and home plate are level.

The pitcher's plate shall be level with the ground. The infield and outfield, including the boundary lines, are fair territory and all other area is foul territory.

It is desirable that the line from home base through the pitcher's plate to second base shall run east-northeast.

It is recommended that the distance from home base to the backstop, and from the base lines to the nearest fence, stand, or other obstruction in foul territory should be 25 feet or more (see Diagram 1).

When the location of home base is determined, with a steel tape measure 84 feet, 10 inches in the desired direction to establish second base. From home base, measure 60 feet towards first base; from second base, measure 60 feet towards first base, the intersection

RULE 1.00 — OBJECTIVES OF THE GAME

of these lines establishes first base. From home base, measure 60 feet towards third base; from second base, measure 60 feet towards third base; the intersection of these lines establishes third base. The distance between first base and third base is 84 feet, 10 inches. All measurements from home base shall be taken from the point where the first and third base lines intersect.

The catcher's box, the batter's boxes, the coach's boxes, and the three-foot runner's lane shall be laid out as shown in Diagrams 1 and 2.

The catcher's box extends approximately 6 feet 4-3/8 inches to the rear of home plate. It is determined by extending each foul line 9 feet beyond the back point of home plate. **Junior/Senior/Big League:** The catcher's box shall be 10 feet in length from the rear outside corners of the batter's boxes and shall be 8 feet, 5 inches wide.

The batter's box shall be rectangular 7 feet by 3 feet. The inside line, if used, shall be parallel to and 4 inches (6 inches for **Junior/Senior/Big League**) away from the side of home plate. It shall extend forward from the center of home plate 4 feet and to the rear 3 feet.

The coach's boxes shall be 4 feet by 8 feet and shall not be closer than 6 feet from the foul lines.

The foul lines and all other playing lines indicated in the diagrams by solid black lines shall be marked with chalk or other white material. Caustic lime must not be used.

The grass and skinned dimensions shown on the diagrams are those used in many fields but they are not mandatory. Each league shall determine the size and shape of the grassed and skinned areas of its playing field.

1.05 - Home base shall be marked by a five-sided slab of whitened rubber. It shall be a 17-inch square with two of the corners filled in so that one edge is 17 inches long, two 8½ inches and two are 12 inches. It shall be set in the ground with the point at the intersection of the lines extending from home base to first base and to third base; with the 17 inch edge facing the pitcher's plate and the two 12-inch edges coinciding with the first and third base lines. The top edges of home base shall be beveled and the base shall be fixed in the ground level with the ground surface. The black beveled edge is not considered part of home plate.

1.06 - First, second, and third bases shall be marked by white canvas or rubber covered bags, securely attached to the ground. The first and third base bags shall be entirely within the infield. The second base bag shall be centered on second base. The base bags shall not be less than fourteen (14) nor more than fifteen (15) inches square and the outer edges shall not be more than two and one-fourth (2¼) inches thick and filled with a soft material. **Leagues are required to ensure that first, second, and third bases will disengage their anchor.**

NOTE 1: If a base is dislodged from its position during a play, any following runner on the same play shall be considered as touching or occupying the base if, in the umpire's judgment, that runner touches or occupies the dislodged bag or the point marked by the original location of the dislodged bag.

NOTE 2: Use of the "Double First Base" is permissible at all levels of play. See Rule 7.15.

1.07 - The pitcher's plate shall be a rectangular slab of whitened rubber 24 inches by 6 inches. It shall be set in the ground as shown in Diagrams 1 and 2, so that the distance between the front side of the pitcher's plate and home base (the rear point of home plate)

RULE 1.00 — OBJECTIVES OF THE GAME

shall be — (1) **Minor League**: 35 feet; (2) **Little League (Majors):** 40 feet; and (3) **Junior/Senior/Big League**: 43 feet.

Diagram No. 1

Diagram showing Tee Ball/Minor League/Little League/Junior/Senior/Big League Softball field layout.

All dimensions are compulsory unless marked "optional" or "recommended."

NOTE 1: The eight-foot (8') radius circle is to be properly marked — measured from the center of the front side of the pitcher's plate.

NOTE 2: Tee Ball base paths may be 50 feet.

NOTE 3: Minor League pitching distance is 35 feet.

NOTE 4: Junior, Senior League, and Big League pitching distance is 43 feet.

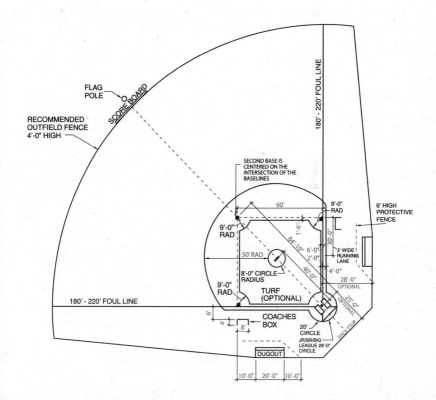

NOTE: A "skinned" infield is recommended.

RULE 1.00 — OBJECTIVES OF THE GAME

Diagram No. 2

Diagram showing layout of batter's box and compulsory dimensions.

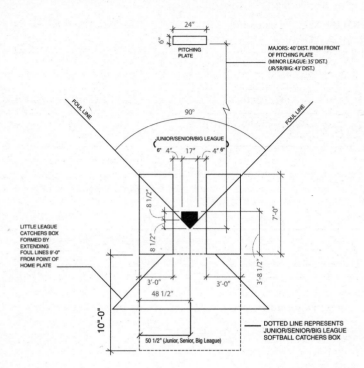

Diagram No. 3

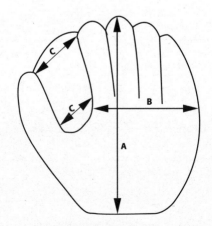

See Rule 1.13 and 1.14

RULE 1.00 — OBJECTIVES OF THE GAME

1.08 - The league shall furnish players' benches, one each for the home and visiting teams. Such benches should be not less than 25 feet from the base lines. They shall be protected by wire fencing.

NOTE 1: The on-deck position is not permitted in **Tee Ball, Minor League, or Little League (Major) Division**.

> A.R.—Fenced-in areas MAY NOT be used for an on-deck batter.

NOTE 2: Only the first batter of each half-inning will be permitted outside the dugout between half-innings in **Tee Ball, Minor League, or Little League (Major) Division**.

> A.R.—The next batter should be ready with a helmet on, but may not pick up a bat until it is his/her turn at bat.

1.09 - The softball used must meet Little League specifications and standards. The ball shall be not less than 11–7/8" nor more than 12-1/8" in circumference and shall weigh not less than 6¼ ounces nor more than 7 ounces. **Tee Ball/Minor League:** The ball shall be not less than 10-7/8" nor more than 11-1/8" in circumference and shall weigh not less than 5½ ounces nor more than 6 ounces.

> A.R.—Optic yellow, white or other colors of softballs are legal for use during regular season and tournament.

1.10 - The bat must be a softball bat which meets Little League specifications and standards as noted in this rule. It shall be a smooth, rounded stick and made of wood or a material tested and proved acceptable to Little League standards. The bat shall be no more than 33 inches (34 inches for **Junior/Senior/Big League**) in length, not more than two and one-quarter (2¼) inches in diameter, and if wood, not less than fifteen-sixteenth (15/16) inches in diameter (7/8 inch for bats less than 30 inches) at its smallest part. Non-wood bats shall be printed with a BPF (bat performance factor) of 1.20. Bats may be taped or fitted with a sleeve for a distance not exceeding 16 inches from the small end. Colored bats are acceptable. A non-wood bat must have a grip of cork, tape, or composition material, and must extend a minimum of 10 inches from the small end. Slippery tape or similar material is prohibited. **An illegal or altered bat must be removed. Penalty** – See Rule 6.06(d).

> A.R.—If the specification mark(s) on a bat are not legible, that bat cannot be used and shall be removed from the game.

NOTE 1: The traditional batting donut is not permissible.

NOTE 2: The bat may carry the mark "Little League Tee Ball."

NOTE 3: Non-wood bats may develop dents from time to time. Bats that have cracks or sharp edges, or cannot pass through the approved Little League bat ring must be removed from play. The 2¼ inch bat ring must be used for bats in all softball divisions. Any bat that has been altered shall be removed from play.

RULE 1.00 — OBJECTIVES OF THE GAME

1.11 -

(a) (1) All players on a team shall wear numbered uniforms identical in color, trim, and style. The wearing of hats or visors is optional for each player while on defense.

(2) The Little League Official Shoulder Patch must be affixed to the upper left sleeve of the uniform blouse. Patches are worn 3" below the left shoulder seam on raglan sleeve; 1" below the seam on set-in sleeve; over the left breast on sleeveless style.

Patches worn 3" below left shoulder seam on raglan sleeve;

1" below seam on set-in sleeve; over left breast on sleeveless style.

(3) Any part of the pitcher's undershirt or T-shirt exposed to view shall be of a solid color. A pitcher shall not wear any items on his/her hands, wrists, or arms which may be distracting to the batter.

(b) A league must provide each team with a distinctive uniform. Uniforms are the property of the league. **Tee Ball/Minor League:** T-shirts and caps/visors are recommended, but hand-me-down uniforms may be worn.

(c) Sleeve lengths may vary for individual players, but the sleeves of each individual shall be approximately the same length. No player shall wear ragged, frayed, or slit sleeves.

(d) No players shall attach to a uniform tape or other material of a different color than the uniform.

(e) No part of the uniform shall include a pattern that imitates or suggests the shape of a softball.

(f) Glass buttons and polished metal shall not be used on a uniform.

(g) No player shall attach anything to the heel or toe of the shoe other than a toe plate.

(h) Shoes with metal spikes or cleats are not permitted. Shoes with molded cleats are permissible. **Junior/Senior/Big League:** Shoes with metal spikes or cleats are permitted.

> A.R.—**Tee Ball/Minors/Majors:** Removable spikes or cleats are permitted if, when removed, no metal remains exposed.

(i) Managers and coaches must not wear conventional softball uniforms or shoes with metal spikes but may wear cap, slacks, and shirt. **Junior/Senior/Big League:** Managers and coaches may wear conventional softball uniforms or cap, slacks, and shirt. They may not wear shoes with metal spikes.

(j) Players must not wear jewelry such as, but not limited to, rings, watches, earrings, bracelets, necklaces, nor any hard cosmetic/decorative items. This rule applies regardless of the composition of such jewelry, hard cosmetic item, or hard decorative item. (**EXCEPTION:** Jewelry that alerts medical personnel to a specific condition is permissible.)

> A.R.—Managers, coaches, players and umpires may not wear metal items on their uniforms.

(k) Casts may not be worn during the game by players and umpires.
NOTE: Persons wearing casts, including managers and coaches, must remain in the dugout during the game.

1.12 - The catcher must wear a mitt of any shape, size, or weight consistent with protecting the hand. This may be a first baseman's mitt or a fielder's glove.

1.13 - The first baseman must wear a glove or mitt of any weight with the following maximum specifications:
(a) not more than 14 inches long (measured from the bottom edge or heel straight up across the center of the palm to a line even with the highest point of the glove or mitt), and;
(b) not more than eight inches wide across the palm (measured from the bottom edge of the webbing farthest from the thumb in a horizontal line to the outside of the little finger edge of the glove or mitt) and;
(c) webbing not more than 5¾ inches wide (measured across the top end or along any line parallel to the top). See Diagram No. 3.

1.14 - Each defensive player (other than the first baseman and catcher) must wear a glove of any weight, with the same maximum specifications as noted in Rule 1.13.

1.15 -
(a) The pitcher's glove shall be of one solid color other than white, gray, or optic yellow, or if multi-colored, white, gray, or optic yellow shall not be included in the colors. A glove that is judged to be distracting is illegal.

> A.R.—Multi-colored gloves are permitted to be worn by the pitcher which includes the manufacturer's label or the lacing of the glove unless, in the umpire's judgment, these would be distracting to the batter. The umpire can remove a glove from the game if he/she determines the glove is a distraction to the batter.

(b) No pitcher shall attach to the glove any foreign material of a color different from the glove. The pitcher may wear a batting glove on the non-pitching hand under the pitcher's glove provided the batting glove is not white, gray, or optic yellow.
(c) No pitcher shall wear sweat bands on his/her wrists or arms.
(d) A pitcher may not wear a catcher's mitt or first baseman's mitt.

1.16 - Each league shall provide in the dugout or bench of the offensive team six (6) protective helmets (7 protective helmets for **Junior/Senior/Big League**) which must meet NOCSAE (National Operating Committee on Standards for Athletic Equipment) specifications and standards. Use of the helmet by the batter, all base runners, and base

RULE 1.00 — OBJECTIVES OF THE GAME

coaches is mandatory. Use of a helmet by an adult base coach or any defensive player is optional. Helmets must have a non-glare surface and cannot be mirror-like in nature. Each helmet must bear the NOCSAE stamp and shall have an exterior warning label. **Warning!** Manufacturers have advised that altering helmets in any way can be dangerous. Altering the helmet in any form, including painting or adding decals (by anyone other than the manufacturer or authorized dealer) may void the helmet warranty. Helmets may not be re-painted and may not contain tape or re-applied decals unless approved in writing by the helmet manufacturer or authorized dealer.

> A.R.—If a player, during play, removes his/her helmet or causes his/her helmet to come off, he/she shall NOT be called out, but shall be warned not to intentionally remove his/her helmet and, if it continues, the player may be removed for unsportsmanlike conduct, as this can cause an unsafe condition.

1.17 - All male players must wear athletic supporters. Male catchers must wear the metal, fibre, or plastic type cup, and approved long or short-model chest protector. Female catchers must wear long or short model chest protectors. All catchers must wear chest protectors with neck collars, throat guard, shin guards, catcher's helmet, and mask, all of which must meet Little League specifications and standards. The catcher's helmet must meet NOCSAE specifications and standards and bear the NOCSAE stamp. All catchers must wear a mask, "dangling" type throat protector, and catcher's helmet during infield/outfield practice, pitcher warm up, and games. **NOTE:** Skull caps are not permitted. **Warning!** Manufacturers have advised that altering helmets in any way can be dangerous. Altering the helmet in any form, including painting or adding decals (by anyone other than the manufacturer or authorized dealer) may void the helmet warranty. Helmets may not be re-painted and may not contain tape or re-applied decals unless approved in writing by the helmet manufacturer or authorized dealer.

> A.R.—Wearing of a catcher's helmet with mask and dangling throat guard (even if the mask has a wire extension) is required during games, pitcher warm-up and any form of infield or infield/outfield practice. The "Hockey Style" helmet is authorized for use at all levels of play. The "dangling" throat guard still must be attached properly.

Rule 2.00

Definition of Terms

(All definitions in Rule 2.00 are listed alphabetically)

ADJUDGED is a judgment decision by an umpire.

An **APPEAL** is the act of a fielder in claiming a violation of the rules by the offensive team.

An **AT-BAT**, for the purposes of meeting the requirements of Mandatory Play (if applicable), is when a batter assumes the position of a batter with no count and is retired or reaches base. An at-bat for scorekeeping/statistical purposes is defined in the publication, "What's the Score?"

A **BACKSTOP** is the barrier erected behind the catcher in order to allow the catcher to retrieve passed balls easily.

A **BALL** is a pitch which does not enter the strike zone in flight and is not struck at by the batter. (**NOTE:** If the pitch touches the ground and bounces through the strike zone it is a "ball." If such a pitch touches the batter, the batter shall be awarded first base. If the batter swings at such a pitch and misses, it is a strike. If the batter hits such a pitch, the ensuing action shall be the same as if the batter hit the ball in flight.) **Majors/Juniors/Senior/Big League**: If the batter swings at such a pitch after two strikes, the ball cannot be caught for the purposes of Rule 6.05(b)(2) and 6.09(b).

A **BASE** is one of four points which must be touched by a runner in order to score a run; more usually applied to the canvas bags and the rubber plate which mark the base points.

A **BASE COACH** is a team member in uniform or an adult manager and/or coach who is stationed in the base coach's box at first and third base to direct the batter and the runners. **NOTE:** Two (2) adult base coaches are permitted at all levels. The second coach may be age 16 years or older. See Rule 4.05 for restrictions.

A **BASE ON BALLS** is an award of first base granted to batters who during their time at bat received four pitches outside the strike zone.

A **BATTER** is an offensive player who takes a position in the batter's box.

BATTER-RUNNER is a term that identifies the offensive player who has just finished a time at bat until that player is retired or until the play on which that player becomes a runner ends.

The **BATTER'S BOX** is the area within which the batter must stand during a time at bat.

The **BATTERY** is the pitcher and catcher.

The **BATTING ORDER** is the list of current defensive players (and designated hitter in Senior/Big League) in the order in which they are to bat. **Exceptions:** In all divisions, the batting order may contain the entire roster of players. In **Tee Ball and Minor League**, the batting order shall contain the entire roster of players.

BENCH or **DUGOUT** is the seating facilities reserved for players, substitutes, one manager, and not more than two coaches when they are not actively engaged on the playing field. Batboys and/or batgirls are not permitted.

A.R.—Bench or dugout is not for additional coaches or scorekeepers.

RULE 2.00 — DEFINITION OF TERMS

BUNT is a batted ball not swung at but intentionally met with the bat and tapped slowly. Holding the bat in the strike zone is considered an attempted bunt. In order to take a pitch, the batter must withdraw the bat backwards away from the ball. (**Tee Ball**: Bunts are not permitted. Batters are not permitted to take a half-swing. If the umpire feels the batter is taking a half-swing, the batter may be called back to swing again.)

A **CALLED GAME** is one in which, for any reason, the Umpire-in-Chief terminates play.

A **CATCH** is the act of a fielder in getting secure possession in the hand or glove of a ball in flight and firmly holding it before it touches the ground; providing such fielder does not use cap, protector, pocket, or any other part of the uniform in getting possession. It is not a catch however, if simultaneously or immediately following contact with the ball the fielder collides with a player, or with a wall, or if that fielder falls down, and as a result of such collision or falling, drops the ball. It is not a catch if a fielder touches a fly ball which then hits a member of the offensive team or an umpire and then is caught by another defensive player. If the fielder has made the catch and drops the ball while in the act of making a throw following the catch, the ball shall be adjudged to have been caught. In establishing the validity of the catch, the fielder shall hold the ball long enough to prove complete control of the ball and that release of the ball is voluntary and intentional. A catch is legal if the ball is finally held by any fielder, even though juggled, or held by another fielder before it touches the ground. Runners may leave their bases the instant the first fielder touches the ball.

The **CATCHER** is the fielder who takes the position back of the home base.

The **CATCHER'S BOX** is that area within which the catcher shall stand until the pitcher delivers the ball. The lines are considered inside the catcher's box.

A **COACH** is an adult appointed to perform such duties as the manager may designate. **NOTE**: If two (2) coaches are appointed, the second coach may be age 16 years or older.

CROW HOP is defined as the act of a pitcher who steps, drags, or hops off the front of the pitcher's plate, replants the pivot foot, establishing a second starting point, pushes off from the newly established starting point, and completes the delivery. (Illegal Pitch - See Rule 8.05)

A **DEAD BALL** is a ball out of play because of a legally created temporary suspension of play.

The **DEFENSE** (or **DEFENSIVE**) is the team, or any player of the team, in the field.

A **DOUBLE HEADER** is two regularly scheduled or rescheduled games, played by the same team(s) on the same day.

A **DOUBLE PLAY** is a play by the defense in which two offensive players are retired as a result of continuous action, providing there is no error between putouts.

(a) A force double play is one in which both putouts are force plays.

(b) A reverse force double play is one in which the first out is made at any base and the second out is made by tagging a runner who originally was forced, before the runner touches the base to which that runner was forced.

DROPPED BALL is a ball which slips from the pitcher's hand after the pitcher takes a position on the pitcher's plate, or goes directly from the pitcher's hand straight to the ground during the pitcher's motion. This can be while the pitcher is just standing on the pitcher's plate, during the back swing, or up to the delivery of the pitch in the windmill motion. A drop is distinguished from a pitch in that a pitch must have lift and carry past the release of the hip and a drop slips from the hand and/or goes straight and direct to the ground. **Penalty**: See Rule 8.07(a).

DUGOUT (see definition of "BENCH").

A **FAIR BALL** is a batted ball that settles on fair ground between home and first base or between home and third base, or that is on or over fair territory when bounding to the outfield past first or third base or that touches first, second, or third base, or that first falls on fair territory on or beyond first base or third base, or that while in or over fair territory touches the person of an umpire or player, or that, while over fair territory, passes out of the playing field in flight.

NOTE: A fair fly shall be adjudged according to the relative position of the ball and the foul line, including the foul pole, and not as to whether the fielder is in fair or foul territory at the time such fielder touches the ball.

FAIR TERRITORY is that part of the playing field within, and including the first base and third base lines, from home base to the bottom of the playing field fence and perpendicularly upwards. Home plate, first base and third base and all foul lines are in fair territory.

A **FIELDER** is any defensive player.

FIELDER'S CHOICE is the act of a fielder who handles a fair grounder and, instead of throwing it to first base to put out the batter-runner, throws to another base in an attempt to retire a preceding runner. The term is also used by scorers (a) to account for the advance of the batter-runner who takes one or more extra bases when the fielder who handles the safe hit attempts to put out a preceding runner; (b) to account for the advance of a runner (other than by error) while a fielder is attempting to put out another runner; and (c) to account for the advance of a runner made solely because of the defensive team's indifference (undefended steal).

A **FLY BALL** is a batted ball that goes high in the air in flight.

A **FORCE PLAY** is a play in which a runner legally loses the right to occupy a base by reason of the batter becoming a runner. (**NOTE:** Confusion regarding this play is removed by remembering that frequently the "force" situation is removed during the play. **Example**: Runner on first, one out, ground ball hit sharply to first baseman, who touches the base and the batter-runner is out. The force is removed at that moment and runner advancing to second must be tagged. If there had been a runner at second or third, and either of these runners scored before the tag-out at second, the run(s) would count. Had the first baseman thrown to second and the ball had been returned to first, the play at second would have been a force-out, making two outs, and the return throw to first would have made the third out. In that case, no run would score.)

A.R.—Runners forced to advance as a result of the batter-runner being awarded first base

A **FORFEITED GAME** is a game declared ended by the Umpire-in-Chief in favor of the offended team by the score of 6 to 0, (7 to 0 **Junior/Senior/Big League**) for violation of the rules. (**Tee Ball/Instructional Minor League:** There shall be no forfeits.)

A **FOUL BALL** is a batted ball that settles in foul territory between home and first base, or between home and third base or that bounds past first or third base in or over foul territory, or that first falls in foul territory beyond first or third base, or that while in or

RULE 2.00 — DEFINITION OF TERMS

over foul territory, touches the person of an umpire or player, or any object foreign to the natural ground.

NOTE 1: A foul fly shall be adjudged according to the relative position of the ball and the foul line, including the foul pole, and not as to whether the fielder is in foul or fair territory at the time that fielder touches the ball.

NOTE 2: In Tee Ball, the ball is foul if it travels less than 15 feet in fair territory from home plate. The ball is also foul if the batter hits the tee with the bat.

FOUL TERRITORY is that part of the playing field outside the first and third base lines extended to the fence and perpendicularly upwards.

A **FOUL TIP** is a batted ball that goes sharp and direct from the bat to the catcher's hands and is legally caught. It is not a foul tip unless caught and any foul tip that is caught is a strike, and the ball is in play. It is not a catch if it is a rebound, unless the ball has first touched the catcher's glove or hand. A foul tip can only be caught by the catcher.

A **GROUND BALL** is a batted ball that rolls or bounces close to the ground.

The **HOME TEAM** is the team which takes the field first at the start of the game. Adopted schedules will determine which team this will be.

ILLEGAL (or **ILLEGALLY**) is contrary to these rules.

An **ILLEGAL BAT** is a bat that has been altered or a bat that is not approved for play because it does not meet specifications with regard to length, weight, barrel diameter, labeling, or performance standard for the division which it is being used. **Penalty:** See Rule 6.06(d).

An **ILLEGAL PITCH** is (1) a pitch delivered to the batter when the pitcher does not have the pivot foot in contact with the pitcher's plate; (2) when the pitcher delivers the pitch with a foreign substance applied to the ball. Rosin can be applied to the hand; (3) a quick return pitch; or (4) a pitch not made in accordance with the pitching rule. **Penalty**: The pitch shall be called a ball, unless the batter reaches first base safely on a hit, an error, a base on balls, a hit batter, fielder's choice, or otherwise, and all base runners advance at least one base safely, in which case the play stands and the illegal pitch is nullified. **Junior/Senior/Big League:** The pitch shall be called a ball and all base runners advance one base, unless the batter reaches first base safely on a hit, an error, a base on balls, a hit batter, fielder's choice, or otherwise, and all base runners advance at least one base safely, in which case the play stands and the illegal pitch is nullified.

An **ILLEGALLY BATTED BALL** is one hit by the batter with one or both feet on the ground entirely outside the batter's box when contact is made with the ball.

INELIGIBLE PITCHER - Applies to regular season violations of Regulation VI. (See also Rule 4.19.)

INELIGIBLE PLAYER - Applies to regular season violations of regulations regarding league age, residence or school attendance (as defined by Little League International), and participation on the proper team within the local league. (See also Rule 4.19.)

The **INFIELD** is that portion of the field in fair territory, which includes areas normally covered by infielders.

An **INFIELDER** is a fielder who occupies a position in the infield.

An **INFIELD FLY** is a fair fly ball (not including a line drive nor an attempted bunt) which can be caught by an infielder with ordinary effort, when first and second, or first, second and third bases are occupied, before two are out. The pitcher, catcher, and any outfielder stationed in the infield on the play shall be considered infielders for the purpose of this rule.

When it seems apparent that a batted ball will be an Infield Fly the umpire shall immediately declare "Infield Fly," for the benefit of the runners. If the ball is near the baseline, the umpire shall declare "Infield fly, if fair."

The ball is alive and runners may advance at the risk of the ball being caught, or retouch and advance after the ball is touched, the same as on any fly ball. If the hit becomes a foul ball, it is treated the same as any foul.

NOTE 1: If a declared Infield Fly is allowed to fall untouched to the ground, and bounces foul and remains foul before passing first or third base, it is a foul ball. If a declared Infield Fly falls untouched to the ground outside the baseline and bounces fair before passing first or third base, it is an Infield Fly.

NOTE 2: The Infield Fly Rule does not apply in Tee Ball.

> A.R.—The infield dirt and the outfield grass do not form a boundary line for infield fly purposes.

IN FLIGHT describes a batted, thrown or pitched ball which has not yet touched the ground or some object other than a fielder. If the pitch touches the ground and bounces through the strike zone, without being struck at by the batter, it is a "ball". If such a pitch touches the batter, that batter shall be awarded first base. **Majors/Junior/Senior/Big League:** If the batter swings at such a pitch after two strikes, the ball cannot be caught for the purpose of Rule 6.05(b). If the batter hits such a pitch, the ensuing action shall be the same as if the ball was hit in flight.

IN JEOPARDY is a term indicating that the ball is in play and an offensive player may be put out.

An **INNING** is that portion of a game within which the teams alternate on offense and defense and in which there are three put outs for each team. It will be held that an inning starts the moment the third out is made completing the preceding inning. **(Minor League Only — A five-run limit is to be imposed which would complete the half inning.)**

INTERFERENCE

(a) Offensive interference is an act by a member of the team at bat which interferes with, obstructs, impedes, hinders, or confuses any fielder attempting to make a play. If the umpire declares the batter, batter-runner, or a runner out for interference, all other runners shall return to the last base that was, in the judgment of the umpire, legally touched at the time of the interference, unless otherwise provided by these rules.

(b) Defensive interference is an act by a fielder which hinders or prevents a batter from hitting a pitch.

(c) Umpire's interference occurs (1) when an umpire hinders, impedes, or prevents

RULE 2.00 — DEFINITION OF TERMS

a catcher's throw attempting to retire a runner, or (2) when a fair ball touches an umpire in fair territory before passing a fielder.

> A.R.—Only the plate umpire may interfere with the catcher and only on a cleanly caught ball or a pitched ball that doesn't cause the catcher to move from his/her position. If the catcher errs on the ball, the umpire will be considered part of the field, and no interference results.

(d) Spectator interference occurs when a spectator reaches out of the stands or goes on the playing field, and touches a live ball.

(e) On any interference the ball is dead.

The **LEAGUE** is a group of teams who play each other in a pre-arranged schedule under these rules for the league championship.

LEAPING is an act by the pitcher when both feet become airborne on the initial move and push from the pitcher's plate. (Illegal Pitch, See Rule 8.05).

LEGAL or (**LEGALLY**) is in accordance with these rules.

A **LINE DRIVE** is a batted ball that goes sharp and direct from the bat to a fielder without touching the ground.

A **LIVE BALL** is a ball which is in play.

The **MANAGER** is an adult appointed by the president to be responsible for the team's actions on the field, and to represent the team in communications with the umpire and the opposing team.

(a) The manager shall always be responsible for the team's conduct, observance of the official rules. and deference to the umpires.

(b) If a manager leaves the field, that manager shall designate an adult coach as a substitute, and such substitute manager shall have the duties, rights, and responsibilities of the manager. If no adult coach is available, the Umpire-in-Chief shall designate a temporary adult manager. If no adult is available, the game or team activities shall be terminated. (See Rule 4.16)

OBSTRUCTION is the act of a fielder who, while not in possession of the ball, impedes the progress of any runner. A fake tag is considered obstruction. (**NOTE**: Obstruction shall be called on a defensive player who blocks off a base, base line or home plate from a base runner while not in possession of the ball.)

OFFENSE is the team, or any player of the team at bat.

OFFICIAL RULES - The rules contained in this book.

OFFICIAL SCORER - See Rule 10.00 in "What's the Score" publication.

An **OUT** is one of the three required retirements of an offensive team during its time at bat.

The **OUTFIELD** is that portion of the field in fair territory which is normally covered by outfielders.

An **OUTFIELDER** is a fielder who occupies a position in the outfield, which is the area of the playing field most distant from home base.

RULE 2.00 — DEFINITION OF TERMS

OVERSLIDE or (**OVERSLIDING**) is the act of an offensive player when the slide to a base, other than when advancing from home to first base, is with such momentum that the player loses contact with the base.

PENALTY is the application of these rules following an illegal act.

The **PERSON** of a player or an umpire is any part of the body, the clothing, or equipment.

A **PITCH** is a ball delivered to the batter by the pitcher.

A **PITCHER** is the fielder designated to deliver the pitch to the batter.

The pitcher's **PIVOT FOOT** is that foot which is in contact with the pitcher's plate prior to pushing off, as opposed to the non-pivot foot with which the pitcher steps toward home plate.

"**PLAY**" is the umpire's order to start the game or to resume action following any dead ball.

A **QUICK RETURN** is a pitch made with the obvious intent to catch a batter off balance. It is an illegal pitch. (Penalty: See Rule 8.05)

REGULATION GAME - See Rules 4.10 and 4.11.

A **RETOUCH** is the act of a runner returning to a base as legally required.

A **RUN** (or **SCORE**) is the score made by an offensive player who advances from batter to runner and touches first, second, third, and home bases in that order.

A **RUNDOWN** is the act of the defense in an attempt to retire a runner between bases.

A **RUNNER** is an offensive player who is advancing toward, touching, or returning to any base.

"**SAFE**" is a declaration by the umpire that a runner is entitled to the base for which that runner was trying.

A **STRIKE** is a legal pitch which meets any of these conditions -

(a) Is struck at by the batter and is missed;

(b) Is not struck at, if any part of the ball passes through any part of the strike zone;

(c) Is fouled by the batter when there is less than two strikes;

(d) Is bunted foul. (The batter is out and the ball is dead, if the batter bunts foul on the third strike);

(e) Touches the batter's person as the batter strikes at it (dead ball);

(f) Touches the batter in flight in the strike zone; or

(g) Becomes a foul tip. (Ball is live and in play.)

NOTE: In Tee Ball, the local league will determine whether or not strikeouts will be permitted.

The **STRIKE ZONE** is that space over home plate which is between the batter's armpits and the top of the knees when the batter assumes a natural stance. The umpire shall determine the strike zone according to the batter's usual stance when that batter swings at a pitch.

A **SUSPENDED GAME** is a called game which is to be completed at a later date.

RULE 2.00 — DEFINITION OF TERMS

A **TAG** is the action of a fielder in touching a base with the body while holding the ball securely and firmly in the hand or glove; or touching a runner with the ball, or with the hand or glove holding the ball, while holding the ball securely and firmly in the hand or glove.

A **THROW** is the act of propelling the ball with the hand and arm to a given objective and is to be always distinguished from the pitch.

A **TIE GAME** is a regulation game which is called when each team has the same number of runs.

"TIME" is the announcement by the umpire of a legal interruption of play, during which the ball is dead.

To **TOUCH** a player or umpire is to touch any part of the player or umpire's body, clothing, or equipment.

A **TRIPLE PLAY** is a play by the defense in which three offensive players are retired as a result of continuous action, providing there is no error between putouts.

A **WILD PITCH** is one so high, so low, or so wide of the plate that it cannot be handled with ordinary effort by the catcher. The ball is alive and in play. Runners may advance with liability to be put out.

Rule 3.00

Game Preliminaries

3.01 - Before the game begins the umpires shall -
(a) require strict observance of all rules governing team personnel, implements of play, and equipment of players;
(b) be sure that all playing lines (heavy lines in Diagrams No. 1 and No. 2) are marked with non-caustic lime, chalk, or other white material easily distinguishable from the ground and grass;
(c) receive from the league a supply of softballs which meet Little League specifications and standards. The umpire shall be the sole judge of the fitness of the balls to be used in the game;
(d) be assured by the league that additional softballs are immediately available for use if required;
(e) have possession of at least two alternate balls and shall require replenishment of such supply of alternate balls as needed throughout the game. Such alternate balls shall be put in play when -
  (1) a ball has been batted out of the playing field or into the spectator area;
  (2) a ball has become discolored or unfit for further use;
  (3) the pitcher requests such alternate ball.

3.02 - No player shall intentionally discolor or damage the ball by rubbing it with soil, rosin, paraffin, licorice, sand paper, emery paper, or other foreign substance.

PENALTY: The umpire shall demand the ball and remove the offender from the pitching position. In case the umpire cannot locate the offender, and if the pitcher delivers such discolored or damaged ball to the batter, the pitcher shall be removed from the pitching position at once.

3.03 - A player in the starting line-up who has been removed for a substitute may re-enter the game once, in any position in the batting order, provided:
(a) his or her substitute has completed one time at bat and;
(b) has played defensively for a minimum of six (6) consecutive outs;
(c) a pitcher remaining in the game, but moving to a different position, can return as a pitcher anytime in the remainder of the game, but only once in the same inning as he/she was removed. **NOTE:** A pitcher, withdrawn from the game for a substitute offensively or defensively, may not re-enter the game as a pitcher. This applies to continuous batting order. **EXCEPTION:** A pitcher may re-enter the game as a pitcher, if withdrawn for a pinch-hitter or pinch-runner, and then returned to the game at the beginning of the next half-inning.
(d) only a player in the starting line-up may re-enter the game.
(e) a starter (S1) re-entering the game as a substitute for another starter (S2) must then fulfill all conditions of a substitute (one at bat and six defensive outs) before starter (S2) can re-enter the game.
(f) Defensive substitutions must be made while the team is on defense. Offensive

substitutions must be made at the time the offensive player has her/his turn at bat or is on base.

NOTE 1: A substitute may not be removed from the game prior to completion of his/her mandatory play requirements.

NOTE 2: When two or more substitute players of the defensive team enter the game at the same time, the manager shall, immediately before they take their positions as fielders, designate to the Umpire-in-Chief such player's positions in the team's batting order and the Umpire-in-Chief shall notify the official scorer. The Umpire-in-Chief shall have authority to designate the substitute's place in the batting order, if this information is not immediately provided.

NOTE 3: If during a game either team is unable to place nine (9) players on the field due to illness, injury, ejection, or inability to make a legal substitution, the opposing manager shall select a player previously used in the line-up to re-enter the game, but only if use of all eligible players has exhausted the roster. A player ejected from the game is not eligible for re-entry.

3.03 - Big League

(a) Any player in the starting line-up, including the designated hitter, who has been removed for a substitute may re-enter the game once, provided such player occupies the same batting position as he or she did in the starting lineup.

(b) A pitcher, withdrawn from the game for a substitute offensively or defensively, may not re-enter the game as a pitcher. (**EXCEPTION**: A pitcher may re-enter the game as a pitcher, if withdrawn for a pinch-hitter or pinch-runner, and then returned to the game at the beginning of the next half-inning.)

(c) A pitcher remaining in the game, but moving to a different position, can return as a pitcher anytime in the remainder of the game, but only once in the same inning as he/she was removed.

(d) A substitute who is withdrawn may not re-enter the game. (**NOTE**: This means that a starter and his/her substitute must not be in the line-up at the same time, except as provided in this rule.)

Defensive substitutions must be made while the team is on defense. Offensive substitutions must be made at the time the offensive player has her/his turn at bat or is on base.

NOTE 1: When two or more substitute players of the defensive team enter the game at the same time, the manager shall, immediately before they take their positions as fielders, designate to the Umpire-in-Chief such players' positions in the team's batting order and the Umpire-in-Chief shall notify the official scorer. The Umpire-in-Chief shall have authority to designate the substitutes' places in the batting order, if this information is not immediately provided.

NOTE 2: If during a game either team is unable to place nine (9) players on the field due to illness, injury, or ejection, the opposing manager shall select a player previously used in the line-up to re-enter the game, but only if the use of all other eligible players has exhausted the roster. A player ejected from the game is not eligible for re-entry. This provision does not apply to injury, illness, or ejection of the designated hitter or the player for whom he or she is batting, in which case the role of the designated hitter must be terminated.

Senior/Big League Designated Hitter Rule:
(a) At the beginning of a game, each manager may list on the line-up card a designated hitter to bat throughout the game for a designated player in the regular line-up.
(b) Only a player not in the regular batting order may be used as a designated hitter.
(c) In the event a manager decides to use the designated hitter as a defensive player, the player must remain in the same position in the batting order, unless otherwise replaced by a substitute. If so, the player for whom the designated hitter was batting must be removed from the game. Such player may re-enter the game once, but only in the batting order position of the former designated hitter, who must be removed.

3.04 - A player whose name is on the team's batting order may not become a substitute runner for another member of the team. "Courtesy runner" not permitted.

3.05 -

(a) The pitcher named in the batting order handed to the Umpire-in-Chief, as provided in Rules 4.01(a) and 4.01(b) shall pitch to the first batter or any substitute batter until such batter or any substitute batter is retired or reaches first base, unless the pitcher sustains an injury or illness which, in the judgment of the Umpire-in-Chief, incapacitates the pitcher from further play as a pitcher.

(b) If the pitcher is replaced, the substitute pitcher shall pitch to the batter then at bat, or any substitute batter, until such batter is retired or reaches first base, or until the offensive team is put out, unless the substitute pitcher sustains an injury or illness, which in the Umpire-in-Chief's judgment, incapacitates the pitcher from further play as a pitcher.

3.06 - The manager shall immediately notify the Umpire-in-Chief of any substitution and shall state to the Umpire-in-Chief the substitute's place in the batting order.

3.07 - The Umpire-in-Chief after having been notified, shall immediately announce, or cause to be announced, each substitution.

3.08 -
(a) If no announcement of a substitution is made, the substitute shall be considered to have entered the game when -
  (1) if a pitcher, the substitute takes a position on the pitcher's plate and throws one warm-up pitch to the catcher;
  (2) if a batter, the substitute takes a position in the batter's box;
  (3) if a fielder, the substitute reaches the position usually occupied by the fielder being replaced and play commences;
  (4) if a runner, the substitute takes the place of the runner being replaced.
(b) Any play made by, or on, any of the above mentioned, unannounced substitutes shall be legal.

3.09 - Players, managers, and coaches of the participating teams shall not address or mingle with spectators, nor sit in the stands during a game in which they are engaged. Managers or coaches must not warm up a pitcher at home plate or in the bull pen or elsewhere at any time. They may, however, stand by to observe a pitcher during warm-up

RULE 3.00 — GAME PRELIMINARIES

in the bullpen.

3.10 -
(a) The managers of both teams shall agree on the fitness of the playing field before the game starts. In the event that the two managers cannot agree, the president or a duly delegated representative shall make the determination.

(b) The Umpire-in-Chief shall be the sole judge as to whether and when play shall be suspended during a game because of unsuitable weather conditions or the unfit condition of the playing field; as to whether and when play shall be resumed after such suspension; and as to whether and when a game shall be terminated after such suspension. Said umpire shall not call the game until at least thirty minutes after play has been suspended. The umpire may continue the suspension as long as there is any chance to resume play.

3.11 - Double Headers

Minor League/Little League (Major) Division: A team may play two (2) doubleheaders in a seven-day period. No team shall play three games in a day. (Exception under condition of Rule 4.12.)

Tee Ball: No team shall be scheduled to play two games in one day. (See Rule 4.12.)

Junior/Senior/Big League: A team may play three (3) games in a day.

3.12 - When the umpire suspends play, "Time" shall be called. At the umpire's call of "Play" the suspension is lifted and play resumes. Between the call of "Time" and call of "Play" the ball is dead.

3.13 - The local league will establish ground rules to be followed by all teams in the league.

> A.R.—Local ground rules should pertain to particular situations or field conditions that are not specifically covered in the rulebook, but at no time should they supersede or change the rulebook.

3.14 - Members of the offensive team shall carry all gloves and other equipment off the field and to the dugout while their team is at bat. No equipment shall be left lying on the field, either in fair or foul territory.

3.15 - No person shall be allowed on the playing field during a game except uniformed players, managers and coaches, umpires, and news photographers authorized by the league. In case of intentional interference with play by any person authorized to be on the playing field, the ball is dead at the moment of the interference and no runners on base may advance. Should an overthrown ball accidentally touch an authorized person, it will not be considered interference and the ball will remain live.

3.16 - When there is spectator's interference with any thrown or batted ball, the ball shall be dead at the moment of interference and the umpire shall impose such penalties as in the umpire's opinion will nullify the act of interference.

> A.R.—If spectator interference clearly prevents a fielder from catching a fly ball, the umpire shall declare the batter out.

3.17 - Players and substitutes shall sit on their team's bench or in the dugout unless participating in the game or preparing to enter the game. No one except eligible players

RULE 3.00 — GAME PRELIMINARIES

in uniform, a manager, and not more than two coaches shall occupy the bench or dugout. When batters or base runners are retired, they must return to the bench or dugout at once. Batboys and/or batgirls are not permitted. The use of electronic communication equipment during the game is restricted. No team shall use electronic communication equipment, including walkie-talkies, cellular telephones, etc., for any communication with on-field personnel, including those in the dugout, bullpen, or field.

Penalty: If, in the umpire's judgment, any player, manager, or coach uses an electronic communications device during the game, the penalty is ejection from the game.

NOTE: A manager or coach is permitted to use a scorekeeping and/or pitch-counting application on an electronic device without penalty, provided such device is not used to receive messages of any sort.

3.18 - The local league shall provide proper protection sufficient to preserve order and to prevent spectators from entering the field. Either team may refuse to play until the field is cleared.

RULE 4.00 — STARTING AND ENDING THE GAME

Rule 4.00

Starting and Ending the Game

4.01 - The umpires shall proceed directly to home plate where they shall be met by the managers of the opposing teams, just preceding the established time to begin the game. In sequence -

(a) The home team manager shall give the batting order in duplicate to the Umpire-in Chief;

(b) Next, the visiting manager shall give the batting order in duplicate to the Umpire-in-Chief;

(c) The Umpire-in-Chief shall make certain that the original and duplicate copies are the same, then provide a copy of each batting order to the opposing manager. The original copy retained by the umpire shall be the official batting order;

(d) As soon as the home team's batting order is handed to the Umpire-in-Chief, the umpires are in charge of the playing field and from that moment shall have sole authority to determine when a game shall be called, halted, or resumed on account of weather or the conditions of the playing field.

NOTE 1: In Tee Ball and non-competitive Minor Leagues, all players on the roster may be given a defensive position. Only one player may occupy the catcher's position.

NOTE 2: Rostered players who arrive at the game site after a game begins may be inserted in the lineup, if the manager so chooses. This applies even when a suspended game is resumed at a later date.

4.02 - The players of the home team shall take their defensive positions, the first batter of the visiting team shall take a position in the batter's box, the umpire shall call "Play" and the game shall start.

4.03 - When the ball is put in play at the start of, or during a game, all fielders other than the catcher shall be in fair territory.

(a) The catcher shall be stationed in the catcher's box. The catcher may leave that position at any time to catch a pitch or make a play except that when the batter is being given an intentional base on balls, the catcher must stand with both feet within the lines of the catcher's box until the ball leaves the pitcher's hand.

PENALTY: No pitch.

(b) The pitcher, while in the act of delivering the ball to the batter, shall take the legal position.

(c) Except the pitcher and catcher, any fielder may be stationed anywhere in fair territory.

4.04 - The batting order shall be followed throughout the game unless a player is substituted for another. Substitutes must take the place of the replaced player's position in the batting order except as covered by Rule 3.03. A league may adopt a policy of a continuous batting order that will include all players on the team roster present for the game batting in order. If this option is adopted, each player would be required to bat in his/her respective

RULE 4.00 — STARTING AND ENDING THE GAME

spot in the batting order. However, a player may be entered and/or re-entered defensively in the game anytime provided he/she meets the requirements of mandatory play. **NOTE 1: The continuous batting order is mandatory for all Tee Ball and Minor League divisions.** **NOTE 2:** For the Tee Ball and Minor League Divisions (and when the continuous batting order is adopted for other divisions), when a child is injured, becomes ill, or must leave the game site after the start of the game, the team will skip over him/her when his/her time at bat comes up without penalty. If the injured, ill, or absent player returns he/she is merely inserted into their original spot in the batting order and the game continues. Also, if a child arrives late to a game site, if the manager chooses to enter him/her in the lineup (see Rule 4.01 NOTE), he/she would be added to the end of the current lineup.

4.05 - The offensive team shall station two base coaches on the field during its time at bat, one near first base and one near third base. The coaches shall not leave their respective dugouts until the pitcher has completed his/her preparatory pitches to the catcher. Base coaches shall -

(a) be eligible players in the uniform of their team; a manager and/or coach. Both base coaches may be managers or coaches.

(b) be a manager or coach only if there is at least one other adult manager or coach in the dugout.

(c) remain within the base coaches' boxes at all times, except as provided in Rule 7.11;

> A.R.—Once an inning starts, coaches shall not alternate between the first and third base coaches boxes.

(d) talk to members of their own team only.

An offending base coach shall be removed from the base coach's box.

4.06 - No manager, coach, or player, shall at any time, whether from the bench or the playing field or elsewhere -

(1) incite, or try to incite, by word or sign, a demonstration by spectators;

(2) use language which will in any manner refer to or reflect upon opposing players, manager, coach, an umpire, or spectators;

(3) make any move calculated to cause the pitcher to commit an illegal pitch;

(4) take a position in the batter's line of vision, with the deliberate intent to distract the batter.

The umpire may first warn the player, coach, and/or manager. If continued, remove the player, coach, and/or manager from the game or bench. If such action causes an illegal pitch, it shall be nullified.

4.07 - When the manager, coach, or a player is ejected from a game, they shall leave the field immediately and take no further part in that game. They may not sit in the stands and may not be recalled. **A manager or coach ejected from a game must not be present at the game site for the remainder of that game.** Any manager, coach, or player ejected from a game is suspended for his or her team's next physically played game and may not be in attendance at the game site from which they were suspended. This includes pregame and postgame activities.

RULE 4.00 — STARTING AND ENDING THE GAME

4.08 - When the occupants of a player's bench show violent disapproval of an umpire's decision, the umpire shall first give warning that such disapproval shall cease. If such action continues -

PENALTY: The umpire shall order the offender out of the game and away from the spectators' area. If the umpire is unable to detect the offender or offenders, the bench may be cleared of all players. The manager of the offending team shall have the privilege of recalling to the playing field only those players needed for substitution in the game.

4.09 - HOW A TEAM SCORES

(a) One run shall be scored each time a runner legally advances to and touches first, second, third, and home base before three players are retired to end the inning.

EXCEPTIONS: A run is not scored if the runner advances to home base during a play in which the third out is made (1) by the batter-runner before touching first base; (2) by any runner being forced out; or (3) by a preceding runner who is declared out because that runner failed to touch one of the bases (appeal play).

> A.R.—One out, Jones on third, Smith on first and Brown flies out to right field for the second out. Jones tags up and scores after the catch. Smith attempted to return to first but the right fielder's throw beat Smith to the base for the third out. But Jones scored before the throw to catch Smith reached first base. Hence, Jones' run counts. It was not a force play.

(b) When the winning run is scored in the last half inning of a regulation game or in the last half of an extra inning as the result of a base on balls, hit batter, or any other play with the bases full which forces the runner on third to advance, the umpire shall not declare the game ended until the runner forced to advance from third has touched home base and the batter-runner has touched first base.

4.10 -

(a) A regulation game consists of six innings (**Junior/Senior/Big League:** seven innings), unless extended because of a tie score or shortened (1) because the home team needs none of its half of the sixth inning (**Junior/Senior/Big League:** seventh), or only a fraction of it; or (2) because the umpire calls the game.

(b) If the score is tied after six completed innings (**Junior/Senior/Big League:** seven innings), play shall continue until (1) the visiting team has scored more total runs than the home team at the end of a complete inning; or (2) the home team scores the winning run in an uncompleted inning.

(c) If a game is called, it is a regulation game:

   (1) if four innings (**Junior/Senior/Big League:** five innings) have been completed;

   (2) if the home team has scored more runs in three-and-a-half innings (**Junior/Senior/Big League:** four-and-a-half innings) than the visiting team has scored in four completed half innings (**Junior/Senior/Big League:** five completed half innings);

   (3) if the home team scores one or more runs in its half of the fourth inning (**Junior/Senior/Big League:** fifth inning) to tie the score.

RULE 4.00 — STARTING AND ENDING THE GAME

(d) If a game is called before it has become a regulation game, but after one (1) or more innings have been played, it shall be resumed exactly where it left off. **NOTE:** All records, including pitching, shall be counted.

(e) If after four (4) innings (**Junior/Senior/Big League**: five innings), three-and-a-half innings if the home team is ahead (**Junior/Senior/Big League:** four-and-a-half innings), one team has a lead of ten (10) runs or more, the manager of the team with the least runs shall concede the victory to the opponent. **NOTE:** (1) If the visiting team has a lead of ten (10) runs or more, the home team must bat in its half of the inning. (2) The local league may adopt the option of not utilizing this rule.

(f) **Tee Ball:** The local league may determine appropriate game length but shall not exceed 6 innings. It is recommended that Tee Ball games be 4 innings or 1-1/2 hour time limit or less.

4.11 - The score of a regulation game is the total number of runs scored by each team at the moment the game ends.

(a) The game ends when the visiting team completes its half of the sixth inning (**Junior/Senior/Big League**: seventh inning) if the home team is ahead.

(b) The game ends when the sixth inning (**Junior/Senior/Big League:** seventh inning) is completed, if the visiting team is ahead.

(c) If the home team scores the winning run in its half of the sixth inning (**Junior/Senior/Big League:** seventh inning), or its half of an extra inning after a tie, the game ends immediately, when the winning run is scored.

NOTE: Once a game becomes regulation and it is called with the home team taking the lead in an incomplete inning, the game ends with the home team the winner.

EXCEPTION: If the last batter in a game hits a home run out of the playing field, the batter-runner and all runners on base are permitted to score, in accordance with the base-running rules, and the game ends when the batter-runner touches home plate.

> A.R.—The batter hits a home run out of playing field to win the game in the last half of the sixth (**Junior/Senior/Big League:** seventh inning), or an extra inning, but is called out for passing a preceding runner. The game ends immediately when the winning run is scored.

(d) A called game ends at the moment the umpire terminates play.

EXCEPTION: If the game is called during an incomplete inning, the game ends at the end of the last previous completed inning in each of the following situations:
(1) The visiting team scores one or more runs to tie the score in the incomplete inning, and the home team does not score in the incomplete inning.
(2) The visiting team scores one or more runs to take the lead in the incomplete inning, and the home team does not tie the score or retake the lead in the incomplete inning.

(e) A regulation game that is tied after four or more completed innings (**Junior/**

RULE 4.00 — STARTING AND ENDING THE GAME

Senior/Big League: five innings) and halted by the umpire, shall be resumed from the exact point that play was halted. The game shall continue in accordance with Rule 4.10(a) and 4.10(b).

NOTE: When the TIE game is halted, the pitcher of record may continue pitching in the same game on any subsequent date provided said pitcher has observed the required day of rest and has pitching eligibility in the calendar day in which the game is resumed. For scorekeeping purposes, it shall be considered the same game, and all batting, fielding, and pitching records will count.

LITTLE LEAGUE AND MINOR LEAGUE EXAMPLE:
Rule 4.11

	1	2	3	4	5	6
VISITORS	0	0	0	4	1	
HOME	0	0	0	5		

Game called in top of 5th inning on account of rain. Score reverts to last completed inning (4th) and the home team is the winner 5 to 4.

JUNIOR/SENIOR/BIG LEAGUE EXAMPLE:
Rule 4.11

	1	2	3	4	5	6
VISITORS	0	0	0	0	4	1
HOME	0	0	0	0	5	

Game called in top of 6th inning on account of rain. Score reverts to last completed inning (5th) and the home team is the winner 5 to 4.

4.12 - TIE games halted due to weather, curfew, or light failure shall be resumed from the exact point at which they were halted in the original game. It can be completed preceding the next scheduled game between the same teams. A pitcher can pitch in both games on same day subject to Regulation VI(b). The lineup and batting order of both teams shall be the same as the lineup and batting order at the moment the game was halted, subject to the rules governing substitution. Any player may be replaced by a player who was not in the game prior to halting the original game.

No player once removed before the game was halted may be returned to the lineup unless covered by Rule 3.03.

NOTE: When the TIE game is halted, the pitcher of record may continue pitching in the same game on any subsequent date provided said pitcher has observed the required day of rest and has pitching eligibility in the calendar day in which the game is resumed. For scorekeeping purposes, it shall be considered the same game, and all batting, fielding, and pitching records will count.

RULE 4.00 — STARTING AND ENDING THE GAME

LITTLE LEAGUE AND MINOR LEAGUE EXAMPLE:

Rule 4.12

Tie games halted due to weather, curfew, or light failure shall be resumed from the exact point at which they were halted in the original game.

	1	2	3	4	5	6
VISITORS	0	0	0	0	4	5
HOME	0	0	0	0	4	

Game called in top of 6th inning, visiting team batting with two out, no base runners this is a tie game. Resume the game in the top of the 6th, visiting team at bat, two out.

JUNIOR/SENIOR/BIG LEAGUE EXAMPLE:

Rule 4.12

Tie games halted due to weather, curfew, or light failure shall be resumed from the exact point at which they were halted in the original game.

	1	2	3	4	5	6	7
VISITORS	0	0	0	0	0	4	5
HOME	0	0	0	0	0	4	

Game called in top of 7th inning, visiting team batting with two out, no base runners this is a tie game. Resume the game in the top of the 7th, visiting team at bat, two out.

4.13 - Double Headers

Minors/Little League (Majors): A team may play two (2) doubleheaders in a seven-day period. No team shall play three games in a day. (Exception under condition of Rule 4.12.)

Tee Ball: No team shall be scheduled to play two games in one day. (See Rule 4.12).

Junior/Senior/Big League: A team may play three (3) games in a day.

4.14 - The Umpire-in-Chief shall order the playing field lights turned on whenever in such umpire's opinion darkness makes further play in daylight hazardous.

4.15 - A game may be forfeited by the Umpire-in-Chief of the game in progress to the opposing team when a team -

(1) being upon the field, refuses to start play within 10 minutes after the appointed hour for beginning the game, unless such delay is unavoidable;

(2) refuses to continue play unless the game was terminated by the umpire;

(3) fails to resume play, after the game was halted by the umpire, within one minute after the umpire has called "Play";

(4) fails to obey within a reasonable time the umpire's order to remove a player from the game;

(5) after warning by the umpire, willfully and persistently violates any rules of the game;

(6) employs tactics designed to delay, shorten, or make a travesty of the game.

RULE 4.00 — STARTING AND ENDING THE GAME

4.16 - If a game cannot be played because of the inability of either team to:
(1) place nine players on the field before the game begins, and/or,
(2) place at least one adult in the dugout as manager or acting manager. This shall not be grounds for automatic forfeiture, but shall be referred to the Board of Directors for a decision.

NOTE: A game may not be started with less than nine (9) players on each team, nor without at least one adult as manager or substitute manager.

4.17 - If during a game either team is unable to place nine (9) players on the field due to injury or ejection, the opposing manager shall select the player to re-enter the lineup. A player ejected from the game is not eligible for re-entry. If no players are available for re-entry, or if a team refuses to place nine (9) players on the field, this shall not be grounds for automatic forfeiture but shall be referred to the Board of Directors for a decision.

NOTE: A game may not be continued with less than nine (9) players on each team.

4.18 - Forfeited games shall be recorded in the scorebook and the book signed by the Umpire-in-Chief. A written report stating the reason for the forfeiture shall be sent to the league president within 24 hours but failure of the umpire to file this report shall not affect the forfeiture.

4.19 - PROTESTING GAME

(a) Protest shall be considered only when based on the violation or interpretation of a playing rule, use of an ineligible pitcher or the use of an ineligible player. No protest shall be considered on a decision involving an umpire's judgment. Equipment which does not meet specifications must be removed from the game. **Exception:** Illegal bat [see Rule 6.06 (d)].

(b) The managers of contesting teams only shall have the right to protest a game (or in their absence, coaches). However, the manager or acting manager may not leave the dugout until receiving permission from an umpire.

(c) Protests shall be made as follows:
  (1) The protesting manager shall immediately, and before any succeeding play begins, notify the umpire that the game is being played under protest.
  (2) Following such notice the umpire shall consult with the other umpire(s). If the umpire is convinced that the decision is in conflict with the rules, the umpire shall reverse that decision. If, however, after consultation, the umpire is convinced that the decision is not in conflict with the rules, said umpire shall announce that the game is being played under protest. Failure of the umpire to make such announcement shall not affect the validity of the protest.

(d) Protest made due to the use of an ineligible pitcher or an ineligible player may be considered only if made to the umpire before the umpire(s) leave the field at the end of the game. Whenever it is found that an ineligible pitcher or ineligible player is being used, said pitcher shall be removed from the pitcher's plate, or said player shall be removed from the game, and the game shall be continued under protest or not as the protesting manager decides.

(e) Any protest for any reason whatsoever must be submitted by the manager first to the umpire on the field of play and then in writing to the local league president

RULE 4.00 — STARTING AND ENDING THE GAME

within 24 hours. The Umpire-in-Chief shall also submit a report immediately.

(f) A committee composed of the president, player agent, league's Umpire-in-Chief, and one or more other officers or directors who are not managers or umpires shall hear and resolve any such protest as above, including playing rules. If protest is allowed, resume game from exact point when the infraction occurred.

NOTE 1: This rule does not pertain to charges of infractions of regulations such as field decorum or actions of the league personnel or spectators which must be considered and resolved by the Board of Directors.

NOTE 2: All Little League officials are urged to take precautions to prevent protests. When a protest situation is imminent, the potential offenders should be notified immediately. **Example:** Should a manager, official scorer, league official, or umpire discover that a pitcher is ineligible at the beginning of the game, or will become ineligible during the game or at the start of the next inning of play, the fact should be brought to the attention of the manager of the team involved. Such action should not be delayed until the infraction has occurred. However, failure of personnel to notify the manager of the infraction does not affect the validity of the protest.

> A.R.—A substitute pitcher who is ineligible DOES NOT have to pitch to a batter. It is not a violation until the ineligible pitcher has delivered a "Pitch" as defined in Rule 2.00.

(g) **Minor League:** A local league may adopt a rule that protests must be resolved before the next pitch or play.

(h) There are no protests in Tee Ball.

Rule 5.00

Putting the Ball in Play - Live Ball

5.01 - At the time set for beginning the game, the Umpire-in-Chief shall order the home team to take its defensive positions and the first batter of the visiting team to take a position in the batter's box. As soon as all players are in position, the Umpire-in-Chief shall call "Play."

5.02 - After the umpire calls "Play," the ball is alive and in play and remains alive and in play until, for legal cause, or at the umpire's call of "Time" suspending play, the ball becomes dead. While the ball is dead, no player may be put out, no bases may be run, and no runs may be scored, except that runners may advance one or more bases as the result of acts which occurred while the ball was alive (such as, but not limited to an overthrow, interference, or a home run or other fair ball hit out of the playing field).

5.03 - The pitcher shall deliver the pitch to the batter who may elect to strike the ball, or who may not offer at it, as such batter chooses.

5.04 - The offensive team's objective is to have its batter become a runner, and its runners advance.

5.05 - The defensive team's objective is to prevent offensive players from becoming runners, and to prevent their advance around the bases.

5.06 - When a batter becomes a runner and touches all bases legally, one run shall be scored for the offensive team.

5.07 - When three offensive players are legally put out, that team takes the field and the opposing team becomes the offensive team (side retired). (**Minor League:** The side is retired when three offensive players are legally put out, called out by an umpire, or when all players on the roster have batted one time in the half-inning or when the offensive team scores five (5) runs. (**OPTION:** The local league Board of Directors may suspend the five-run rule in the last half-inning for either team.) **Tee Ball:** The side is retired when three offensive players are legally put out, called out by an umpire, or when all players on the roster have batted one time in the half-inning.)

5.08 - If a thrown ball accidentally touches a base coach, or a pitched or thrown ball touches an umpire, the ball is alive and in play. However, if the base coach interferes with a thrown ball, the runner is out.

5.09 - The ball becomes dead and runners advance one base, or remain on their bases, without liability to be put out, when -
(a) a pitched ball touches a batter, or the batter's clothing, while in a legal batting position; runners, if forced, advance (See 6.08);
(b) the plate umpire interferes with the catcher's act of throwing (when the throw is in an attempt to retire a runner); runners return. If the catcher's throw gets the runner out, the out stands. No umpire interference.
(c) an illegal pitch is committed (see Penalty 8.05). The ball is dead at the end of playing action, if the ball is pitched;
(d) a ball is illegally batted either fair or foul. Runners return;

RULE 5.00 — PUTTING THE BALL IN PLAY - LIVE BALL

(e) a foul ball is not caught, runners return. The umpire shall not put the ball in play until all runners have retouched their bases;

(f) a fair ball touches a runner or an umpire in fair territory before it touches an infielder including the pitcher, or touches an umpire before it has passed an infielder other than the pitcher. A runner hit by a fair batted ball is out.

NOTE: If a fair ball goes through, or by an infielder and touches a runner immediately back of said infielder, or touches a runner after being deflected by an infielder, the ball is in play and the umpire shall not declare the runner out. In making such a decision, the umpire must be convinced that the ball passed through, or by, the infielder and that no other infielder had the chance to make a play on the ball; runners advance, if forced.

(g) a pitched ball lodges in the catcher's or umpire's mask or paraphernalia; runners advance;

> A.R.—If a pitched ball lodges in the umpire's or catcher's mask or paraphernalia, and remains out of play, on the third strike (**Little League (Majors)/Junior/Senior/Big League**) or fourth ball, then the batter is entitled to first base and all runners advance one base. If the count on the batter is less than three balls, runners advance one base.

5.10 - The ball becomes dead when an umpire calls "Time". The Umpire-in-Chief shall call "Time" -

(a) when in said umpire's judgment, weather, darkness, or similar conditions make immediate further play impossible;

(b) when light failure makes it difficult or impossible for the umpires to follow the play.

NOTE: A league may adopt its own regulations governing games interrupted by light failure.

(c) when an accident incapacitates a player or an umpire:
  (1) if an accident to a runner is such as to prevent said runner from proceeding to an entitled base, as on a home run hit out of the playing field or an award of one or more bases, a substitute runner shall be permitted to complete the play.

(d) when a manager requests "Time" for a substitution, or for a conference with one of the players; (**NOTE:** Only one offensive time-out, for the purpose of a visit or conference, will be permitted each inning.)

(e) when the umpire wishes to examine the ball, to consult with either manager, or for any similar cause;

(f) when a fielder, after catching a fly ball, falls into a stand, or falls across ropes into a crowd when spectators are on the field, or other dead-ball area. As pertains to runners, the provisions of 7.04(b) shall prevail. If a fielder after making a catch steps into a dead ball area, but does not fall, the ball is alive and in play and runners may advance at their own peril;

(g) when an umpire orders a player or any other person removed from the playing field;

(h) except in the cases stated in paragraphs (b) and (c) (1) of this rule, no umpire shall call "Time" while a play is in progress;

RULE 5.00 — PUTTING THE BALL IN PLAY - LIVE BALL

(i) the ball remains live until the umpire calls "Time."

5.11 - After the ball is dead, play shall be resumed when the pitcher takes a position on the pitcher's plate with a new ball or the same ball in said pitcher's possession and the plate umpire calls "Play." The plate umpire shall call "Play" as soon as the pitcher takes a position on the pitcher's plate with possession of the ball.

Rule 6.00
The Batter

6.01 -
(a) Each player of the offensive team shall bat in the order that their name appears in the team's batting order.

(b) The first batter in each inning after the first inning shall be the player whose name follows that of the last player who legally completed a time at bat in the preceding inning.

NOTE: In the event that while a batter is in the batter's box, the third out of an inning is made on a base runner, the batter then at bat shall be the first batter of the next inning and the count of balls and strikes shall start over.

6.02 -
(a) The batter shall take a position in the batter's box promptly when it is said batter's time at bat.

(b) The batter shall not leave that position in the batter's box after the pitcher starts the windup.

PENALTY: If the pitcher pitches, the umpire shall call "Ball" or "Strike" as the case may be.

(c) If the batter refuses to take a position in the batter's box during a time at bat, the umpire shall call a strike on the batter without the need for a pitch to be delivered. The ball is dead and no runner may advance. After the penalty, the batter may take a proper position, and the regular ball and strike count shall continue, but if the batter does not take his/her proper position before three strikes are called, that batter shall be declared out.

6.03 - The batter's legal position shall be with both feet within the batter's box.

> A.R.—The lines defining the box are within the batter's box.

6.04 - A batter has legally completed a time at bat when he/she is retired or becomes a runner.

6.05 - A batter is out when -
(a) a fair or foul fly ball (other than a foul tip) is legally caught by a fielder;

> A.R.—A fielder may reach into, but not step into, a dugout to make a catch, and if he/she holds the ball, the catch shall be allowed. A fielder, in order to make a catch on a foul ball nearing a dugout or other out-of-play area (such as the stands), must have one or both feet on or over the playing surface (including the dugout) and neither foot on the ground inside the dugout or in any other out-of-play area. Ball is in play, unless the fielder, after making a legal catch, falls into a dugout or other out-of-play area, in which case the ball is dead.

(b) **Majors/Junior/Senior Big League:**
   (1) a third strike is legally caught by the catcher; or,
   (2) a third strike is not caught by the catcher when first base is occupied before two are out; **Minor League and Tee Ball:** A third strike is caught or not caught by catcher.

RULE 6.00 — THE BATTER

> **A.R.—Majors/Junior/Senior/Big League:** When a batter becomes a runner on a third strike that is not caught, and starts for the bench or his/her position, that batter may advance to first base at any time before entering the dugout or any other dead ball area. To put the batter out, the defense must tag the batter or first base before the batter touches first base.

(c) bunting foul on the third strike;

(d) an Infield Fly is declared;

(e) the batter attempts to hit a third strike and is touched by the ball;

(f) a fair ball touches said batter before touching a fielder;

(g) after hitting or bunting a fair ball, the bat hits the ball a second time in fair territory. The ball is dead and no runners may advance. If the batter-runner drops the bat and the ball rolls against the bat in fair territory and, in the umpire's judgment there was no intention to interfere with the course of the ball, the ball is alive and in play;

> **A.R.**—If a bat is thrown into fair or foul territory and interferes with a defensive player attempting to make a play, interference shall be called, whether intentional or not.

(h) after hitting or bunting a foul ball, the batter-runner intentionally deflects the course of the ball in any manner while running to first base. The ball is dead and no runners may advance;

(i) after hitting a fair ball, the batter-runner or first base is tagged before said batter-runner touches first base; or **Majors/Junior/Senior/Big League:** after a third strike as defined in 6.09(b), the batter-runner or first base is tagged before said batter-runner touches first base;

(j) in running the last half of the distance from home base to first base, while the ball is being fielded to first base, the batter-runner runs outside (to the right of) the three-foot line, or inside (to the left of) the foul line, and in the umpire's judgment in so doing interferes with the fielder taking the throw at first base; except that the batter runner may run outside (to the right of) the three-foot line or inside (to the left of) the foul line to avoid a fielder attempting to field a batted ball;

> **A.R.**—The lines marking the three-foot lane are a part of that lane and a batter-runner is required to have both feet within the three foot lane or on the lines marking the lane.

(k) an infielder intentionally drops a fair fly ball or line drive, with first; first and second; first and third; or first, second, and third bases occupied before two are out. The ball is dead and runner or runners shall return to their original base or bases;

> **A.R.**—In this situation, the batter is not out if the infielder permits the ball to drop untouched to the ground, except when the Infield Fly rule applies.

(l) a preceding runner shall, in the umpire's judgment, intentionally interfere with a fielder who is attempting to catch a thrown ball or to throw a ball in an attempt to complete a play;

RULE 6.00 — THE BATTER

6.06 - A batter is out for illegal action when –

(a) hitting the ball with one or both feet on the ground entirely outside the batter's box.

> A.R.—If a batter hits a ball fair or foul while out of the batter's box, he/she shall be called out.

(b) stepping from one batter's box to the other while the pitcher is in position ready to pitch;

(c) interfering with the catcher's fielding or throwing by:
  (1) stepping out of the batter's box, or;
  (2) making any other movement that hinders the catcher's actions at home plate or the catcher's attempt to play on a runner, or;
  (3) failing to make a reasonable effort to vacate a congested area when there is a throw to home plate and there is time for the batter to move away.

  EXCEPTION: Batter is not out if any runner attempting to advance is retired or if the runner trying to score is called out for batter's interference.

(d) the batter enters the batter's box with one or both feet entirely on the ground with an illegal bat (see bat specifications rule 1.10) or is discovered having used an illegal bat prior to the next player entering the batter's box.

> A.R.—When an illegal bat is discovered, it MUST be removed from the game at that point.

NOTE: If the infraction is discovered before the next player enters the batter's box following the turn at bat of the player who used an illegal bat:

(1) The manager of the defense may advise the plate umpire of a decision to decline the penalty and accept the play. Such election shall be made immediately at the end of the play.
(2) For the first violation, the offensive team will lose one eligible adult base coach for the duration of the game.

> A.R.—Any of the three adults in the dugout may be used as the one adult base coach at any time during the duration of the game.

(3) For the second violation, the manager of the team will be ejected from the game. Any subsequent violation will result in the newly designated manager being ejected.

6.07 - BATTING OUT OF TURN

(a) A batter shall be called out, on appeal, when failing to bat in the proper turn, and another batter completes a time at bat in place of the proper batter.
  (1) The proper batter may take a position in the batter's box at any time before the improper batter becomes a runner or is retired, and any balls and strikes shall be counted in the proper batter's time at bat.

(b) When an improper batter becomes a runner or is retired, and the defensive team appeals to the umpire before the first pitch to the next batter of either team, or before any play or attempted play, the umpire shall –

RULE 6.00 — THE BATTER

   (1) declare the proper batter out; and
   (2) nullify any advance or score made because of a ball batted by the improper batter or because of the improper batter's advance to first base on a hit, an error, a base on balls, a hit batter, or otherwise.

   NOTE: If a runner advances while the improper batter is at bat, on a stolen base, wild pitch, or passed ball, such advance is legal.

(c) When an improper batter becomes a runner or is retired, and a pitch is made to the next batter of either team before an appeal is made, the improper batter thereby becomes the proper batter, and the results of such time at bat become legal.

(d) (1) When the proper batter is called out for failing to bat in turn, the next batter shall be the batter whose name follows that of the proper batter thus called out;
   (2) When an improper batter becomes a proper batter because no appeal is made before the next pitch, the next batter shall be the batter whose name follows that of such legalized improper batter. The instant an improper batter's actions are legalized, the batting order picks up with the name following that of the legalized improper batter.

BATTING OUT OF TURN APPROVED RULINGS

To illustrate various situations arising from batting out of turn, assume a first-inning batting order as follows:

Ann - Becky - Cher - Dianne - Erin - Fran - Ginny - Heather - Irene

PLAY (1). Becky bats. With the count 2 balls and 1 strike, (a) the offensive team discovers the error or (b) the defensive team appeals.
   RULING: In either case, Ann replaces Becky, with the count 2 balls and 1 strike.

PLAY (2). Becky bats and doubles. The defensive team appeals (a) immediately or (b) after a pitch to Cher.
   RULING: (a) Ann is called out and Becky is the proper batter; (b) Becky stays on second and Cher is the proper batter.

PLAY (3). Ann walks. Becky walks. Cher forces Becky. Erin bats in Dianne's turn. While Erin is at bat, Ann scores and Cher goes to second on a wild pitch. Erin grounds out, sending Cher to third. The defensive team appeals (a) immediately or (b) after a pitch to Dianne.
   RULING: (a) Ann's run counts and Cher is entitled to second base since these advances were not made because of the improper batter batting a ball or advancing to first base. Cher must return to second base because the advance to third resulted from the improper batter batting a ball. Dianne is called out and Erin is the proper batter; (b) Ann's run counts and Cher stays on third. The proper batter is Fran.

PLAY (4). With the bases full and two out, Heather bats in Fran's turn, and triples, scoring three runs. The defensive team appeals (a) immediately or (b) after a pitch to Ginny.

RULING: (a) Fran is called out and no runs scored. Ginny is the proper batter to lead off the second inning; (b) Heather stays on third and three runs scored. Irene is the proper batter.

PLAY (5). After Play (4) (b) above, Ginny continues to bat. (a) Heather is picked off third base for the third out, or (b) Ginny flies out, and no appeal is made. Who is the proper leadoff batter in the second inning?

RULING: (a) Irene became the proper batter as soon as the first pitch to Ginny legalized Heather's triple; (b) Heather. When no appeal was made, the first pitch to the leadoff batter of the opposing team legalized Ginny's time at bat.

PLAY (6). Dianne walks and Ann comes to bat. Dianne was an improper batter and if an appeal is made before the first pitch to Ann, Ann is out, Dianne is removed from base, and Becky is proper batter. There is no appeal and a pitch is made to Ann. Dianne's walk is now legalized, and Erin thereby becomes the proper batter. Erin can replace Ann at any time before Ann is put out, or becomes a runner. Erin does not do so. Ann flies out, and Becky comes to bat. Ann was an improper batter and if an appeal is made before the first pitch to Becky, Erin is out, and the proper batter is Fran. There is no appeal, and a pitch is made to Becky. Ann's out is now legalized, and the proper batter is Becky. Becky walks. Cher is the proper batter. Cher flies out. Now Dianne is the proper batter, but Dianne is on second base. Who is the proper batter?

RULING: The proper batter is Erin. When the proper batter is on base, that batter is passed over, and the following batter becomes the proper batter.

(**NOTE:** The umpire and scorekeeper shall not direct the attention of any person to the presence in the batter's box of an improper batter. This rule is designed to require constant vigilance by the players and managers of both teams. There are two fundamentals to keep in mind: 1. When a player bats out of turn, the proper batter is the player called out. 2. If an improper batter bats and reaches base or is out and no appeal is made before a pitch o the next batter, or before any play or attempted play, that improper batter is considered to have batted in proper turn and establishes the order that is to follow.)

Tee Ball: The scorekeeper shall inform the manager that a player has batted out of order. There shall be no penalty and that player shall not have another turn at bat, but shall resume the normal position next time up.

6.08 - The batter becomes a runner and is entitled to first base without liability to be put out (provided said runner advances to and touches first base) when -
(a) four "Balls" have been called by the umpire; the ball is live and in play. Base runners may advance;
(b) the batter is touched by a pitched ball which the batter is not attempting to hit unless (1) the ball is in the strike zone when it touches the batter, or (2) the batter makes no attempt to avoid being touched by the ball.

RULE 6.00 — THE BATTER

NOTE: If the ball is in the strike zone when it touches the batter, it shall be called a strike, whether or not the batter tries to avoid the ball. If the ball is outside the strike zone when it touches the batter, it shall be called a ball if that batter makes no attempt to avoid being touched.

> A.R.—When the batter is touched by a pitched ball which does not entitle that batter to first base, the ball is dead and no runner may advance.

(c) The catcher or any fielder interferes with the batter. If a play follows the interference, the manager of the offense may advise the plate umpire of a decision to decline the interference penalty and accept the play. Such election shall be made immediately at the end of the play. However, if the batter reaches first base on a hit, an error, a base on balls, a hit batter, or otherwise, and all other runners advance at least one base, the play proceeds without reference to the interference;

(d) A fair ball touches an umpire or a runner on fair territory before touching a fielder.

> A.R.—Ball is dead. Runner(s) who are forced advance and any runners not forced will return to their bases at the time of the pitch.

NOTE: If a fair ball touches an umpire after having passed a fielder other than the pitcher, or having touched a fielder, including the pitcher, the ball is in play.

6.09 - The batter becomes a runner when -

(a) a fair ball is hit;

(b) **Majors/Junior/Senior/Big League:** the third strike called by the umpire is not caught, providing (1) first base is unoccupied or (2) first base is occupied with two out. **NOTE:** A batter forfeits his/her opportunity to advance to first base when he/she enters the dugout or any other dead ball area.

(c) a fair ball, after having passed a fielder other than the pitcher, or after having been touched by a fielder, including the pitcher, shall touch an umpire or runner in fair territory;

(d) a fair fly ball passes over a fence or into the stands at a distance from home base of 165 feet or more. Such hit entitles the batter to a home run when all bases have been legally touched. A fair fly ball that passes out of the playing field at a point less than 165 feet from home base shall entitle the batter to advance to second base only;

(e) a fair ball, after touching the ground, bounds into the stands; passes through, over, or under a fence; through or under a scoreboard; or through or under shrubbery or vines in the fence, in which case the batter and runners shall be entitled to advance two bases;

(f) any fair ball which, either before or after touching the ground, passes through or under a fence, through or under a scoreboard, through any opening in the fence or scoreboard, through or under shrubbery or vines on the fence, or which sticks in a fence or scoreboard in which case the batter and runners shall be entitled to two bases;

RULE 6.00 — THE BATTER

(g) any bounding fair ball is deflected by the fielder into the stands, or over or under a fence in fair or foul territory, in which case the batter and all runners shall be entitled to advance two bases;

(h) any fair fly ball is deflected by the fielder into the stands or over the fence into foul territory, in which case the batter shall be entitled to advance to second base, but if deflected into the stands or over the fence in fair territory, the batter shall be entitled to a home run. However, should such a fair fly be deflected at a point less than 165 feet from home plate, the batter shall be entitled to two bases only.

Rule 7.00

The Runner

7.01 - A runner acquires the right to an unoccupied base when that runner touches it before being retired. The runner is then entitled to it until put out or forced to vacate it for another runner legally entitled to that base. If a runner legally acquires title to a base, and the pitcher has control of the ball within the eight (8) foot radius circle and is not making a play, the runner may not return to a previously occupied base.

7.02 - In advancing, a runner shall touch first, second, third, and home base in order. If forced to return, the runner shall retouch all bases in reverse order, unless the ball is dead under any provision of Rule 5.09. In such cases, the runner may go directly to the original base.

7.03 - Two runners may not occupy a base, but if, while the ball is alive, two runners are touching the base, the following runner shall be out when tagged. The preceding runner is entitled to the base.

(a) If two runners are on a base and both are tagged, then the lead runner is out if forced.

7.04 - Each runner, other than the batter, may without liability to be put out, advance one base when -

(a) the batter's advance without liability to be put out, forces the runner to vacate a base, or when the batter hits a fair ball that touches another runner or the umpire before such ball has been touched by, or has passed a fielder, if the runner is forced to advance;

(b) a fielder, after catching a fly ball, falls into a stand, falls across ropes into a crowd when spectators are on the field, or falls into any other dead-ball areas;

NOTE: When a runner is entitled to a base without liability to be put out, while the ball is in play, or under any rule in which the ball is in play after the runner reaches an entitled base, and the runner fails to touch the base to which that runner is entitled before attempting to advance to the next base, the runner shall forfeit the exemption from liability to be put out and may be put out by tagging the base or by tagging the runner before that runner returns to the missed base.

> A.R.—A runner forced to advance without liability to be put out, may advance past the base to which he/she is entitled at his/her own risk.

(c) **Majors/Junior/Senior/Big League:** While the runner is attempting to steal a base, the batter is interfered with by the catcher or any other fielder.

(d) **Junior/Senior/Big League:** A pitcher makes an illegal pitch, providing the offensive coach does not take the result of the play. See Rule 8.01 Penalty.

7.05 - Each runner including the batter-runner may, without liability to be put out, advance -

(a) to home base scoring a run, if a fair ball goes out of the playing field in flight and the runner touches all bases legally; or if a fair ball which in the umpire's judgment, would have gone out of the playing field in flight (165 feet from home plate), is deflected by the act of a fielder in throwing a glove, cap, any article of apparel;

RULE 7.00 — THE RUNNER

(b) three bases, if a fielder deliberately touches a fair ball with a cap, mask, or any part of that fielder's uniform detached from its proper place on the person of said fielder. The ball is in play and the batter may advance to home plate at the batter's peril;

(c) three bases, if a fielder deliberately throws a glove and touches a fair ball. The ball is in play and the batter may advance to home base at that batter's peril;

(d) two bases, if a fielder deliberately touches a thrown ball with a cap, mask, or any part of the uniform detached from its proper place on the person of said fielder. The ball is in play;

(e) two bases, if a fielder deliberately throws a glove at and touches a thrown ball. The ball is in play;

(f) two bases if a fair ball bounces or is deflected into the stands outside the first or third base foul line; if it goes through or under a field fence; through or under a scoreboard; through or under shrubbery or vines on the fence; or if it sticks on such fence, scoreboard, shrubbery, or vines;

(g) two bases when, with no spectators on the playing field, a thrown ball goes into the stands; into a bench (whether or not the ball rebounds into the field); over, under, or through a field fence; on a slanting part of the screen above the backstop; or remains in the meshes of wire screen protecting spectators. The ball is dead. When such wild throw is the first play by an infielder, the umpire, in awarding such bases shall be governed by the position of the runners at the time the ball was pitched; in all other cases the umpire shall be governed by the position of the runners at the time the wild throw was made;

> A.R.—If all runners, including the batter-runner have advanced at least one base when an infielder makes a wild throw on the first play after the pitch, the award shall be governed by the position of the runners when the wild throw was made.

(h) one base, if a ball, pitched to the batter, goes into a stand or bench, or over or through a field fence or backstop. The ball is dead;

(i) one base, if the batter becomes a runner on a ball four when the pitch passes the catcher and lodges in the umpire's mask or paraphernalia.

NOTE 1: If the batter becomes a runner on a wild pitch which entitled the runners to advance one base, the batter-runner shall be entitled to first base only but can advance beyond first base at their own risk if the ball stays in play.

NOTE 2: In Tee Ball, the runner or runners will be permitted to advance at their own risk on an overthrow that remains in play, but not more than one base.

(j) one base, if a fielder deliberately touches a pitched ball with his/her cap, mask, or any part of his/her uniform detached from its proper place on his/her person. The ball is in play, and the award is made from the position of the runner at the time the ball was touched.

7.06 - When the obstruction occurs, the umpire shall call or signal "Obstruction."

RULE 7.00 — THE RUNNER

(a) If a play is being made on the obstructed runner, or if the batter-runner is obstructed before touching first base, the ball is dead and all runners shall advance without liability to be put out, to the bases they would have reached, in the umpire's judgment, if there had been no obstruction. The obstructed runner shall be awarded at least one base beyond the base last legally touched by such runner, before the obstruction. Any preceding runners forced to advance by the award of bases as the penalty for obstruction shall advance without liability to put out;

(b) If no play is being made on the obstructed runner, the play shall proceed until no further action is possible. The umpire shall then call "Time" and impose such penalties, if any, as in that umpire's judgment will nullify the act of obstruction. (**NOTE 1:** When the ball is not dead on obstruction and an obstructed runner advances beyond the base which, in the umpire's judgment, the runner would have been awarded because of being obstructed, the runner does so at his/her own risk and may be tagged out. This is a judgment call. **NOTE 2:** If the defensive player blocks the base (plate) or base line clearly without possession of the ball, obstruction shall be called. The runner is safe and a delayed dead ball shall be called.)

7.08 - Any runner is out when -

(a) (1) running more than three feet away from his/her baseline to avoid being tagged, unless such action is to avoid interference with a fielder fielding a batted ball. A runner's baseline is established when the tag attempt occurs and is a straight line from the runner to the base to which he/she is attempting to reach; or

(2) after touching first base the runner leaves the baseline obviously abandoning all effort to touch the next base; or

(3) the runner does not slide or attempt to get around a fielder who has the ball and is waiting to make the tag; or

(4) the runner slides head first while advancing (**Tee Ball, Minor, or Major Divisions only**); or

(5) (a) **Major/Junior/Senior/Big League Divisions:** the runner fails to keep contact with the base to which that runner is entitled until the ball has been released by the pitcher on the delivery.
NOTE: Major Division: A local league may adopt a rule that requires the runner to keep in contact with the base to which that runner is entitled until the ball has been batted or reaches the batter, or be called out.

(b) **Minor League/Tee Ball**: the runner fails to keep in contact with the base which that runner is entitled until the ball has been batted or reaches the batter.

NOTE 1: If the ball slips from the pitcher's hand before, during, or up to the delivery of a pitch, the ball will remain in play and the runner(s) may advance at their own risk (see 8.07(a) Dropped Ball). When a runner is off a base after a pitch or as a result of a batter completing a turn at bat, and while the pitcher has the ball within the eight (8) foot radius circle, the runner must immediately attempt to advance to the next base or return to the base the runner is entitled.

NOTE 2: If the pitcher has possession of the ball within the pitcher's circle, and is not making a play (a fake throw is considered a play), runners not in contact with their bases must immediately attempt to advance or return to base.

RULE 7.00 — THE RUNNER

PENALTY: The ball is dead. "No Pitch" is declared and the runner is out. Eight (8) foot radius circle must be properly marked.

> A.R.—After making a decision, should the runner stop again without a play being made before reaching the base, he/she shall be called out. The responsibility for the runners to advance or return is removed if the pitcher attempts a play on a runner.

(b) intentionally interferes with a thrown ball; or hinders a fielder attempting to make a play on a batted ball (**NOTE:** A runner who is adjudged to have hindered a fielder who is attempting to make a play on a batted ball is out whether it was intentional or not);

(c) that runner is tagged, when the ball is alive, while off a base;

EXCEPTION: A batter-runner cannot be tagged out after overrunning or over sliding first base if said batter-runner returns immediately to the base.

> A.R. 1—This includes a batter-runner who over runs first after being issued a base on balls.
>
> A.R. 2—If the impact of a runner breaks a base loose from its position, no play can be made on that runner at that base if the runner had reached the base safely.
>
> A.R. 3—If a base is dislodged from its position during a play, any following runner on the same play shall be considered as touching or occupying the base if, in the umpire's judgment, that runner touches or occupies the dislodged bag, or the point marked by the original location of the dislodged bag.

(d) failing to retouch the base after a fair or foul ball is legally caught before that runner or the base is tagged by a fielder. The runner shall not be called out for failure to retouch the base after the first following pitch, or any play or attempted play. This is an Appeal Play;

NOTE: Base runners can legally retouch their base once a fair ball is touched in flight and advance at their own risk if a fair ball or foul ball is caught.

(e) failing to reach the next base before a fielder tags said runner or the base after that runner has been forced to advance by reason of the batter becoming a runner. However, if a following runner is retired on a force play, the force is removed and the runner must be tagged to be put out. The force is removed as soon as the runner touches the base to which that runner is forced to advance, and if sliding or overrunning the base, the runner must be tagged to be put out. However, if the forced runner, after touching the next base, retreats for any reason towards the base last occupied, the force play is reinstated and the runner can again be put out if the defense tags the base to which the runner is forced;

(f) touched by a fair ball in fair territory before the ball has touched or passed an infielder. The ball is dead and no runner may score, no runners may advance, except runners forced to advance;

EXCEPTION: If a runner is touching a base when touched by an Infield Fly, that runner is not out although the batter is out.

RULE 7.00 — THE RUNNER

NOTE 1: If a runner is touched by an Infield Fly when not touching a base, both runner and batter are out.

NOTE 2: If two runners are touched by the same fair ball, only the first one is out because the ball is instantly dead.

(g) attempting to score on a play in which the batter interferes with the play at home base before two are out. With two out, the interference puts the batter out and no score counts;

(h) passes a preceding runner before such runner is out;

(i) after acquiring legal possession of a base, the runner runs the bases in reverse order for the purpose of confusing the defense or making a travesty of the game. The umpire shall immediately call "Time" and declare the runner out;

(j) failing to return at once to first base after overrunning or over sliding that base. If attempting to run to second the runner is out when tagged. If after overrunning or over sliding first base, the runner starts toward the dugout, or toward a position, and fails to return to first base at once, that runner is out on appeal, when said runner or the base is tagged;

(k) in running or sliding for home base, the runner fails to touch home base and makes no attempt to return to the base, when a fielder holds the ball in hand, while touching home base, and appeals to the umpire for the decision. (**NOTE:** This rule applies only where the runner is on the way to the bench and a fielder would be required to chase the runner to tag him/her. It does not apply to the ordinary play where the runner misses the plate and then immediately makes an effort to touch the plate before being tagged. In that case, the runner must be tagged.)

7.09 - It is an interference by a batter or a runner when -

(a) the batter hinders the catcher in an attempt to field the ball.

(b) the batter intentionally deflects the course of a foul ball in any manner;

(c) before two are out and a runner on third base, the batter hinders a fielder in making a play at home base; the runner is out;

(d) any member or members of the offensive team stand or gather around any base to which a runner is advancing, to confuse, hinder, or add to the difficulty of the fielders. Such runner shall be declared out for the interference of a teammate or teammates;

(e) any batter or runner who has just been retired hinders or impedes any following play being made on a runner. Such runner shall be declared out for the interference of a teammate;

(f) if, in the judgment of the umpire, a base runner willfully and deliberately interferes with a batted ball or a fielder in the act of fielding a batted ball with the obvious intent to break up a double play, the ball is dead. The umpire shall call the runner out for interference and also call out the batter-runner because of the action of the runner. In no event may bases be run or runs scored because of such action by a runner;

RULE 7.00 — THE RUNNER

(g) if, in the judgment of the umpire, a batter-runner willfully and deliberately interferes with a batted ball or a fielder in the act of fielding a batted ball, with the obvious intent to break up a double play, the ball is dead; the umpire shall call the batter-runner out for interference and shall also call out the runner who advanced closest to home plate regardless where the double play might have been possible. In no event shall bases be run because of such interference;

(h) in the judgment of the umpire, the base coach at third base or first base, by touching or holding the runner, physically assists that runner in returning to or leaving third base or first base;

> A.R.—When a play is being made on the assisted runner, the runner is out and all runners return to the bases occupied at the time of the interference (dead ball). If no play is being made on the assisted runner, the runner is out and play continues (delayed dead ball).

(i) with a runner on third base, the base coach leaves the box and acts in any manner to draw a throw by a fielder;

(j) the runner fails to avoid a fielder who is attempting to field a batted ball, or intentionally interferes with a thrown ball, provided that if two or more fielders attempt to field a batted ball, and the runner comes in contact with one or more of them, the umpire shall determine which fielder is entitled to the benefit of this rule, and shall not declare the runner out for coming in contact with a fielder other than the one the umpire determines to be entitled to field such a ball;

(k) a fair ball touches the batter or runner in fair territory before touching a fielder. If a fair ball goes through or by an infielder and touches a runner immediately back of said infielder or touches the runner after having been deflected by a fielder, the umpire shall not declare the runner out for being touched by a batted ball. In making such decision, the umpire must be convinced that the ball passed through or by the infielder and that no other infielder had the chance to make a play on the ball. If in the judgment of the umpire, the runner deliberately and intentionally kicks such a batted ball on which the infielder had missed a play, then the runner shall be called out for interference;

PENALTY FOR INTERFERENCE: The runner is out and the ball is dead.

7.10 - Any runner shall be called out on appeal if -

(a) after a fly ball is caught the runner fails to retouch the base before said runner or the base is tagged. (**NOTE:** "Retouch" in this rule means to tag up and start from a contact with the base after the ball is caught. A runner is not permitted to take a flying start from a position in back of, and not touching, the base);

(b) with the ball in play, while advancing or returning to a base, the runner fails to touch each base in order before said runner or a missed base is tagged.

> A.R.—(1) No runner may return to touch a missed base after a following runner has scored. (2) When the ball is dead, no runner may return to touch a missed base or one abandoned after said runner has advanced to and touched a base beyond the missed base.

RULE 7.00 — THE RUNNER

Play A - Batter hits the ball out of the park, or hits a ground rule double, and misses first base (ball is dead). The runner may return to first base to correct the mistake before touching second. But if the runner touches second, he/she may not return to first and if the defensive team appeals, the runner is declared out at first. **(Appeal play.)**

Play B - Batter hits a ground ball to shortstop, who throws wild into the stands (ball is dead). Batter-runner is awarded second base on the overthrow out of play, but misses first base. The runner must touch first base before proceeding to touch second base. **(Appeal play.)**

(c) the runner overruns or over slides first base and fails to return to the base immediately, and said runner or the base is tagged;

(d) the runner fails to touch home base and makes no attempt to return to that base, and home base is tagged. **NOTE:** A runner forfeits his/her opportunity to return to home base when he/she enters the dugout or any other dead ball area.

Any appeal under this rule must be made before the next pitch, or any play or attempted play. No appeal can be made if the ball is dead. If the violation occurs during a play which ends a half-inning, the appeal must be made before all the defensive players have left fair territory.

An appeal is not meant to be interpreted as a play or an attempted play.

In making an appeal, the pitcher shall not throw to a base while the foot is in contact with the pitcher's plate. In putting the ball back into play, after taking the pitching position, the pitcher shall step backwards off the pitcher's plate (with the pivot foot first) to begin the appeal. **PENALTY:** Illegal pitch (8.05(e)).

Successive appeals may not be made on a runner at the same base. If the defensive team on its first appeal errs, a request for a second appeal on the same runner at the same base shall not be allowed by the umpire. (Intended meaning of the word "err" is that the defensive team in making an appeal threw the ball out of play. For example, if the pitcher threw to first base to appeal and threw the ball into the stands, no second appeal would be allowed).

NOTE 1: Appeal plays may require an umpire to recognize an apparent "fourth out." If the third out is made during a play in which an appeal play is sustained on another runner, the appeal play decision takes precedence in determining the out. If there is more than one appeal during a play that ends a half-inning, the defense may elect to take the out that gives it the advantage. For the purposes of this rule, the defensive team has "left the field" when all players have left fair territory on their way to the bench or dugout. **EXCEPTION:** If an otherwise proper appeal is being made by a player who has to go into foul territory to retrieve the ball in order to make an appeal or if the appeal is being made by the catcher (who may never have been in fair territory at all), the appeal will be adjudged to have been properly executed.

NOTE 2: An appeal should be clearly intended as an appeal, either by a verbal request by the player or an act that unmistakably indicates an appeal to the umpire. A player, inadvertently stepping on the base with a ball in hand, would not constitute an appeal. The ball must be live to make an appeal.

RULE 7.00 — THE RUNNER

7.11 - The players, coaches, or any member of an offensive team shall vacate any space (including both dugouts) needed by a fielder who is attempting to field a batted or thrown ball.

PENALTY: Interference shall be called and the batter or runner on whom the play is being made shall be declared out.

7.12 - Unless two are out, the status of a following runner is not affected by a preceding runner's failure to touch or retouch a base. If upon appeal, the preceding runner is the third out, no runners following the preceding runner shall score. If such third out is the result of a force play, neither preceding nor following runners shall score.

7.13 – Majors/Junior/Senior/Big League: When the pitcher is in the eight (8) foot radius circle and in possession of the ball, the base runner(s) shall not leave their base(s) until the pitched ball has been released by the pitcher. See Rule 7.08(a) for penalty.

NOTE 1: Minor League: When the pitcher is in the eight (8) foot radius circle and in possession of the ball, the base runner(s) shall not leave their base(s) until the pitched ball has been batted or reaches the batter. See Rule 7.08(a) for penalty. Local leagues may adopt this rule for their Major Division.

NOTE 2: Tee Ball: Base runners must stay in contact with the base until the ball is hit. When players have advanced as far as possible without being put out or having been retired the umpire shall call "time" and place the ball on the tee.

7.14 - Once each inning a team may utilize a player who is not in the batting order as a special pinch-runner for any offensive player. A player may only be removed for a special pinch runner one time during a game. The player for whom the pinch runner runs is not subject to removal from the lineup. If the pinch runner remains in the game as a substitute defensive or offensive player, the player may not be used again as a pinch-runner while in the batting order. However, if removed for another substitute that player or any player not in the lineup, is again eligible to be used as a pinch runner. **NOTE: Does not apply if the local league adopts the continuous batting order. See Rule 4.04.**

7.15 - Procedures for Use of a Double First Base: The double base may be used for first base only. The base must be rectangular, with two sides not less than 14 inches and not more than 15 inches, and the other two sides not less than 29 inches and not more than 30 inches. The longer sides shall face toward home plate and the right field corner. The outer edges shall not be more than two and one-fourth (2¼) inches thick, filled with soft material, and covered with canvas or rubber. Half the base shall be white (entirely over fair territory) and half shall be orange or green (entirely over foul territory). When using the double first base, the following rules must be observed:

(a) A batted ball that hits the white section of the double base shall be declared fair. A batted ball that hits the colored (orange or green) section without first touching or bounding over the white section shall be declared foul.

(b) Whenever a play is being made on the batter-runner, the defense must use the white section of the double first base. **NOTE 1:** A play is being made on the batter-runner when he or she is attempting to reach first base while the defense is attempting to retire him/her at that base. **NOTE 2:** If there is a play on the batter-runner, and the batter-runner touches only the white portion and the defense appeals prior to the batter-runner returning to first base, it is treated the same as missing the base. **Penalty:** Batter-runner is out.

RULE 7.00 — THE RUNNER

(c) Whenever a play is being made on the batter-runner, the batter-runner must use the colored (orange or green) section on his/her first attempt to tag first base. **NOTE:** On extra-base hits or other balls hit to the outfield when there is no chance for a play to be made at the double first base, the batter-runner may touch either the white or colored (orange or green) section of the base. Should, however, the batter-runner reach and go beyond first base, he/she may only return to the white section of the base. **PENALTY:** If there is a play on the batter-runner, and the batter-runner touches only the white portion and the defense appeals prior to the batter-runner returning to first base, it is treated the same as missing the base. If properly appealed, the batter-runner is out.

(d) When tagging up on a fly ball, the white section of the base must be used by the runner. One foot is permitted to extend behind or on the base into foul territory, as long as the front foot is touching the white section of the base. **PENALTY:** If properly appealed, runner is out.

(e) When leaving base on a pitched ball in **Majors, Junior, Senior, and Big League**, the runner must maintain contact with the white section of the base until the ball has been released by the pitcher on the delivery (**Minors:** the pitched ball has reached the batter). Runners may extend a foot behind the white portion of the base, but must maintain contact with the white section until the ball has reached the batter.

PENALTY: See Rule 7.08(a)(5).

(f) On an attempted pick-off play, the runner must return to the white section of the base only. This includes a throw from the pitcher, catcher, or any other player, in an attempt to retire the runner at the double first base.

(g) In **Majors, Junior, Senior, and Big League** divisions, when the batter becomes a runner on a third strike not caught by the catcher, the batter-runner and the defensive player may use either the colored (orange or green) or the white section:
1) On any force out attempt from the foul side of first base, or;
2) On any errant throw pulling the defense off the base into foul territory, or;
3) When the defensive player used the colored portion of the double base, the batter-runner can run in fair territory when the throw is coming from the foul side of first base, and if hit by the thrown ball, it is not interference. If intentional interference is ruled, the runner is out.

(h) Use of the double first base does not change any other rule concerning interference or obstruction at first base. (An errant throw into the three-foot running lane could still result in an obstruction call. Also, the batter-runner must still avoid interference with the fielder attempting to field a batted ball.)

Rule 8.00

The Pitcher

8.01–

(a) A legal pitching delivery shall be a ball that is delivered to the batter in an underhand motion.

(b) Both feet must be on the ground within or partially within the 24-inch length of the pitcher's plate.

(c) The shoulders shall be in line with first and third bases. When taking the pitching position, the pitcher must have his/her hands separated and must have the ball in either the glove or the pitching hand.

(d) Prior to pitching, the pitcher shall take a position with his/her pivot foot in contact with the pitcher's plate. This contact must be on or partially on the top surface of the pitcher's plate. The non-pivot foot must be on or behind the pitcher's plate.

(e) While on the pitching plate, the pitcher shall take the signal or appear to be taking a signal with the hands separated. The ball must remain in either the glove or pitching hand.

(f) After completing (e) above, the pitcher shall bring the hands together in front of the body for not less than one second and not more than 10 seconds before starting the delivery.

(g) A backward step may be taken before or simultaneous with the hands being brought together. The pivot foot must remain in contact with the pitching plate at all times prior to the forward step.

> A.R.—If the hands are together while in the pitching position, the pitcher may not step back.

(h) In the act of delivering the ball, the pitcher may take one step with the non-pivot foot simultaneously with the release of the ball. The step must be forward and toward the batter within or partially within the 24-inch length of the pitcher's plate. **NOTE:** It is not a step if the pitcher slides the pivot foot across the pitcher's plate toward the batter, or if the pivot foot turns or slides in order to push off the pitcher's plate, provided contact is maintained with the plate. Raising the foot off the pitching plate and returning it to the plate creates a rocking motion and is an illegal act.

(i) The pitcher shall not be considered in the pitching position unless the catcher is in position to receive the pitch.

> A.R.—The catcher is considered to be in position to receive a pitch when his/her mask is on and is facing the pitcher. It is not necessary to be in a squatting position.

(j) The pitcher may not take the pitching position on the pitcher's plate without having the ball in his/her possession.

(k) The pitch starts when one hand is taken off the ball after the hands have been placed together.

RULE 8.00 — THE PITCHER

(l) The pitcher must not make any motion to pitch without immediately delivering the ball to the batter.

(m) The pitcher must not use a pitching motion in which, after bringing the hands together, the pitcher removes one hand from the ball, and returns the ball to both hands in front of the body.

(n) The pitcher must not make a stop or reversal of the forward motion after separating the hands.

(o) The pitcher must not make two revolutions of the arm in the windmill motion. A pitcher may drop the arm to the side and to the rear before starting the windmill motion. If the windmill motion is not used the ball must be delivered toward home plate on the first forward swing of the pitching arm past the hip.

(p) The delivery must be an underhanded motion with the hand below the hip and the wrist not farther from the body than the elbow.

(q) The release of the ball and follow through of the hand and wrist must be forward and past the straight line of the body.

(r) Pushing off with the pivot foot from a place other than the pitcher's plate is illegal. This includes a "crow hop" as defined under Rule 2.00.

(s) The pivot foot must remain in contact with or push off and drag away from the pitching plate prior to the front foot touching the ground, as long as the pivot foot remains in contact with the ground. When the pivot foot leaves the ground it is considered a "leap" and is considered an illegal pitch. See definition under Rule 2.00.

(t) The pitcher must not make another revolution after releasing the ball.

(u) The pitcher shall not deliberately drop, roll, or bounce the ball in order to prevent the batter from hitting it.

(v) The pitcher has 20 seconds to release the next pitch after receiving the ball or after the umpire indicates "play ball."

PENALTY: The penalty imposed for violation of all subsections of rule 8.01, with the exception of subsection (i), is an illegal pitch. Violation of (i) is ruled as a No Pitch. **Minor/Major Divisions:** The pitch shall be called a ball. **Junior/Senior/Big League:** The pitch shall be called a ball and all base runners advance one base without liability to be put out. If a play follows the illegal pitch, the manager of the offense may advise the plate umpire of a decision to decline the illegal pitch penalty and accept the play. Such election shall be made immediately at the end of the play. However, if the batter hits the ball and reaches first base safely, and if all base runners advance at least one base on the action resulting from the batted ball, the play proceeds without reference to the illegal pitch. **NOTE:** A batter hit by a pitch shall be awarded first base without reference to the illegal pitch.

8.02 - The pitcher shall not -
(a) (1) apply a foreign substance of any kind to the ball, pitching hand, or fingers. Under the supervision of the umpire, powder rosin may be used to dry the hands; **NOTE:** A pitcher may use a rosin bag for the purpose of applying rosin to the bare hand or hands. Neither the pitcher nor any other player shall dust the ball with the rosin bag; neither shall the pitcher nor any other

player be permitted to apply rosin from the bag to their glove or dust any part of the uniform with the rosin bag.

(2) wear a sweatband, bracelet, or similar type items on the wrist or forearm of either arm;

(3) deface the ball in any manner;

(b) intentionally delay the game by throwing the ball to players other than the catcher, when the batter is in position.

PENALTY: If, after a warning by the umpire, such delaying action is repeated, the pitcher can be removed from the game.

8.03 -
(a) At the beginning of each inning or when a pitcher relieves another, no more than one minute may be used to deliver not more than eight preparatory pitches to the catcher or other teammate acting in the capacity of catcher.

> A.R.—If a sudden emergency causes a pitcher to be summoned into the game without any opportunity to warm-up, the umpire-in-chief shall allow the pitcher as many pitches as the umpire deems necessary.

(b) The catcher shall return the ball directly to the pitcher after each pitch, except after a strikeout or putout made by the catcher, or to make a play on a base runner.

(c) If the pitcher desires to walk a batter intentionally, all pitches must be legally delivered to the batter.

8.04 - "No Pitch" shall be declared and the ball is dead when -
(a) the pitcher pitches during the suspension of play;

(b) the runner is called out for leaving the base too soon;

(c) a catcher's feet (both) are not within the catcher's box while the pitcher has the ball and is ready to pitch. Once the ball is released, the catcher may step outside the box.

8.05 - An Illegal Pitch is -
(a) pushing off with the pivot foot from a place other than the pitcher's plate. The pivot foot may remain in contact with or may push off and drag away from the pitching plate prior to the front foot touching the ground, as long as the pivot foot remains in contact with the ground and within or partially within the 24-inch length.

(b) when the pitcher delivers the pitch with a foreign substance applied to the ball; (Rosin can be applied to the hand.)

(c) a "quick" return pitch; Umpires will judge a quick pitch as one delivered before the batter is reasonably set in the batter's box.

(d) a pitch not made in accordance with the pitching rules.

(e) a throw to a base while the pivot foot is in contact with the pitcher's plate.

PENALTY: Minor/Major Divisions: The pitch shall be called a ball. **Junior/Senior/Big League:** The pitch shall be called a ball and all base runners advance one base

RULE 8.00 — THE PITCHER

without liability to be put out. If a play follows the illegal pitch, the manager of the offense may advise the plate umpire of a decision to decline the illegal pitch penalty and accept the play. Such election shall be made immediately at the end of the play. However, if the batter hits the ball and reaches first base safely, and if all base runners advance at least one base on the action resulting from the batted ball, the play proceeds without reference to the illegal pitch. **NOTE 1:** A batter hit by a pitch shall be awarded first base without reference to the illegal pitch. **NOTE 2:** There is no balk in softball.

8.06 - This rule, which applies to each pitcher who enters a game, governs the visits of the manager or coach to the pitcher in the circle**.**

(a) A manager or coach may come out twice in one inning to visit with the pitcher, but the third time out, the player must be removed as a pitcher. **Example**: If a manager visits Pitcher A once in the first inning, then makes a pitching change in the same inning, Pitcher B would be allowed two visits in that inning before being removed on the third visit.

(b) A manager or coach may come out three times in one game to visit with the pitcher, but the fourth time out, the player must be removed as a pitcher. **Example**: If a manager visits Pitcher A twice in the first three innings, then makes a pitching change in the fourth inning, Pitcher B would be allowed three visits in that game before being removed on the fourth visit, subject to the limits in (a) above.

(c) The manager or coach is prohibited from making a third visit while the same batter is at bat.

(d) A manager or coach may confer with **any other player(s),** including the catcher, during the visit with the pitcher. A manager or coach who is granted a time out to talk to any defensive player will be charged with a visit to the pitcher.

> A.R. 1— At the time a pitcher is removed, a visit shall not be charged to the new pitcher.
>
> A.R. 2—A conference with the pitcher or any other fielder to evaluate the player's condition after an injury shall not be considered a visit for the purposes of this rule. The manager or coach should advise the umpire of such a conference, and the umpire should monitor same.

8.07 - Dropped Ball

(a) If a ball slips from the pitcher's hand before, during, or up to the delivery of a pitch, a ball is declared on the batter. The ball will remain in play and the runner(s) may advance at their own risk. See 2.00 - Dropped Ball.

Rule 9.00

The Umpire

9.01 -

(a) The league president shall appoint one or more adult umpires to officiate at each league game. The umpire shall be responsible for the conduct of the game in accordance with these official rules and for maintaining discipline and order on the playing field during the game.

NOTE 1: It is highly recommended all umpires attach a "dangling" type throat protector to their mask.

NOTE 2: Male umpires working the game behind the plate must wear mask, chest protector, and protective cup.

NOTE 3: Female umpires working the game behind the plate must wear mask and chest protector.

NOTE 4: Use of protective shin guards is strongly recommended as a safety precaution for both male and female umpires working behind the plate.

(b) Each umpire is the representative of the league and of Little League International, and is authorized and required to enforce all of these rules. Each umpire has authority to order a player, coach, manager, or league officer to do or refrain from doing anything which affects the administering of these rules and to enforce the prescribed penalties.

(c) Each umpire has authority to rule on any point not specifically covered in these rules.

(d) Each umpire has authority to disqualify any player, coach, manager, or substitute for objecting to decisions or for unsportsmanlike conduct or language and to eject such disqualified person from the playing field. If an umpire disqualifies a player while a play is in progress, the disqualification shall not take effect until no further action is possible in that play.

(e) All umpires have authority at their discretion to eject from the playing field (1) any person whose duties permit that person's presence on the field, such as ground crew members, photographers, newsmen, broadcasting crew members, etc. and (2) any spectator or other person not authorized to be on the playing field.

(f) **Umpires may order both teams into their dugouts and suspend play until such time as league officials deal with unruly spectators. Failure of league officials to adequately handle an unruly spectator can result in the game remaining suspended until a later date.**

9.02 -

(a) Any umpire's decisions which involves judgment, such as, but not limited to, whether a batted ball is fair or foul, whether a pitch is a strike or a ball, or whether a runner is safe or out, is final. No player, manager, coach, or substitute shall object to any such judgment decisions.

(b) If there is reasonable doubt that any umpire's decision may be in conflict with the rules, the manager may appeal the decision and ask that a correct ruling be made. Such appeal shall be made only to the umpire who made the protested decision.

RULE 9.00 — THE UMPIRE

(c) If a decision is appealed, the umpire making the decision, may ask another umpire for information before making a final decision. No umpire shall criticize, seek to reverse, or interfere with another umpire's decision unless asked to do so by the umpire making it.

(d) No umpire may be replaced during a game unless injured or ill.

9.03 -

(a) If there is only one umpire, that umpire must be an adult and shall have complete jurisdiction in administering the rules. This umpire may take any position on the playing field which will enable said umpire to discharge all duties (usually behind the catcher, but sometimes behind the pitcher if there are runners.)

(b) If there are two or more umpires, one shall be designated Umpire-in-Chief and the others field umpires, or a plate umpire.

(c) The Umpire-in-Chief may be a plate umpire or a field umpire. The Umpire-in-Chief's duties, in addition to any field or plate duties, shall be to:
  (1) take full charge of, and be responsible for, the proper conduct of the game;
  (2) make all decisions except those commonly reserved for the other field umpires or plate umpire;
  (3) decide when a game shall be forfeited; and
  (4) announce any special ground rules.

(d) If no adult umpire is available for a game, and non-adult umpires are used exclusively for that game, the local Little League must assign an adult as Game Coordinator, or the game cannot be played. The Game Coordinator must not be a manager or coach of either team in the game, and cannot be assigned as Game Coordinator for more than one game at a time. The Game Coordinator's duties shall be:
  (1) To be included in the pregame meeting as noted in Rule 4.01;
  (2) To remain at the game at all times, including between half innings, in a position to see all actions on the field and in close proximity to the field (not in any enclosure). If, for some reason, the Game Coordinator is not present or is unable to perform his/her duties for any reason, the game must be suspended until the Game Coordinator returns, or until a new adult Game Coordinator is present and assumes the duties of Game Coordinator for the remainder of the game;
  (3) To oversee the conduct of all players, managers, coaches, and umpires in the game;
  (4) To have the authority to disqualify any player, coach, manager, or substitute for objecting to the decisions of an umpire, for unsportsmanlike conduct or language, or for any of the reasons enumerated in these Playing Rules, and to eject such disqualified person from the playing field. If the Game Coordinator disqualifies a player while a play is in progress, the disqualification shall not take effect until no further action is possible in that play;
  (5) To have the sole ability to judge as to whether and when play shall be suspended during a game because of inclement weather conditions or the unfit condition of the playing field; as to whether and when play shall be resumed after such suspension; and as to whether and when a game shall

RULE 9.00 — THE UMPIRE

be terminated after such suspension. Said Game Coordinator shall not call the game until at least thirty minutes after play as suspended. The Game Coordinator may continue suspension as long as there is any chance to resume play. (This supersedes Rule 3.10.)

> A.R.—The Game Coordinator should not interrupt or stop a game until all play and action ends. At that time, the Game Coordinator can alert the plate umpire to stop the game, and at that time enforce any part of 9.03(d).

9.04 -

(a) The plate umpire shall stand behind the catcher. This umpire usually is designated as the Umpire-in-Chief. The plate umpire's duties shall be to:
   (1) call and count ball and strikes;
   (2) call and declare fair balls and fouls except those commonly called by field umpires;
   (3) make all decisions on the batter except those specifically reserved to the Umpire-in-Chief, or the field umpire;
   (4) inform the official scorer of the official batting order; and any changes in the lineups and batting order, on request.

(b) A field umpire may take any position (see Little League Umpire Manual) on the playing field best suited to make impending decisions on the bases. A field umpire's duties shall be to:
   (1) make all decisions on the bases except those specifically reserved to the Umpire-in-Chief, or the plate umpire;
   (2) take concurrent jurisdiction with the Umpire-in-Chief in calling "Time," illegal pitches, or defacement or discoloration of the ball by any player;
   (3) aid the Umpire-in-Chief in every manner in enforcing the rules, excepting the power to forfeit the game, shall have equal authority with the Umpire-in-Chief in administering and enforcing the rules and maintaining discipline.

(c) If different decisions should be made on one play by different umpires, the Umpire-in-Chief shall call all the umpires into consultation, with no manager or player present. After consultation, the Umpire-in-Chief shall determine which decision shall prevail, based on which umpire was in the best position and which decision was most likely correct. Play shall proceed as if only the final decision had been made.

9.05 -

(a) The umpire shall report to the league president within 24 hours after the end of a game, all violations of rules and other incidents worthy of comment, including the disqualification of any manager, coach, or player, and the reason therefore.

(b) When any manager, coach, or player is disqualified for a flagrant offense such as the use of obscene or indecent language, or an assault upon an umpire, manager, coach, or player, the umpire shall forward full particulars to the league president within 24 hours after the end of the game.

(c) After receiving the umpire's report that a manager, coach, or player has been disqualified, the league president shall require such manager, coach, or player to appear before at least three members of the Board of Directors to explain their

RULE 9.00 — THE UMPIRE

conduct. In the case of a player, the manager shall appear with the player in the capacity of an advisor. The members of the Board present at the meeting shall impose such penalty as they feel is justified. **NOTE**: The Board may impose such penalties that it feels are warranted, but may not lessen the requirements of Rule 4.07.

9.06 - Umpires shall not wear shoes with metal spikes or cleats.

IMPORTANT

Carry your Rulebook. It is better to consult the rules and hold up the game long enough to decide a knotty problem than to have a game protested and possibly replayed.

TOURNAMENT RULES AND GUIDELINES

Tournament Rules and Guidelines
Little League Softball®, 9- and 10-Year-Old Division Softball, 10- and 11-Year-Old Division Softball, Junior League Softball, Senior League Softball, and Big League Softball

Points of Emphasis in Bold Italics

Tournament play started in Little League in 1947. Conduct of tournament play by District Administrators began in 1956 following the first Little League International Congress. Today, responsibility for scheduling and supervising all District tournament games comes under jurisdiction of the District Administrator. Little League International has the right to appoint Tournament Directors at other levels of tournament play.

The Tournaments of Little League have grown year by year until today they have become the outstanding, in fact, the only exposure that the majority of the public sees. In many cases, they are the criterion by which Little League is judged. Proper conduct at tournament time imposes a large responsibility upon all concerned. Good judgment and exemplary disciplines are demanded if Little League tournaments of the future are to remain worthwhile in the public esteem.

The Little League Softball Tournament, 9- and 10-Year-Old Division Softball Tournament, 10- and 11-Year-Old Division Softball Tournament, Junior League Softball, Senior League Softball and Big League Softball Tournaments are authorized by the Little League International Board of Directors. Leagues which exercise the option to participate in Tournament Play must pledge they will do so with full knowledge of the rules and in agreement that the rules will be upheld.

RULES: Except where noted in these Tournament Rules and Guidelines, the Little League Softball Official Regulations and Playing Rules will be used in the conduct of the 9- and 10-Year-Old Division Tournament, the 10- and 11-Year-Old Division Tournament, the Little League Softball Tournament, the Junior League Softball Tournament, Senior League Softball Tournament and Big League Softball Tournament.

9- and 10-Year-Old Division and 10- and 11-Year-Old Division: The objective of the 9- and 10-Year-Old Division and 10- and 11-Year-Old Division Tournament is to provide nine, ten and eleven-year-old players the opportunity to participate in a softball tournament at the District, Sectional and State levels at the conclusion of the regular season. Leagues are strongly encouraged to place the maximum number of players (14) on the Tournament Affidavit, thereby giving more players the opportunity to participate.

Responsibility and Chain of Command

It should be clearly understood by Tournament Directors and league presidents that operation of the annual tournaments in Little League come under a different authority and jurisdiction from that normally observed during the playing season. It is, in fact, a whole new ball game. Once the tournament season starts, authority is vested solely in the Tournament Committee at Williamsport.

There will be no waivers, resorting to local rules, or other variation unless granted explicitly from Williamsport. To administer the tournament properly and scale down thousands of teams to two finalists in the limited time afforded by the tournament season is an undertaking requiring considerable disciplines. Once the tournament starts, it must

TOURNAMENT RULES AND GUIDELINES

proceed without interruption. If protests or disputes occur which cannot be settled by the umpires or Tournament Director through immediate and concise application of the rules, an appeal must be made through proper channels promptly to prevent a major blockage or loss of momentum.

Revocation of tournament privileges or forfeiture of a tournament game may be decided only by the Tournament Committee at Williamsport. Should a problem arise that cannot be resolved while a game is in progress, the game must be suspended by the Umpire-in-Chief and the problem referred immediately to the Tournament Director. If not resolved, it must be referred to the Regional Director. If still unresolved, it will be referred to the Tournament Committee in Williamsport. If the Tournament Committee deems any player to be ineligible, by league age, residency or school attendance, participation in other programs, or participation in less than sixty (60) percent [Big League: forty (40) percent] of the regular season games, it may result in forfeiture of tournament game(s), and/or suspension or removal of personnel from tournament play, and/or suspension or removal of personnel or teams from further Little League activities, and/or suspension or revocation of the local league's charter. These actions can only be taken by the Tournament Committee in Williamsport.

The Tournament Committee and the individual Regional Directors may appoint agents to act on their behalf, and any person so appointed shall have the authority to act as, and exercise the duties of, the Tournament Committee or the individual Regional Directors.

The Tournament Committee also reserves the right in its sole discretion to impose any of the above penalties if, in its judgment, any player, manager, or coach displays unsportsmanlike conduct, "makes a travesty of the game," or repeatedly/willfully violates any rules, regulations, or policies contained herein during the game, at the game site, or at any event related to the International Tournament. The decision of the Tournament Committee is final and binding. The Committee also reserves the right to impose any penalty the Committee deems appropriate if the Committee determines action is necessary to correct a situation brought to its attention, regardless of the source of that information. The decision of the Tournament Committee is final and binding.

Knowledge of the rules must be guaranteed before a Tournament Director is declared qualified. All Tournament Directors will undergo a thorough and instructive briefing session prior to taking on their duties, must signify that they understand the rules, and regardless of personal feelings, they are in full agreement and can interpret them properly. At the time of the District tournament meeting, it will be required that each league president or the representative in attendance signify that the league and tournament team managing personnel are knowledgeable of Tournament Rules and are in full agreement with these conditions.

Selection of Tournament Teams (Recommended Method)

Little League would gain immeasurably in esteem of the public if all tournament teams were selected by the players themselves. Players relish the challenge of competition, but their anxiety to excel is in balance with an intuitive respect and admiration for teammate and opponent alike who demonstrate superior ability and skill.

1. It is not required that players be selected for the position they occupy during the regular season. For example, a pitcher who is also a good outfielder or infielder may be placed on the roster and used in whatever position the manager deems to be of advantage.

TOURNAMENT RULES AND GUIDELINES

2. Tournament team candidates should be selected upon their playing ability and eligibility. The roster should include sufficient pitching strength to meet tournament schedules.

3. The following plan was presented to the International Congress, Washington, D.C., 1965, as a guideline, taken from the experience of the International Advisory Council. The principle is to have all components of a league determine and participate in fair and democratic selection of the tournament team. This would eliminate many of the complaints, abuses, pressures, and charges of favoritism which are directed toward the league president. The following groups should each select its tournament team.

> Group 1 - Players
> Group 2 - League Officers
> Group 3 - Team Managers
> Group 4 - Team Coaches
> Group 5 - Volunteer Umpires

Every player on the eligible teams is entitled to vote. Each group submits its list of players at a meeting of the Board of Directors of the league. The names are to be read and counted from each of the groups, and the players in the order of total votes received will become eligible for the tournament team. Where more than one player has an equal number of votes to qualify for the last position or positions, final selection should be made by a majority vote of the Board of Directors at the time of the meeting.

NOTE: Method of selection is to be determined by the local league Board of Directors.

Tournament Organization

Teams

Each chartered league shall be eligible to enter a team. Alternates are not authorized.

(**NOTE**: In the 9- and 10-Year-Old Division and 10- and 11-Year-Old Division, a league may enter more than one tournament team with the District Administrator's approval.)

Where two or more charters have combined to form a single program, a tournament team must be selected for each charter composed of players from within its own chartered area. Exceptions can only be made by the Charter Committee.

Tournament teams and Eligibility Affidavit shall consist of, and must be limited to, a maximum of fourteen (14) players, one (1) manager, and a maximum of two (2) coaches.

Senior League: Tournament teams may be selected from all league teams in a district or may be regular season unit team. Teams and Eligibility Affidavit shall consist of, and must be limited to, a maximum of sixteen (16) players, one (1) manager, and a maximum of two (2) coaches.

Big League: Tournament teams may be selected from all league teams in a district or may be a regular season unit team. Teams and Eligibility Affidavit shall consist of, and must be limited to, a maximum of seventeen (17) players, one (1) manager, and a maximum of two (2) coaches.

Managers and Coaches

The president of the league, the District Administrator, or District Staff shall not serve as manager or coach.

TOURNAMENT RULES AND GUIDELINES

Little League: The manager and coach(es) shall be regular season team managers and/or coaches from the Little League Softball (Major) Division.

9- and 10-Year-Old Division & 10- and 11-Year-Old Division: The manager and coach(es) shall be regular season team managers and/or coaches from the Little League Softball (Major) Division or Minor League Division.

Junior League: The manager and coach(es) shall be regular season team managers and/or coaches from the Junior Division or Senior Division.

Senior League: The manager and coach(es) shall be regular season team managers and/or coaches from the Junior Division, Senior Division, or Big League Division.

Big League: The manager and coach(es) shall be regular season team managers and/or coaches from the Senior Division or Big League Division.

Umpires

The Tournament Director shall have full responsibility for providing volunteer Little League umpires for tournament play. Umpires from leagues involved in the game should not be assigned. The District Administrator shall not umpire.

There should be at least two umpires in each game. More are recommended when available.

The designated Umpire-in-Chief for each game must be an adult.

Tournament Eligibility Affidavit

It shall be the league president's responsibility to review and certify the birth records (league age) by viewing the original birth record and residence or school attendance (as defined by Little League Baseball, Incorporated) of all players. When the league finally decides on the makeup of the team, names must be entered on the league's Eligibility Affidavit. Once the District Administrator certifies the Eligibility Affidavit, the tournament team will be required to have in its possession:

1. the Eligibility Affidavit;
2. a map, signed and dated by the league president and District Administrator, showing the actual boundaries of the league, with locations noted for the residences of the parent or legal guardian (court-appointed) or location of the school for every participant named on the affidavit;
3. tournament verification form for each player (strongly recommended);
4. three or more documents to determine residency of the parent(s) or legal guardian (court-appointed) or a document to support school attendance/enrollment for each player named on the tournament affidavit;
5. **waivers (i.e. II(d), IV(h), Charter Committee, etc...)**

IMPORTANT: Alternates are not authorized. They shall not accompany the team and shall not be listed on the Eligibility Affidavit.

Eligibility Affidavit must be certified by the District Administrator or his or her designated appointee and presented by the team manager to the Tournament Director before every game. Each Tournament team must have twelve (12) eligible players for the District Administrator to certify. **EXCEPTION**: A District Administrator may certify the

TOURNAMENT RULES AND GUIDELINES

Eligibility Affidavit for those teams that provide a justifiable reason for not having twelve (12) players. **NOTE:** The Eligibility Affidavit becomes official once the team plays its first tournament game.

Player Participation in Other Programs
Player participation in other programs during the International Tournament is permitted, subject to the provisions of Regulation IV(a)Note 2.

Release of Names
The release of names of players selected for the tournament team shall not be made before June 15, or two weeks prior to the start of the tournament within their respective division (whichever is earlier), and not until the availability and eligibility of all prospective team members have been established. (The Little League group accident insurance program underwritten by an AIG member company for tournament teams will not go into effect until June 15, or the date of the release of the names of Tournament team members, whichever is earlier).

Violation of this rule may be cause for revocation of tournament privilege by the Tournament Committee.

League Eligibility
In order for a Little League program to be eligible to enter a team or teams into the International Tournament (including 9- and 10-Year-Old Division and 10- and 11-Year-Old Division) the following must be accomplished as indicated:
1) The league must be chartered in an age appropriate division(s) for which it wishes to enter a tournament team(s), no later than June 1, 2016. **Examples**: Chartered in Little League Majors to enter a Major Division team (11- and 12-year-olds); chartered in Senior League to enter a Junior, Senior, or Big League team, etc.
2) The league must have scheduled and played, at a minimum, a 12-game (per team) regular season, exclusive of playoffs and tournament games, for each division entering tournament prior to the first game in their respective tournament. See Reg. VII.
3) All waiver requests (for the league, team, player, manager, and/or coach) of any kind must be submitted and approved not later than June 1, 2016.
4) Team number revisions and fees incurred by the league must be paid in full by June 1, 2016.
5) All combined team and interleague play requests that may involve tournament play must be submitted and approved not later than June 1, 2016.

Failure to meet any of the listed requirements could result in a team or teams being declared ineligible by the Tournament Committee at Little League International.

Player Eligibility
Players are eligible for Tournament Play, provided they meet the criteria established by the Little League "Residency and School Attendance Player Eligibility Requirement," "Player Participation In Other Programs," and the following:
9- and 10-Year-Old Division - Any player League Age 9 or 10, with amateur status, who has participated as an eligible player in 60 percent (60%) of the regular season games as of June 15, with the exception of the school softball season, on a:

TOURNAMENT RULES AND GUIDELINES

1. Little League Softball (Major Division) team, or;
2. Minor League Softball team.

10- and 11-Year-Old Division - Any player League Age 10 or 11, with amateur status, who has participated as an eligible player in 60 percent (60%) of the regular season games as of June 15, with the exception of the school softball season, on a:
1. Little League Softball (Major Division) team, or;
2. Minor League Softball team.

Little League (Major Division) - Any player League Age 11 or 12, with amateur status, who has participated as an eligible player in 60 percent (60%) of the regular season games as of June 15 on a Little League Softball (Major Division) team, with the exception of the school softball season.

Junior League - Any player League Age 12, 13, or 14, with amateur status, who has participated as an eligible player in 60 percent (60%) of the regular season games (**Special Games may be counted toward this requirement - See Regulation IX**) as of June 15, with the exception of the middle school, junior high school or high school softball season, on a:
1. Junior League Softball team, or;
2. Senior League Softball team, or;
3. Big League Softball team.

Senior League - Any player League Age 13, 14, 15, or 16, with amateur status, who has participated as an eligible player in 60 percent (60%) of the regular season games (**Special Games may be counted toward this requirement - See Regulation IX**) as of June 15 or by the start of Tournament Play in their respective District (whichever is later), with the exception of the middle school, junior high school or high school softball season, on a:
1. Junior League Softball team, or;
2. Senior League Softball team, or;
3. Big League Softball team.

Big League - Any player League Age 14, 15, 16, 17, and 18, with amateur status, who has participated as an eligible player in 40 percent (40%) of the regular season games (**Special Games may be counted toward this requirement - See Regulation IX**) by the start of Tournament Play in their respective District, with the exception of the high school or college softball season, on a:
1. Junior League Softball team, or;
2. Senior League Softball team, or;
3. Big League Softball team.

NOTE: For the purpose of qualifying for a Big League International Tournament team under this rule, participation is considered as having completed one or more of the following:
1. The player completed one (1) at bat as defined in Regulation IV(i); or,
2. The player enters the game in one of nine defensive positions and occupies such for one (1) defensive out or one (1) at-bat; or,
3. The player is entered as a special pinch runner and scores, is retired or three (3) outs end the inning.

TOURNAMENT RULES AND GUIDELINES

Exception: The local league Board of Directors may permit a player to be eligible for selection, who does not meet the 60 percent (60%) requirement [**Big League:** 40 percent (40%) requirement], if they provide a physician's note documenting an injury or illness prior to or during the current season prohibiting his/her participation and such note releases the player for the balance of the Regular Season and/or Tournament Play.

NOTE 1: Consistent with a manager's ability to conduct the affairs of his or her team, a manager may disqualify a player from the team for the current season, subject to Board of Directors approval, if the player repeatedly misses practice or games.

NOTE 2: The Big League Softball, Senior League Softball, and Junior League Softball Tournaments are divided by age, without regard to the regular season division in which a player participates, as noted above.

CONDITION 1: Participation must be within the chartered league/district named on the Eligibility Affidavit unless written approval is granted by the respective Regional Director and Charter Committee.

CONDITION 2: A player who is not able to participate in a number of local league regular season games because of participation in a school softball program will receive an adjustment on the minimum participating in games required under this rule.

EXAMPLE: If, for any given division, Team A played 20 regular season games before June 15, and a player missed 10 games because of participation in a school softball program, that player is required to have participated in only six (6) regular season games to be eligible for the Tournament Team.

CONDITION 3: A player may be named to the roster of, and practice with, only ONE Little League International Tournament Team. Once the affidavit is signed by the local league president, player agent, and District Administrator (or their representatives), the players listed on the affidavit shall not be eligible to participate on any other Little League International Tournament Team for the current year.

Softball players league age 10, 11, 12, 13, 14, 15, and 16 may be eligible for selection to multiple tournament teams. These players may only be selected to one tournament team. Under no circumstances may these players be chosen for, practice with, or participate with more than one tournament team. *Violation of this rule may be cause for revocation of tournament privilege by the Tournament Committee.*

Tournament Requirement for Non-Citizens

A participant who is not a citizen of the country in which he/she wishes to play, but meets residency or school attendance requirements as defined by Little League, may participate in that country if:

1. his/her visa allows that participant to remain in that country for a period of at least one year, or;
2. the prevailing laws allow that participant to remain in that country for at least one year, or;
3. the participant has an established bona fide residence in that country for at least two years prior to the start of the regular season.

Exceptions can only be made by action of the Charter Committee in Williamsport.

TOURNAMENT RULES AND GUIDELINES

Insurance

Accident: A league or district Senior/Big League team shall not be accepted for tournament play unless covered by accident insurance, which includes tournament play. It is strongly recommended that a medical release for each player on the Affidavit be carried by the team manager.

Liability: Liability Insurance must be carried by the league on whose field tournaments are played as well as all leagues who participate in the tournament. Minimum coverage of $1,000,000 single limit, bodily injury, and property damage. The policy must include coverage for claims arising out of athletic participants.

If insurance is purchased locally, a copy of the policy must be on file at Little League International.

Replacement of Player, Manager or Coach

Any player, manager, or coach listed on the Eligibility Affidavit who is unable to participate because of injury, illness, vacation, or other justifiable reason may be replaced by another eligible person. If a player, manager, or coach is replaced, that person may not be returned to the Tournament Affidavit. Permanent replacements must be from the league's regular season teams and shall be recorded and approved by the District Administrator or Tournament Director in the space provided on the back of the Eligibility Affidavit. **Exception: If a manager or coach is unable to attend a game for a justifiable reason, a Tournament Director could approve a temporary replacement as outlined in the Little League Tournament Team Eligibility Affidavit. Temporary replacement of a manager or coach must be entered on the Eligibility Affidavit. A manager or coach who is ejected from a game may not be replaced for the team's next physically played game. (See Rule 4.07)**

Playing Equipment

The dimensions and other specifications of all playing equipment used must conform to those set forth in the Little League, Junior League, Senior League, and Big League Softball Playing Rules except for those noted below:

Every member of the team must wear a conventional uniform which includes shirt, pants or shorts, socks, and cap or visor. This may be a regular season uniform.

NOTE: The wearing of caps or visors is optional for each player while on defense.

Each team must provide at least six (6) [seven (7) for **Junior/Senior/Big League**] NOCSAE approved safety helmets with warning labels. The batter, all base runners, (on-deck batters for **Junior/Senior/Big League**, and player base coaches must wear approved helmets.

All male players must wear athletic supporters. Catchers (male) must wear the metal, fibre, or plastic type cup.

Catchers must wear a mask with (NOCSAE) approved catchers helmet (**skull cap type not acceptable**) and "dangling" type throat guard during practice, infield/outfield, pitcher warm-up, and games. All catchers must wear chest protector and shin guards.

Shoes with metal spikes or cleats are not permitted. Shoes with molded cleats are permissible. **Junior/Senior/Big League Players:** Shoes with metal spikes or cleats are permitted.

TOURNAMENT RULES AND GUIDELINES

Schedules

Each District Administrator must finalize tournament schedules prior to the start of the tournament or by June 15 (whichever is earliest). Schedules for each level (District, Section, Division, State, Regional) must utilize Little League International approved single elimination brackets, double elimination brackets, or pool play format with pool play tie breaker format as noted in this section. All other tournament formats must be approved by the Tournament Committee.

9- and 10- & 10- and 11-Year-Old Division, Little League: A team may play in up to two (2) doubleheaders in a seven (7) day period.

Junior/Senior/Big League: Teams may participate in a maximum of three (3) games in a day.

NOTE 1: Inclement weather may be justification to revert to single elimination in order to complete a tournament on schedule, with the approval of the Regional Director.

NOTE 2: The 9- and 10- and 10- and 11-Year-Old Divisions advances to state level only.

NOTE 3: Consult approved schedules for specific dates. Tournament dates may vary.

Tournament Team Practice

Try-outs or practices by tournament teams shall not be held before June 15 or two weeks prior to the start of the tournament within their respective division (whichever is earlier). Tournament team practice may only take place against other teams within the same or contiguous districts in the same division, providing such practice is done out of uniform. (The Little League group accident insurance program underwritten by an AIG member company for tournament teams will not go into effect until June 15, or the date of the release of the names of tournament team members, whichever is earlier.)

Violation of this rule may be cause for revocation of tournament privileges by the Tournament Committee.

Selection of Fields

Local leagues selected to host a Section, State, Division, Region, or World Series tournament must have an approved ASAP safety plan.

All games shall be played upon Little League fields approved by the Tournament Director. Exception to this rule can only be made with the consent of the Regional Director.

Fields must be enclosed with an outfield fence. The distance to the outfield fence should be 200 feet from home plate. The outfield fence must be a minimum of 180 feet and a maximum of 225 feet from home plate. Tournament Directors should not permit portable outfield fences to exceed 200 feet. The Tournament Director or assistant shall judge fitness of the playing field before the game starts.

9- and 10-Year-Old Division, 10- and 11-Year-Old Division and Little League: The on-deck batter's position is not permitted.

NOTE: For additional information about field selection, see "Physical Conditions."

TOURNAMENT RULES AND GUIDELINES

Games Under Lights
Games under lights may be scheduled at all levels of tournament play. The District Administrator having jurisdiction must determine that lighting installations meet minimum standards approved by Little League International.

Curfew
No inning shall start after midnight prevailing time (12:30 a.m. prevailing time for **Junior League;** 1:00 a.m. prevailing time for **Senior/Big League**).

NOTE 1: An inning starts the moment the third out is made completing the previous inning.

NOTE 2: Neither Tournament Directors and officials nor tournament teams are permitted to circumvent the curfews established above by continuing, suspending and restarting, or starting a game after curfew has been reached and play is required to be terminated. If the curfew noted above occurs during a game suspended in accordance with Tournament Rule 11, that game must not be continued after the curfew. It must either be resumed on a subsequent day, or declared ended, as determined by rule.

Starting Time of Games
A game shall not be started unless the Tournament Director or assistant judge there is adequate time to complete the game before darkness or curfew.

Admission Charge
There shall be no charge for admission to Little League, 9- and 10-, or 10- and 11-Year-Old Division Tournament games.

Junior/Senior/Big League: An admission charge is permitted.

Conditions of Tournament Play

Protests
This rule replaces Rule 4.19.

No protest shall be considered on a decision involving an umpire's judgment. Equipment which does not meet specifications must be removed from the game.

Protest shall be considered only when based on:

A. The violation or interpretation of a playing rule;
When a manager claims that a decision is in violation of the playing rules, the following steps must be taken:
1. A formal (verbal) protest must be made to the Umpire-in-Chief at once by the manager or coach.
2. The Umpire-in-Chief must immediately call a conference of all umpires working the game.
3. If the problem cannot be resolved to the satisfaction of the managers, the Umpire-in-Chief shall be required to consult with the Tournament Director or District Administrator.

TOURNAMENT RULES AND GUIDELINES

4. If the managers do not accept the decision of the Tournament Director, either manager may elect, without penalty, to discontinue play until the matter is referred to the Regional Headquarters. Either the Umpire-in-Chief, Tournament Director or District Administrator will call the Regional Headquarters at this time.

5. If the managers do not accept the decision of the Regional Director (or his/her designated agent), either may insist that the matter be referred to the Tournament Committee in Williamsport. The decision of the Tournament Committee shall be final and binding.

NOTE 1 - PROTESTS INVOLVING PLAYING RULES NOT RESOLVED BEFORE THE NEXT PITCH OR PLAY SHALL NOT BE CONSIDERED.

NOTE 2 - UMPIRES, TOURNAMENT DIRECTORS, AND DISTRICT ADMINISTRATORS DO NOT HAVE THE AUTHORITY TO DECLARE A FORFEITURE UNDER ANY CIRCUMSTANCES.

B. The use of an ineligible pitcher.
Ineligibility under this rule applies to violations of Tournament Playing Rule 4. If an ineligible pitcher delivers one or more pitches to a batter, that game is subject to protest and action by Tournament Committee in Williamsport. **NOTE: Junior/Senior/Big League:** Does not apply. See Tournament Rule 10(f).

1. If the facts establishing or verifying an ineligible pitcher become known DURING a game, and the ineligible pitcher participates in the game, subject to the following conditions:
   (a) A protest may be lodged by the manager or coach with the Umpire-in-Chief, who shall consult with the Tournament Director or District Administrator.
   (b) The Tournament Director or District Administrator must contact the Regional Director (or his/her appointed agent), who shall contact the Tournament Committee for a decision. The decision of the Tournament Committee shall be final and binding.

2. If the facts establishing or verifying an ineligible pitcher become known AFTER a game, and the ineligible pitcher participated in the game, subject to the following conditions:
   (a) A protest may be lodged by the manager or coach with the Tournament Director or District Administrator. Such protest must be made before either team affected by the protest begins another game.
   (b) The Tournament Director or District Administrator must contact the Regional Director (or his/her appointed agent), who shall contact the Tournament Committee for a decision. The decision of the Tournament Committee shall be final and binding.

PENALTY for 9- and 10-, 10- and 11-, 11- and 12-Year-Old Divisions: See Tournament Rule 4(i).

C. The use of an ineligible player.
Ineligibility under this rule applies to league age, residence or school attendance (as defined by Little League Baseball, Incorporated), participation in other programs,

TOURNAMENT RULES AND GUIDELINES

participation as an eligible player for sixty (60%) percent (**Big League:** forty (40%) percent) of the regular season in the proper division, or violation of Regulation I-XVII.

1. If the facts establishing or verifying the ineligibility of a player are known to the complainant PRIOR TO the game, the following steps must be taken:
   (a) The complainant shall present the matter to the Tournament Director and/or District Administrator.
   (b) The matter SHALL be resolved with the Regional Director and, through the Regional Director and the Tournament Committee BEFORE the first pitch of the game. The decision of the Tournament Committee shall be final and binding.

2. If the facts establishing or verifying the ineligibility of a player become known DURING a game, and the ineligible player participates in the game, that team shall forfeit the game in question, subject to the following conditions:
   (a) A protest may be lodged by the manager or coach with the Umpire-in-Chief, who shall consult with the Tournament Director or District Administrator.
   (b) The Tournament Director or District Administrator must contact the Regional Director (or his/her appointed agent), who shall contact the Tournament Committee for a decision. The decision of the Tournament Committee shall be final and binding.

3. If the facts establishing or verifying the ineligibility of a player become known AFTER a game, and the ineligible player participated in the game, that team shall forfeit the game in question, subject to the following conditions:
   (a) A protest may be lodged by the manager or coach with the Tournament Director or District Administrator. Such protest must be made before either team affected by the protest begins another game.
   (b) The Tournament Director or District Administrator must contact the Regional Director (or his/her appointed agent), who shall contact the Tournament Committee for a decision. The decision of the Tournament Committee shall be final and binding.

In addition to the penalties described above in A, B, and C, the Tournament Committee may disqualify a player, team, or entire league from tournament play. The Tournament Committee may take action as a result of a protest or on its own initiative. Disqualification of a team or player(s) and/or forfeiture of a game must be the decision of the Tournament Committee at Williamsport, and such decisions will be made prior to the continuation of the affected team(s) or player(s) in further tournament play.

NOTE 1: All officials, including all managers, coaches, scorekeepers, umpires, Tournament Directors, District Administrators, etc., should make every effort to prevent a situation that may result in the forfeiture of a game or suspension of tournament privileges. However, failure by any party to prevent such situations shall not affect the validity of a protest.

Must Play To Advance

A team shall not advance from one level of Tournament to a higher level of tournament play without first having competed against and defeated a scheduled opponent at the tournament level from which it is seeking to advance. Any team advancing without play must do so with the approval of the Regional Director.

TOURNAMENT RULES AND GUIDELINES

Tournament Playing Rules

The Little League, Junior League, Senior League, and Big League Softball Playing Rules shall govern tournament play except as noted below:

1. **SOFTBALLS:** Softballs meeting Little League specifications for a 12-inch softball shall be used in 10-11 Year Old Division, Little League, Junior League, Senior League, and Big League play. The 11-inch softball shall be used in the 9-10 Year Old Division.

   NOTE: The preferred ball of tournament play is Little League licensed Dudley® brand softballs. Specific models for tournament play can be found here: **LittleLeague.org/tournamentballs.**

2. **FIELDS:** All fields are considered neutral. The home team shall be determined by the toss of a coin, the winner having the choice. The official pitching distance shall be – (1) **9- and 10-Year-Old Division:** 35 feet; (2) **10- and 11-Year-Old Division** and **Little League (Majors):** 40 feet; and (3) **Junior/Senior/Big League:** 43 feet.

3. **PLAYING RULES:** A copy of the Little League Regulations and Playing Rules and the Tournament Rules and Guidelines must be available at each tournament site and at the time the game is to be played. This is the responsibility of the Tournament Director. Written ground rules established by the Tournament Director or assistant must be reviewed with both managers and the Umpire-in-Chief at least ten (10) minutes before the start of the game. It is suggested the same be available to news media if requested.
   a. In all Tournament levels and divisions, the penalty for use of an illegal bat [see Rule 6.06 (d)], if discovered before the next player enters the batter's box following the turn at bat of the player who used an illegal bat, is:
      i. The batter is out (**NOTE:** The manager of the defense may advise the plate umpire of a decision to decline this portion of the penalty and accept the play. Such election shall be made immediately at the end of the play), and;
      ii. The manager of the team will be ejected from the game, the batter who violated the rule will be ejected from the game, and the offensive team will lose one eligible adult base coach for the duration of the game.
   b. **10- and 11-Year-Old Division**: The batter may advance on an uncaught third strike (6.05/6.09). This rule will not apply for the **9- and 10-Year-Old Division**.
   c. **10- and 11-Year-Old Division**: Base runner(s) must maintain contact with the base in which they are entitled until the ball has been released by the pitcher on delivery [(7.08(a)(5)]. **9- and 10-Year-Old Division:** Base runner(s) must maintain contact with the base in which they are entitled until the ball has been batted or reaches the batter [(7.08(a)(5)].

4. **PITCHING RULES - LITTLE LEAGUE SOFTBALL, 9- AND 10-YEAR-OLD SOFTBALL AND 10- AND 11-YEAR-OLD DIVISION**
   These rules replace the regular season pitching regulations. *Violation of these pitching rules is subject to protest and action by the Tournament Committee in Williamsport if protested or brought to the Tournament Committee's attention.*
   a. Any player on a tournament team may pitch. (**NOTE:** There is no limit to the number of eligible pitchers a tournament team may use in a game.)
   b. A Tournament pitcher may not pitch in regular season or Special Games while the team is still participating in the Tournament.
   c. Delivery of a single pitch constitutes having pitched an inning.

TOURNAMENT RULES AND GUIDELINES

- d. A pitcher remaining in the game, but moving to a different position, can return as a pitcher anytime in the remainder of the game, but only once in the same inning as he/she was removed.
- e. One (1) calendar day of rest must be observed following regular season or Special Games play, and between levels of Tournament Play if a player pitches seven (7) or more innings in a calendar day.
- f. A player may not pitch in more than twelve (12) innings in a day.
- g. If a player pitches in less than seven (7) innings in a calendar day, no rest is required.
- h. If a player pitches in seven (7) or more innings in a calendar day, one day's rest is required. This also applies between regular season games following Tournament elimination or Special Games following the Tournament.

  EXAMPLE 1: A player may pitch on Saturday in regular season play then, after one (1) calendar day's rest, pitch again in the next level of tournament play on Monday.

  EXAMPLE 2: A player may pitch on Saturday in the final district game then, after one (1) calendar day's rest, pitch again in the next level of tournament play on Monday.

  EXCEPTIONS:
  (1) A player may pitch on consecutive calendar days if less than seven (7) innings were pitched in the previous calendar day.
  (2) In a game suspended by darkness, weather or other causes and resumed the following calendar day, the pitchers of record at the time the game was halted may continue to pitch to the extent of the remaining eligibility that pitcher would have had during the previous day. However, in no event shall any pitcher pitch more than twelve (12) innings in any game.

- i. Failure to remove a pitcher who has reached his/her maximum number of innings pitched or use of an ineligible pitcher is basis for protest. Violations protested or brought to the Tournament Committee's attention, shall result (by action of the Tournament Committee) in the suspension of the team's manager for the next two scheduled tournament games, even if those games are played at the next tournament level. Additional penalties (up to and including forfeiture of a game and/or disqualification of the team, managers, or coaches from further tournament participation) may be imposed if, in the opinion of the Tournament Committee:
  1. a manager or coach takes any action that results in making a travesty of the game, or;
  2. a team fails to meet the requirements of this rule more than once during the International Tournament, which begins with District play and ends at the World Series level (State level for 9- and 10- and 10- and 11-), or;
  3. a manager willfully and knowingly disregards the requirements of this rule. A manager or coach suspended for any reason is not permitted to be at the game site and must not take any part in the game, nor have any communications whatsoever with any persons at the game site. **This includes pregame and postgame activities**. Violation may result, by action of the Tournament Committee, in further suspension; forfeiture of a game; and/or disqualification of the team, managers, or coaches from further tournament participation.

TOURNAMENT RULES AND GUIDELINES

JUNIOR/SENIOR/BIG LEAGUE
    a. Any player on a tournament team may pitch. (**NOTE:** There is no limit to the number of eligible pitchers a tournament team may use in a game.)
    b. A Tournament pitcher may not pitch in regular season or Special Games while the team is still participating in the Tournament.
    c. Delivery of a single pitch constitutes having pitched an inning.
    d. A pitcher remaining in the game, but moving to a different position, can return as a pitcher anytime in the remainder of the game, but only once in the same inning as he/she was removed. If a pitcher is removed from the game and is returned to the pitching position, it will be ruled as an improper substitution. **Penalty**: See Rule 10(f).
    e. No pitching restrictions apply.

5. **FORFEITS:** No game may be forfeited or a team disqualified without the authorization of the Tournament Committee. Violations which may result in forfeiture or disqualification must be reported immediately to the Regional Director before further play takes place which would involve a team or teams affected by such action.

6. **BENCH/DUGOUT:** No one except the players, manager, and coach(es) shall occupy the bench or dugout during a game. Base coaches may be players or adults. Two (2) adult base coaches are permitted at all levels subject to playing rule 4.05(2).

7. **VISITS:** A manager or coach may not leave a dugout for any reason during a game without receiving permission from an umpire. The manager or coach may be removed from the field for the remainder of the game for violation of this rule. When permission is granted the manager or coach will be permitted to go to the pitcher's circle to confer with the pitcher or any defensive player(s). A manager or coach who is granted a time out to talk to any defensive player will be charged with a visit to the pitcher.

    A manager or coach may come out twice in one inning to visit with the pitcher, but the third time out, the player must be removed as a pitcher. The manager or coach may come out three times in a game to visit with the pitcher, but the fourth time out, the player must be removed as a pitcher. The rule applies to each pitcher who enters a game. **NOTE:** Only one offensive time-out will be permitted each inning.

8. **INJURY/ILLNESS:** If a player is injured or becomes ill during a game, the decision of a doctor (if present) or medical personnel will be final as to whether or not the player may continue in the game.

9. **MANDATORY PLAY 9- and 10-Year Old Division, 10- and 11-Year-Old Division, Little League, and Junior League: If a tournament team has thirteen (13) or more eligible players in uniform at a game, then every player on a team roster shall participate in each game for a minimum of one (1) at bat. If a tournament team has twelve (12) or fewer eligible players in uniform at a game, then every player on a team roster shall participate in each game for a minimum of six (6) consecutive defensive outs and bat at least one (1) time.**
    a. Managers are responsible for fulfilling the mandatory play requirements.
    b. There is no exception to this rule unless the game is shortened for any reason. **NOTE:** A game is not considered shortened if the home team does not complete the offensive half of the sixth or seventh inning (or any extra inning) due to winning the game.

TOURNAMENT RULES AND GUIDELINES

c. **Failure to meet the mandatory play requirements in this rule is a basis for protest. If one or more players on a roster do not meet this requirement, and if protested or brought to the Tournament Committee's attention, it shall result (by action of the Tournament Committee) in the suspension of the team's manager for the next two scheduled tournament games, even if those games are played at the next tournament level. Additional penalties (up to and including forfeiture of a game and/or disqualification of the team, managers, or coaches from further tournament participation) may be imposed if, in the opinion of the Tournament Committee:**

   1. **a manager or coach takes any action that results in making a travesty of the game, causing players to intentionally perform poorly for the purpose of extending or shortening a game, or;**

   2. **a team fails to meet the requirements of this rule more than once during the International Tournament, which begins with District play and ends at the World Series level (State level for 9- and 10- and 10- and 11-Year-Old Divisions), or;**

   3. **a manager willfully and knowingly disregards the requirements of this rule.**

   A manager or coach suspended for any reason is not permitted to be at the game site and must not take any part in the game, nor have any communications whatsoever with any persons at the game site. This includes pregame and postgame activities.

   Violation may result, by action of the Tournament Committee, in further suspension; forfeiture of a game; and/or disqualification of the team, managers, or coaches from further tournament participation.

d. For the purposes of this rule, "six (6) consecutive defensive outs" is defined as: A player enters the field in one of the nine defensive positions when his/her team is on defense and occupies such position while six consecutive outs are made; "bat at least one (1) time" is defined as: A player enters the batter's box with no count and completes that time at bat by being retired or by reaching base safely.

10. **SUBSTITUTIONS/RE-ENTRY:** This tournament rule replaces regular season Rule 3.03 (re-entry) for all levels of tournament play.

   a. If illness, injury, or the ejection of a player prevents a team from fielding nine (9) players, a player previously used in the lineup may be inserted, but only if there are no other eligible substitutes available. The opposing team manager shall select the player to re-enter the lineup. A player ejected from the game is not eligible for re-entry.

   b. Any player who has been removed for a substitute may re-enter the game in the **SAME** position in the batting order.

   c. **A substitute entering the game for the first time may not be removed prior to completion of her/his mandatory play requirements.**

   NOTE 1: See definitions in Rule 9(d) above on complying with this rule defensively and offensively. Tournament Rule 10(c) does not apply to Senior League or Big League.

   NOTE 2: A player who has met the mandatory play requirements, and is a pitcher at the time she/he is removed, may be removed for a substitute batter

TOURNAMENT RULES AND GUIDELINES

and re-enter the game as a pitcher once, provided the pitcher was not physically replaced on the pitcher's plate. **EXCEPTION: Does not apply to Senior and Big League Softball.**

Example: Player A is a starter and not a pitcher, Player B substitutes into the game for player A. Both players have met mandatory play by completing one time at bat and/or 6 consecutive outs and both occupy the same spot in the batting order. In the fifth inning player A becomes a pitcher and is scheduled to bat in the sixth inning, but player B bats for player A. Both players have met mandatory play requirements and player A was not physically replaced on the pitcher's plate as a pitcher, therefore, player A can return to pitch the sixth inning.

d. Defensive substitutions must be made while the team is on defense. Offensive substitutions must be made at the time the offensive player has her/his turn at bat or is on base.

e. A starter and her/his substitute must not be in the lineup at the same time, except as provided in Rule 10(a).

f. Improper substitution is a basis for protest. Protests involving improper substitution not resolved before the next pitch or play shall not be considered. **Junior/Senior/Big League:** Ineligible pitcher under 1) a Tournament pitcher pitches during the regular season or special games concurrently, 2) a Tournament pitcher is removed from the lineup and then is returned as pitcher later in the game, or 3) a Tournament pitcher moves to another defensive position twice and then returns as pitcher twice in the same inning, will be considered an improper substitution.

g. Rule 7.14, Special Pinch Runner, will apply during tournament.

h. **Senior/Big League only:** Rule 3.03, Designated Hitter, WILL apply during the tournament.

i. **Senior League/Big League Softball:** Any player in the starting lineup, including the designated hitter, who has been removed for a substitute may re-enter the game ONCE, provided such player occupies the same batting position as he or she did in the starting lineup. A substitute (non-starter) may not re-enter the game in any position once they are removed from the lineup.

11. **SUSPENDED GAMES:** Any game in which a winner cannot be determined in accordance with the playing rules shall be resumed from the exact point at which it was suspended regardless of the number of innings played.

EXCEPTION: In the event that the first inning is not completed, the game shall be replayed from the beginning and all records, including pitching, disregarded. Incomplete (not regulation) or tie games are considered suspended games.

NOTE: A contest decided by forfeit does not constitute a "game" for the purposes of this rule, unless one complete inning was physically played before the game was forfeited. (Forfeits are only by decree of the Tournament Committee in Williamsport.)

12. **TEN-RUN RULE:** If at the end of a regulation game one team has a lead of ten (10) runs or more, the manager of the team with the least runs shall concede the victory to the opponent. **NOTE:** If the visiting team has a lead of ten (10) or more runs, the home team must bat in their half of the inning.

TOURNAMENT RULES AND GUIDELINES

13. **REGULATION GAME:** Each tournament game must be played to the point of being an official game:
    a. Regulation games are of four or more innings (five or more innings in **Junior/Senior/Big League**) in which one team has scored more runs than the other (three and one-half (3½) if the home team is ahead or four and one-half (4½) if the home team is ahead in **Junior/Senior/Big League**).
    b. Regulation games (when a winner can be determined) terminated because of weather, darkness, or curfew must be resumed if the visiting team ties the game or takes the lead in their half of the inning and the home team does not complete their at bat or take the lead in an incomplete inning. This does not apply to games suspended or delayed by weather that may still be resumed before darkness or curfew (as defined in Tournament Rules and Guidelines – Curfew) on the same day.
    c. If two games are scheduled for the same site, no "time limit" may be imposed on the first game.

14. **REPLAYING GAMES:** No tournament game may be replayed without specific approval from the Tournament Committee at Williamsport.

15. **UNAUTHORIZED AGREEMENTS:** No agreements shall be made between managers, and/or Tournament Directors, and/or umpires contrary to Tournament Rules.

16. **ALTERCATIONS**: Any player, manager, coach, or official who is involved in a physical or verbal altercation at the game site could be suspended or removed from tournament play by the Tournament Committee.

17. **EJECTIONS:** Any manager, coach, or player ejected from a game will be suspended for the next physically played game (See Rule 4.07). This includes pregame and postgame activities. Ejections shall be noted in the tournament team's affidavit in the Record of Ejections on page 4. Entry should include member's name and date ejected and signed by the Tournament Director or District Administrator.

TOURNAMENT RULES AND GUIDELINES

OFFICIALS

Scorers

The Tournament Director having jurisdiction shall appoint and provide an official scorer for each game.

The official scorer shall, immediately following each game, enter on the reverse side of each team's Eligibility Affidavit:
1. Date of game.
2. Name of each player who pitched.
3. Number of innings pitched.
4. Name of opponent.
5. Score of game.
6. Signature of Tournament Director or assistant. This record shall be accepted as official.

Financial Responsibility

Unless officially notified to the contrary by Williamsport, each league shall assume full responsibility for expenses incurred in tournament competition. Participating teams which choose not to accept housing and/or meals provided by the host shall reside and eat elsewhere at their own expense, and shall be responsible for their own local transportation.

Compensation to defray travel expenses for teams traveling 150 miles or more per one round trip, to Section tournaments and beyond will be paid by Little League Baseball, Incorporated, to local leagues in the form of a credit toward the next year's fees (U.S. leagues only). All Tournament fees and adjustments to Tournament Teams enrolled must be submitted by the local league to Little League International by September 15, 2016.
NOTE: A maximum of one round trip will be compensated per tournament site at each level of play. Mileage forms must be completed and submitted by the local league to Little League International by September 15, 2016, in order for reimbursement to be paid.
EXCEPTION: The local league president may request, in writing, reimbursement by check. This request must accompany the mileage reimbursement form.

Mileage compensation is $1 per mile. Little League International, Williamsport, Pennsylvania, will make all arrangements and reservations for transporting the regional champions to and from the World Series.

Guidelines for Conduct of Tournament

The following standards for the conduct of tournament play are for the guidance and information of Tournament Directors and participating leagues. Experience of hundreds of field directors responsible for the conduct of the tournament at all levels over many years is reflected in these guidelines which should be studied carefully and applied totally to assure successful staging of the various levels of play.

District Administrators

District Administrators or their appointed assistants will direct the tournaments. This responsibility may not be delegated to a local league. The Tournament Director conducts or supervises play up to and including the final game of that level; collects or directs the collection of all funds belonging to the tournament; pays or directs payments from moneys so collected or received; and makes required reports to leagues involved and to the Regional Center.

TOURNAMENT RULES AND GUIDELINES

The league or leagues hosting tournaments may not assume responsibility for, nor physically operate, the tournament. The league or leagues may not retain tournament income, may not make payments from nor obligate tournament funds for any purpose.

At the District tournament meeting the Tournament Rules should be reviewed in briefing league representatives, umpires, and others involved in the tournament. Before assigning tournament games, the District Administrators should inspect all prospective sites. It cannot be emphasized too strongly that providing the best possible playing conditions on regular fields is the obligation of the District Administrator.

Tournament Director
A. District, Sectional, Divisional, State, or Regional Tournament Director may provide appropriate awards to participating teams and players.
B. Each Tournament Director shall report as follows:
 1. Advise each participating league of schedule, time, and site of games.
 2. Forward completed schedule to the Regional Director showing winners at each level of play.
 3. Pay allowable expenses and distribute balance of tournament income to the District Fund and/or leagues on a per-game basis. Where one or more teams travel greater distances than others, a mileage allowance may be paid before distributing the per-game shares.
 4. Forward completed financial report to the Regional Director within ten (10) days following final game of each level of tournament.
 NOTE: 9- and 10- & 10- and 11-Year-Old Divisions advances to State level only.

Physical Conditions
It is essential that the best possible playing conditions be provided at every level of the tournament. The following conditions are recommended for tournament games:
1. Facilities:
 a. Grass outfield (Regional, Divisional, State, and Sectional Tournaments).
 b. Outfield fences should be 200 feet from home plate. The outfield fence must be a minimum of 180 feet and a maximum of 225 feet from home plate.
 c. Outfield fences of safe-type construction, a minimum of 4 feet in height, maximum of 6 feet.
 d. Batter's eye 24 feet wide minimum at center field.
 e. Backstop not less than 20 feet from home plate.
 f. Back drop of 6 to 8 feet of canvas in back of home plate if no press box is in that position.
 g. Two foul poles at least 6 feet above the top of the fence.
 h. A protective screen in front of dugouts.
 i. Lights, if used, must meet minimum Little League standards.
 j. Dirt pitching circles are recommended for tournament play.
 k. Skinned infield recommended.
2. Groundskeeper's services:
 a. Grass cut to proper height. No holes or other unsafe conditions.
 b. Infield dragged and in playable condition.
 c. Markings according to regulations.
 d. Bases must be regulation size and properly secured. A double first base is permitted.

TOURNAMENT RULES AND GUIDELINES

3. Additional Facilities:
    a. Public address system and announcer.
    b. Scoreboard and operator(s).
    c. Adequate seating (Sectional - 500; Divisional/State - 1,000; Regional - 1,500 minimum).
    d. Adequate parking.
    e. Policing. Local police departments should be advised of the event and requested to cooperate with league personnel.
    f. First aid, medical, and ambulance services available.
    g. Rest rooms.
    h. Softballs (if not otherwise provided by Tournament Director).
    i. Adult volunteer insurance should be provided by each league involved.
    NOTE 1: 9- and 10- & 10- and 11-Year-Old Division advances to State level only.
    NOTE 2: Host leagues may retain concession income.

Assistants and Committees

To assure a successful tournament, it is desirable that the director (particularly at Sectional, Divisional, State, and Regional levels) appoint assistants and committee chairperson to undertake the various functions which are essential. The following are suggested:

1. **Finance:** To solicit donations, supervise collections at games, sale of advertising and programs, etc. Host leagues may not conduct fund raising projects unless approved by the Tournament Director.
2. **Housing:** Players, managers, coaches, and umpires may be provided hotel or motel accommodations and food allowance.
3. **Publicity:** Obtain and make available to all news media names of teams, players, time of games and sites, results of games, and other information essential to news media in the interest of promoting the tournament. Addresses and/or telephone numbers of players must not be released to anyone for any purpose.
4. **Transportation:** Arrangements for meeting teams upon arrival and delivery to points of departure. Arrange for transportation of managers and coaches.
5. **Program:** When authorized by Tournament Director as a fund raising project, the Program Chairperson should work with the Finance Chairperson to assemble material, sell ads, etc. Programs should not be published unless self-supporting.
6. **Parking and Police:** If deemed necessary, arrange for traffic control, parking, and related functions.
7. **Medical:** Have names and phone numbers of doctors, nurses, ambulance, and hospital available and arrangements made for their services, if required. If possible, a doctor or nurse should be in attendance.
8. **Ceremonies:** Arrange for flag raising, welcome, introductions, etc. These should be brief and meaningful.
9. **Umpires:** Recommended minimum of two, a maximum of six. Services on a voluntary basis. Normal expenses may be provided.
10. **Official scorekeepers.**

TOURNAMENT RULES AND GUIDELINES

Expenses

Tournament Directors are authorized to pay from tournament income the following costs:
1. Championship pennant.
2. Approved Little League pins for players, managers, coaches (all teams), and umpires.
3. Postage, telephone, and out-of-pocket expenses.
4. Housing and food allowance for players, managers, coaches, and umpires.

   NOTE: Tournament Director should secure, at no cost to the tournament, softballs (if not provided by host league), umpires, scorekeepers, and housing for players.

Radio

Broadcasting of tournament games is permitted with authorization from the Tournament Director. Commercial sponsorship must be consistent with Little League policy. Fees or donations paid for the broadcasting rights must accrue to the tournament fund at that level.

Television

Only Little League International may authorize the televising (live or taped) of tournament games. The District Administrator or Tournament Director may recommend approval, but may not make commitments or sign any agreement or contracts for the televising of games.

Not later than two weeks prior to the start of the tournament at the level to be televised, the director having jurisdiction shall submit in writing complete details of the proposal to Little League International. Videotaping of games is permissible provided tapes are not sold or used for any commercial purposes. Brief, televised reports on tournament games and activities on news programs are permitted.

Programs

The District Administrator or Tournament Director may authorize the publication of a program or scorecard as a means of providing additional financing for the tournament at that level. However, they may not execute contracts or other commitments in the name of, or as agents for, Little League International. All funds (net) realized from advertising and/or sale of programs must be applied to the tournament fund at that level.

TOURNAMENT RULES AND GUIDELINES

Regional Directors

The following Regional Directors or their appointed agents should be contacted by the Tournament Director when protests cannot be resolved at the tournament level.

U.S. OFFICES

U.S. CENTRAL
Director - Nina Johnson-Pitt;
Assistant Director - Scott Spillman

U.S. EAST
Director - Don Soucy;
Assistant Director - Corey Wright; Assistant Director - TBD

U.S. SOUTHEAST
Director - Jennifer Colvin;
Assistant Director - Matt Weber

U.S. SOUTHWEST
Director - Sergio Guzman;
Assistant Director - Douglas Galler

U.S. WEST
Director - Dave Bonham;
Assistant Director - Brian Pickering; Assistant Director - Kia Riley

INTERNATIONAL OFFICES

ASIA-PACIFIC
Director - B.H. Chow

CANADA
Director - Joe Shea;
Assistant Director - Wendy Thomson

EUROPE AND AFRICA
Director - Beata Kaszuba-Baker;
Assistant Director - Bart Sochacki

LATIN AMERICA AND CARIBBEAN
Director - Carlos Pagan;
Assistant - Jose Berrios

TOURNAMENT RULES AND GUIDELINES

International Tournament Pool Play Format
Section I – Guidelines

The Pool Play Format should only be used in divisions in which there is a reasonable expectation for all teams to play all games for which they are scheduled. In divisions in which teams traditionally drop out at the last moment, or partway through the tournament, the standard double-elimination or single-elimination formats should be used instead.

The following conditions must apply to all Pool Play Format tournaments, unless specified as optional:

A. In the event a team or teams drop out of a pool play format tournament before the first game of the tournament is played (by any team in the tournament), the pools must be redrawn. If a team or teams drop out or is/are removed by action of the Tournament Committee after the first game is played, the matter must be referred to the Tournament Committee for a decision.
B. A Pool Play Format tournament may have one or more pools.
C. The pool assignments (or "draw") must either be a blind draw, or must be based on geographic considerations. Pool assignments must never be "seeded" based on the expected ability of the teams.
D. In all cases, the results of Pool Play have no bearing on the next segment of play, with the exception of rules and regulations regarding rest periods for pitchers, (i.e., losses do not "carry over").
E. It is preferable for each team in a given pool to be scheduled to play all other teams in that pool once.
F. Each team within any one pool must be scheduled to play an equal number of games as the other teams in that pool.
G. In the case of a one-pool tournament, one team may advance to become the tournament champion, based solely on the results of pool play, at the discretion of the tournament director. More commonly in a one-pool tournament, however, two teams advance to play each other for the tournament championship.
H. If more than one pool is used, and the total number of teams in the largest and smallest of the pools combined is less than ten (10), the number of teams in largest pool must be no more than one team greater than the number of teams in the smallest pool.

Example:

Acceptable		**Not Acceptable**	
Pool A	**Pool B**	**Pool A**	**Pool B**
4 teams	5 teams	3 teams	6 teams

I. If more than one pool is used, and the total number of teams in the largest and smallest of the pools is ten (10) or more, the number of teams in the largest pool must be no more than two teams greater than the number of teams in smallest pool. Example:

Acceptable		**Not Acceptable**	
Pool A	**Pool B**	**Pool A**	**Pool B**
4 teams	6 teams	3 teams	7 teams

J. In the case of tournaments involving more than one pool, one or more teams may advance out of each pool to the next segment. In most cases, when two teams advance, the schedule may be arranged so that teams will "cross over" for the purpose of seeding in the next round. For example, in a two-pool tournament:
   1. The first-place team in Pool A plays the second-place team in Pool B.
   2. The first-place team in Pool B plays the second-place team in Pool A.

TOURNAMENT RULES AND GUIDELINES

    3. The winners of those two games play each other for the championship.
    4. A consolation game may be scheduled between the losing teams.
       The crossover method, however, is not required. At the discretion of the tournament director, the teams advancing from pool play could be re-drawn for placement in the next round via blind draw.

K. In the case of tournaments involving more than one team advancing out of pool play into a playoff, the playoff format may be single- or double-elimination, at the discretion of the tournament director.

However, if the published format calls for double-elimination, and the tournament director subsequently wishes for it to revert to single-elimination because of delays caused by weather, etc., this can only be approved by the Tournament Committee in Williamsport.

L. The tournament director may, at his/her discretion, use a format in which all teams that finish the pool play round with a specific won-lost record will advance. In the following examples, the format calls for advancing all teams (from a 10-team pool in which each team plays only seven games) that finish pool play with zero or one loss. **EXAMPLE 1:** Among the 10 teams in the pool, two finished with 7-0 records, while two others finished with 6-1 records. Result – These four teams advance and the other six teams are eliminated. **EXAMPLE 2:** Among the 10 teams in the pool, one finished with a 7-0 record, while two others finished with 6-1 records. Result – These three teams advance and the other seven teams are eliminated.

M. The tiebreaker methods published herein by Little League International are the only methods that will be used when a tiebreaker is required. If any question or controversy arises, it must be referred to the Regional Headquarters before advancing a team.

N. A manager is not permitted to purposely forfeit any game for the purpose of engineering the outcome of pool play, and may be removed from the tournament by action of the Tournament Committee in Williamsport. Additionally, the Tournament Committee may remove such a team from further tournament play.

O. Only the Tournament Committee can forfeit a game in the International Tournament, and reserves the right to disregard the results of a forfeited game in computing a team's won-lost record and Runs-Allowed Ratio. (Section IV)

P. When a manager or coach instructs his/her players to play poorly for any reason, such as, but not limited to the following, such action may result in the manager's removal by the Umpire-in-Chief, and/or removal of the manager, coach(es) and/or team from further tournament play. **NOTE:** This policy is not intended to prevent a manager from using lesser-skilled players more frequently if he or she wishes, even if such action may result in losing a game:
    1. losing a game to effect a particular outcome in a Pool Play Format tournament;
    2. so as to lose a game by the 10-run rule;
    3. to delay the game until the curfew;
    4. to allow an opponent to tie the score so that more innings may be played, etc.

Section II – Segments of a Pool Play Tournament

A. Under this format, there are two distinct segments to a pool play format tournament.
    1. In Segment 1 – The Pool Play Round, the teams are divided into a number of pools (usually two to four pools). Each team in each of the pools should play the other teams in that pool once. By decision of the tournament director, one or more teams with the best records(s) in the pool will advance to the next segment.

TOURNAMENT RULES AND GUIDELINES

NOTE: In a one-pool format, one or more teams team may advance to become the tournament champion. If only one team advances, there is no second segment.
    2. In Segment 2 – The Elimination Round, the teams advancing out of Segment 1 are matched up in either a standard single-elimination format, or a standard double-elimination format.
B. Once a segment is completed, games played previously have no bearing on the next segment, with the exception of:
    1. rules and regulations regarding the required rest periods for pitchers;
    2. rules and regulations regarding players, managers and/or coaches that were ejected, and the prescribed penalties resulting from the ejection.

Section III – Tiebreaker Procedures

A. In all cases, the team(s) advancing past Segment 1 must be the team(s) with the best won-lost record(s) during pool play. The tournament director will decide the number of teams that will advance beyond pool play, and such decision must be made available to the leagues/teams involved before the tournament begins.
B. When records are tied, however, the following procedures must be applied in order, so that the tie can be broken. These procedures also apply to determining the seeding for Segment 2 (the playoff round), if seeding for Segment 2 is based on results of pool play.
    1. The first tiebreaker is the result of the head-to-head match-up(s) during pool play (Segment 1) of the teams that are involved in the tie.
        (a) If one of the teams involved in the tie has accomplished EVERY ONE of the following, then that team will advance:
            i   Defeated all of the other teams involved in the tie at least once; AND,
            ii Defeated all of the other teams involved in the tie in every one of the pool play games it played against those teams; AND,
            iii Played each of the teams involved in the tie an equal number of times.
        EXAMPLE: Three teams are tied with identical records for first place at the end of pool play, and one team is to advance to Segment 2. Teams A, B and C played against each other once in pool play. Team A won all of its games against Team B and Team C during pool play. Result – Team A advances, while Team B and Team C are eliminated.
        (b) Each time a tie is broken to advance one team, leaving a tie between two or more teams, the situation reverts to "B. (1.)" (head-to-head results) in this section.
        Example: Three teams are tied with identical records for first place at the end of pool play, and two teams are to advance to Segment 2. Teams A, B and C played against each other once in pool play. Team A won all of its games against Team B and Team C during pool play. Result – Team A advances, which then creates a two-way tie between Team B and Team C. That tie then is broke by reverting to "B. (1)(a)" in this section.
    2. If the results of the head-to-head match-up(s) during pool play of the teams that are involved in the tie cannot break the tie (because no team defeated each of the other teams in the tie each time they played, or because no team has defeated all of the other teams involved in the tie in everyone of the pool play games played between those teams, or because the teams involved in the tie did not play one another an equal number of times during pool play), then the tie is broken using

TOURNAMENT RULES AND GUIDELINES

the Runs Allowed Ratio (see Section IV).

C. In all cases, if the tie-breaking principles herein are correctly applied and fail to break the tie, or if these guidelines are not applied correctly (in the judgment of the Tournament Committee in Williamsport), then the matter will be referred to the Tournament Committee, which will be the final arbiter in deciding the issue. If a tie cannot be broken through the proper application of these guidelines (in the opinion of the Tournament Committee), then a playoff, blind draw or coin flip will determine which team(s) will advance. This is a decision of the Tournament Committee.

Section IV – Runs-Allowed Ratio

A. For each team involved in a tie in which head-to-head results cannot be used (because no team defeated each of the other teams in the tie each time they played, or because no team has defeated all of the other teams involved in the tie in everyone of the pool play games played between those teams, or because the teams involved in the tie did not play one another an equal number of times during pool play), the tournament director will calculate: The total number of runs given up in all pool play games played by that team, divided by the number of half-innings played on defense in pool play games by that team. This provides the number of runs give up per half-inning by that team: the Runs-Allowed Ratio.
   1. **EXAMPLE:** The Hometown Little League team has given up eight (8) runs in all four (4) of its pool play games, and has played 23 innings on defense in those four games. 8 divided by 23 equals .3478.
   2. The Runs-Allowed Ratio for Hometown Little League (.3478 in the example above) is compared to the same calculation for each of the teams involved in the tie.
B. The Runs-Allowed Ratio is used to advance ONLY ONE team.
C. If, after computing the Runs-Allowed Ratio using results of all pool play games played by the teams involved in the tie:
   1. one team has the lowest Runs-Allowed Ratio, that team advances. After one team has advanced using the Runs-Allowed Ratio, the breaking of any other ties must revert to the methods detailed in Section III – Tiebreaker Procedures, before the Runs-Allowed Ratio is used to break the tie.
   2. two or more teams remain tied, and the methods detailed in Section III – Tiebreaker Procedures cannot be used (because no team defeated each of the other teams in the tie each time they played, or because no team has defeated all of the other teams involved in the tie in everyone of the pool play games played between those teams, or because the teams involved in the tie did not play one another an equal number of times during pool play), then the Runs-Allowed Ratio must be recomputed using statistics only from the pool play games played between the teams involved in the tie. The results are used to advance ONE team, and any other ties must revert to the methods detailed in Section III – Tiebreaker Procedures, before the Runs-Allowed Ratio is used to break the tie.
D. Any part of a half-inning played on defense will count as a complete half-inning on defense for the purposes of computing the Runs-Allowed Ratio.
E. If a game is forfeited, in most cases the score of the game will be recorded as 6-0 (for Little League Divisions and below) or 7-0 (for Junior League Divisions and above). However, only the Tournament Committee in Williamsport can decree a forfeit, and the Tournament Committee reserves the right to disregard the results of the game, to assign the score as noted above, or to allow the score to stand (if any part of the

TOURNAMENT RULES AND GUIDELINES

    game was played).

F. If a game is forfeited, in most cases each team involved in the forfeit will be deemed to have played six defensive half-innings (for Little League Divisions and below) or seven defensive innings (for Junior League Divisions and above). However, forfeits and the final score and number of innings charged or credited in forfeits, can only be decreed by the Tournament Committee in Williamsport.

G. In the event a team (defined for this purpose as a minimum of nine players) fails to attend a scheduled game, and it is determined by the Tournament Committee in Williamsport that the failure to attend was designed to cause a forfeit or delay the tournament for any reason, the Tournament Committee reserves the right to remove the team from further play in the International Tournament and/or remove those adults it deems responsible from the team and/or local league.

Appendix A
Lightning Safety Guidelines

Each year across the United States, thunderstorms produce an estimated 25 million cloud-to-ground flashes of lightning - each one of those flashes is a potential killer. According to the National Weather Service, an average of 73 people are killed by lightning each year and hundreds more are injured, some suffering devastating neurological injuries that persist for the rest of their lives. A growing percentage of those struck are involved in outside recreational activities.

Officials responsible for sports events often lack adequate knowledge of thunderstorms and lightning to make educated decisions on when to seek safety. Without knowledge, officials base their decisions on personal experience and, sometimes, on the desire to complete the activity. Due to the nature of lightning, personal experience can be misleading.

While many people routinely put their lives in jeopardy when thunderstorms are nearby, few are actually struck by lightning. This results in a false sense of safety. Unfortunately, this false sense of safety has resulted in numerous lightning deaths and injuries during the past several decades because people made decisions that unknowingly put their lives or the lives of others at risk.

For organized outdoor activities, the National Weather Service recommends those in charge have a lightning safety plan, and that they follow the plan without exception. The plan should give clear and specific safety guidelines in order to eliminate errors in judgment. Prior to an activity or event, organizers should listen to the latest forecast to determine the likelihood of thunderstorms. NOAA Weather Radio is a good source of up-to-date weather information. Once people start to arrive, the guidelines in your league's lightning safety plan should be followed.

A thunderstorm is approaching or nearby. Are conditions safe, or is it time to head for safety? Not wanting to appear overly cautious, many people wait far too long before reacting to this potentially deadly weather threat. The safety recommendations outlined here based on lightning research and the lessons learned from the unfortunate experiences of thousands of lightning strike victims.

Thunderstorms produce two types of lightning flashes, 'negative' and 'positive.' While both types are deadly, the characteristics of the two are quite different. Negative flashes occur more frequently, usually under or near the base of the thunderstorm where rain is falling. In contrast, positive flashes generally occur away from the center of the storm, often in areas where rain is not falling. There is no place outside that is safe in or near a thunderstorm. Consequently, people need to stop what they are doing and get to a safe place immediately. Small outdoor buildings including dugouts, rain shelters, sheds, etc., are NOT SAFE. Substantial buildings with wiring and plumbing provide the greatest amount of protection. Office buildings, schools, and homes are examples of buildings that would offer protection. Once inside, stay away from windows and doors and anything that conducts electricity such as corded phones, wiring, plumbing, and anything connected to these. In the absence of a substantial building, a hard-topped metal vehicle with the windows closed provides good protection. Occupants should avoid contact with metal in the vehicle and, to the extent possible, move away from windows.

APPENDIX A — LIGHTNING SAFETY GUIDELINES

Who should monitor the weather and who is responsible for making the decision to stop activities?

Lightning safety plans should specify that someone be designated to monitor the weather for lightning. The 'lightning monitor' should not include the coaches, umpires, or referees, as they are not able to devote the attention needed to adequately monitor conditions. The 'lightning monitor' must know the plan's guidelines and be empowered to assure that those guidelines are followed.

When should activities be stopped?

The sooner activities are stopped and people get to a safe place, the greater the level of safety. In general, a significant lightning threat extends outward from the base of a thunderstorm cloud about 6 to 10 miles. Therefore, people should move to a safe place when a thunderstorm is 6 to 10 miles away. Also, the plan's guidelines should account for the time it will take for everyone to get to a safe place. Here are some criteria that could be used to halt activities.

1. If lightning is observed. The ability to see lightning varies depending on the time of day, weather conditions, and obstructions such as trees, mountains, etc. In clear air, and especially at night, lightning can be seen from storms more than 10 miles away provided that obstructions don't limit the view of the thunderstorm.
2. If thunder is heard. Thunder can usually be heard from a distance of about 10 miles provided that there is no background noise. Traffic, wind, and precipitation may limit the ability to hear thunder less than 10 miles away. If you hear thunder, though, it's a safe bet that the storm is within ten miles.
3. If the time between lightning and corresponding thunder is 30 seconds or less. This would indicate that the thunderstorm is 6 miles away or less. As with the previous two criteria, obstructions, weather, noise, and other factors may limit the ability to use this criterion. In addition, a designated person must diligently monitor any lightning. In addition to any of the above criteria, activities should be halted if the sky looks threatening. Thunderstorms can develop directly overhead and some storms may develop lightning just as they move into an area.

When should activities be resumed?

Because electrical charges can linger in clouds after a thunderstorm has passed, experts agree that people should wait at least 30 minutes after the storm before resuming activities.

What should be done if someone is struck by lightning?

Most lightning strike victims can survive a lightning strike; however, medical attention may be needed immediately - have someone call for medical help. Victims do not carry an electrical charge and should be attended to at once. In many cases, the victim's heart and/or breathing may have stopped and CPR may be needed to revive them. The victim should continue to be monitored until medical help arrives; heart and/or respiratory problems could persist, or the victim could go into shock. If possible, move the victim to a safer place away from the threat of another lightning strike.

Appendix B
Safety Code for Little League

- Responsibility for safety procedures should be that of an adult member of the local league.
- Arrangements should be made in advance of all games and practices for emergency medical services.
- Managers, coaches, and umpires should have some training in first-aid. First-Aid Kit should be available at the field.
- No games or practice should be held when weather or field conditions are not good, particularly when lighting is inadequate.
- Play area should be inspected frequently for holes, damage, glass, and other foreign objects.
- Dugouts and bat racks should be positioned behind screens.
- Only players, managers, coaches, and umpires are permitted on the playing field during play and practice sessions.
- Responsibility for keeping bats and loose equipment off the field of play should be that of a regular player assigned for this purpose.
- Procedure should be established for retrieving foul balls batted out of the playing area.
- During practice sessions and games, all players should be alert and watching the batter on each pitch.
- During warm up drills, players should be spaced so that no one is endangered by errant balls.
- Equipment should be inspected regularly. Make sure it fits properly.
- Pitching machines, if used, must be in good working order (including extension cords, outlets, etc.) and must be operated only by adult managers and coaches.
- Batters must wear protective NOCSAE helmets during practice, as well as during games.
- Catchers must wear catcher's helmet (with face mask and throat guard), chest protector, and shin guards. Male catchers must wear a protective supporter and cup at all times.
- Except when runner is returning to a base, head first slides are not permitted. This applies only to Little League (Majors), Minor League and Tee Ball.
- During sliding practice bases should not be strapped down.
- At no time should "horse play" be permitted on the playing field.
- Parents of players who wear glasses should be encouraged to provide "Safety Glasses."
- Players must not wear watches, rings, pins, jewelry, hard cosmetic, or hard decorative items.
- Catchers must wear catcher's helmet, face mask, and throat guard in warming up pitchers. This applies between innings and in bullpen practice. Skull caps are not permitted.
- Batting/catcher's helmets should not be painted unless approved by the manufacturer.
- Regulations prohibit on-deck batters. This means no player should handle a bat, even while in an enclosure, until it is his/her time at bat. This applies only to Little League (Majors), Minor League and Tee Ball.
- Players who are ejected, ill, or injured should remain under supervision until released to the parent or guardian.

Appendix C

Communicable Disease Procedures

While risk of one athlete infecting another with HIV/AIDS during competition is close to non-existent, there is a remote risk that other blood born infectious diseases can be transmitted. For example, Hepatitis B can be present in blood as well as in other body fluids. Procedures for reducing the potential for transmission of these infectious agents should include, but not be limited to, the following:

1. The bleeding must be stopped, the open wound covered, and if there is an excessive amount of blood on the uniform it must be changed before the athlete may participate.
2. Routine use of gloves or other precautions to prevent skin and mucous-membrane exposure when contact with blood or other body fluids is anticipated.
3. Immediately wash hands and other skin surfaces if contaminated (in contact) with blood or other body fluids. Wash hands immediately after removing gloves.
4. Clean all contaminated surfaces and equipment with an appropriate disinfectant before competition resumes.
5. Practice proper disposal procedures to prevent injuries caused by needles, scalpels, and other sharp instruments or devices.
6. Although saliva has not been implicated in HIV transmission, to minimize the need for emergency mouth-to-mouth resuscitation, mouthpieces, resuscitation bags, or other ventilation devices should be available for use.
7. Athletic trainers/coaches with bleeding or oozing skin conditions should refrain from all direct athletic care until the condition resolves.
8. Contaminated towels should be properly disposed of/disinfected.
9. Follow acceptable guidelines in the immediate control of bleeding and when handling bloody dressings, mouth guards, and other articles containing body fluids.

Additional information is available from your state high school association and from the National Federation TARGET program.

APPENDIX D — BAT MODIFICATIONS AND ALTERATIONS

Appendix D
Bat Modifications and Alterations

While Little League International has not received any reports of Little League volunteers or players making alterations to bats designed to increase their performance, it has been an issue in some upper levels of play.

In an effort to ensure this does not become a problem in Little League, this policy statement has been prepared.

No bat, in any level of Little League Baseball or Softball play, is permitted to be altered. This is of particular concern especially when it is clearly done to enhance performance and violate bat standards. Making such alterations to bats is clearly an inappropriate attempt to gain an unfair advantage, and cheating has no place in our program. Umpires, managers, and coaches are instructed to inspect bats before games and practices - as they always should - to determine if bats might have been altered.

This includes using the appropriate Little League Bat Ring. If a bat does not clearly pass through the correct size ring, or if it has a flat spot on it, the bat must not be used. (This may simply indicate the bat has become misshapen with use, and does not necessarily indicate it was purposely altered. Still, the bat must be removed.)

Other signs to look for include contorted or mangled end-caps or knobs on non-wood bats. This could indicate that machinery was used to "shave" the inside of the bat to make it lighter. Bats with evidence of this type of tampering also must not be used.

Little League International wishes to make it clear that tampering with bats (or any other piece of equipment) is dangerous, and the equipment must not be used in any Little League game or practice.

Appendix E
Heat Illness Prevention Protection Policy

Take steps to protect your league's members from heat illness. Heat stroke, heat exhaustion, and heat cramps are all highly possible outcomes for your players and volunteers if they are not protected from the sun's power. When games are played in high heat or heat and high humidity, precautions should be in place.

According to the American Association of Pediatrics (AAP), children's bodies can't tolerate heat as well as adults, so don't expect them to perform in the same conditions you can.

Watch for heat illness signs: weakness, dizziness, slow pulse, and clammy skin. If sweating can't cool the body, especially because the player is dehydrated, heat stroke could develop. Signs of this are confusion, collapse, rapid pulse, and dry skin (no longer sweating).

The AAP notes heat stroke may cause convulsions or even unconsciousness. This is a medical emergency and professional help should be sought immediately. In some cases, heat stroke can kill, but it can also cause permanent brain damage in victims who survive.

Drink Early, Drink Often: Remember, the best protection for heat illness is water and rest. The maxim is: drink early, drink often, even when players aren't thirsty. Players should arrive for games/practices adequately hydrated and drink at least five (5) ounces of water every 15-20 minutes while they are active in the heat.

Ask players to bring water or a sports drink with modest amounts of electrolytes, but nothing with caffeine that acts as a diuretic and drains water from the body.

Try to provide water for players wherever possible at your facility.

Evidence shows that sunscreen of at least SPF 15 should be applied to exposed skin every time children will be in the sun for extended periods, to help keep the player cool and to protect against future skin cancer risk.

Take first steps:
- Provide sunshades for all dugouts and spectator areas as possible.
- Provide cool water and wet towels (with or without ice) for players and umpires to apply to necks.
- Recommend participants utilize topical sunscreen on a regular basis and encourage its use on all exposed skin.
- Take breaks in the shade between innings, or every 20 minutes.
- Set up a sprinkler in a grassy or paved area where players can cool off.

Take it to the next level:
- Install a water mister near or in dugouts to boost cooling.
- Provide umpires with a Camelback-style water container for hydrating during innings.
- Develop a "cool room" in your concession stand, or just a tent with walls, with fans or air-conditioning for those overcome by heat.

Anyone who begins to develop cramps, dizziness, or other signs of heat stress should be removed from the game, given cool water, and placed in as cool a place as possible: in a car with air-conditioning or in a cool, shaded area.

Make sure volunteers know to call 9-1-1 if the player becomes disoriented or confused, as this is a sign of the more serious heat stroke.

Appendix F
Privacy Policy

The Little League Privacy Policy has been written to answer questions you might have about this issue. As a youth organization we are very concerned about privacy. Therefore, we have taken measures to tailor our content and offerings to help protect an individual's privacy. This Privacy Policy applies to information collected on Little League International authored websites such as: LittleLeague.org; LittleLeaguestore.net; and our official pages on Facebook, Twitter, YouTube, and Instagram as well as information received from other sources such as charter enrollment and player records reporting.

Our Commitment to Security

Little League International has implemented physical, electronic, and managerial processes to safeguard the privacy of the information it obtains.

Advice to Children and Parents

We strongly advise children to get their parent(s) or guardian(s) to review any information they intend to transmit and get their permission before submitting any kind of personal data to anyone over the Internet. We urge parents to repeatedly discuss with their children the danger of giving personal information to anyone (online or in person) whom they don't personally know. We also encourage parents and guardians to spend time online with their children monitoring and reviewing their children's online activity. As a policy, no person under the age of 13 is permitted to register directly to receive Little League's electronic communications.

What personal information do we collect for our electronic database?

Little League International requires chartered Little Leagues to submit player registration data and coach/manager data to be in compliance with Regulation IV(g) as well as league officer information at the time of chartering annually. Complete data for all players, managers/coaches, and league officers is required. Player registration data must include the date of birth of the player and parent or guardian contact information. The local league must verify the accuracy of such information annually. Submission of previous year information is not acceptable per the Regulation. A player, manager, or coach must be listed be on the data submitted to Little League International in order to be covered by Little League National Accident Insurance, provided it is purchased by the league.

All data is submitted electronically through the secure "Little League Data Center" on LittleLeague.org/datacenter. This website details the acceptable formats including a downloadable spreadsheet.

How do we use personal information collected and received

Any information gathered by Little League International on this website, through the League Player Registration and Coach/Manager registration process and/or by any other means, will be used for the purpose of furthering the mission of Little League International. Little League International does not sell any information collected from you to outside companies.

APPENDIX F — PRIVACY POLICY

On occasion, we may provide special offers or services through Little League International and/or its sponsors, licensees, or other business associates. We also may use the information to fulfill your requests for information or products or to respond to your inquiries about our program. We may use this information to communicate with you, such as to update you on new rules, regulations, or risk management issues, ask your opinion through surveys and research, notify you that you have won a contest, or provide you with the latest news story being covered by Little League International.

The information you provide in connection with our website and email communications, online submissions and surveys, social media sites, and communities is used to create an interactive experience. We may use this information to facilitate conversation and from time to time, offer you information, programs, and services.

Should you receive information from Little League or one of our partners, this information will be clearly identified with Little League International identification marks in adherence with our trademark registration.

The data provided to Little League International is utilized in the following ways:

- To catalog and record each individual player into a yearly listing of participants in the Little League program. These records are maintained in the Little League archives and for historical purposes through the *World of Little League*: Peter J. McGovern Museum and Official Store. This information may also be used for operational issues that may arise with respect to eligibility of the participants in a local league program.
- To maintain a record of the coaches and managers involved in the Little League program and their associated team and/or league. This information is used to provide seasonal training materials, to send the Little League Magazine for their team's players during the season as well as operational issues that may arise requiring contact with Little League International.
- Email addresses provided to Little League International through the league player record sharing process by each player's parent(s) or guardian(s), and coach and/or manager are incorporated into Little League International's electronic database for the current season. Individuals receive an "Opt-In" welcome announcement and are given the choice to opt-in to receive communications from Little League. Every communication sent will provide you an option to "Opt-Out".
- Household mailing addresses reported by leagues are occasionally used to provide information to those residents about the Little League program. Should information be sent, it will be sent under the cover of "Current Resident" or "To the Parent or Guardian of Little League Participant."

Player and coach/manager information must be sent to Little League International in accordance with Regulation IV(g) of the Little League Rulebook.

The privacy policy below describes our process for collecting and using email addresses of our constituents.

At Little League International, we collect information in addition to player registration data and coach/manager data in order to help identify you and/or your child's interests in the Little League program and the associated local league with which you may be affiliated. On our websites and through our various links to resources and information, you can read articles; enter contests; participate in promotions; express your opinion; shop online; or subscribe to our online portals, emails, and newsletters. On occasion, we may ask for personal contact information from you for purposes such as:

APPENDIX F — PRIVACY POLICY

1. to provide you with information that you've requested based on your selected preferences upon Opt-In;
2. to enable us to respond to your inquiry;
3. to register you for a contest or promotion;
4. to take your subscription for a Little League publication or web-based portal, or;
5. for league operation and education.

You also have the opportunity to "Opt-Out" of any Little League controlled electronic large group communication at any time by sending an email to LLInternational@LittleLeague.org and typing "Unsubscribe" in the subject line or by clicking on the "Safe Unsubscribe™" link at the bottom of any email you receive from us.

Please note that some information you receive may direct you to a non-Little League website. Please refer to these web sites for specific Privacy Policies and use of data as we have no control over information that is submitted to, or collected by, these third parties.

We may be required to share your personal information and non-personal information pursuant to judicial or governmental subpoenas, warrants, or orders. If we are required to do so, we will, of course, obey the law. In addition, notwithstanding any term to the contrary in this Privacy Policy, we reserve the right to use, disclose, and/or share your personal and non-personal information in order to investigate, prevent, or take action regarding illegal activities, suspected fraud, situations involving potential threats to the physical safety of any person, violations of this Website's Terms of Use, or as otherwise required by law.

Individual Submissions and Promotions

We may offer coupons, special discounts, contests, games, and promotions on behalf of Little League International and/or our national partners; or invite you to submit stories, photos, comments, or questions to certain areas of our website. On these occasions, we may ask you to voluntarily submit additional information along with your submission so that we can notify you if you are a winner, or to respond to (or ask) questions. No individual under the age of 13 should submit information to any of the situations noted above.

Cookies and Pixel Tags -- What are they?

Cookies and pixel tags are pieces of information that a website transfers to an individual's hard drive for record-keeping purposes. Cookies make Internet surfing easier for you by saving your passwords and preferences while you're at a site. The use of cookies is an industry standard -- you'll find that they are used by most major websites. By showing how and when visitors use the site, cookies can also help website developers see which areas are popular and which are not.

Does the Little League website use cookies or pixel tags?

Yes. As you browse LittleLeague.org or Little League-owned websites, cookies, pixel tags, or similar technology may be placed on your computer so that we can understand what information interests you on our site, in order to continue to provide information in the future. On occasion, we may provide target advertising through partners like AdRoll and Facebook to present you with additional information about our program and its offerings based on your previous interaction with LittleLeague.org. These techniques do **not** collect personal information such as your name, email address, postal address, or telephone number. We also work with third party companies to assist us with website analytics such as evaluating the use and operation of our website so that we can continue to enhance

APPENDIX F — PRIVACY POLICY

the website(s) and the information contained within. You can visit networkadvertising.org/choices/ to opt-out of tracking and targeted advertising using cookies or similar technology.

Questions or Concerns

This policy was last updated on October 19, 2015. Little League International reserves the right to modify this policy from time to time as Little League International determines to be appropriate.

If you have any questions, comments or concerns regarding the Little League International Privacy Policy, please contact us at privacy@LittleLeague.org.

Responsibility of Local Little Leagues

A copy of this privacy policy is available at LittleLeague.org/privacypolicy. We strongly encourage all local Little Leagues to download this policy and distribute it to participant families and volunteers at registration and post on local league websites.

Appendix G
2016 Little League Age Chart

For Softball Divisions Only

Match month (top line) and box with year of birth. League age indicated at right.

Jan	Feb	Mar	Apr	May	Jun	Jul	Aug	Sep	Oct	Nov	Dec	Age
2011	2011	2011	2011	2011	2011	2011	2011	2011	2011	2011	2011	4
2010	2010	2010	2010	2010	2010	2010	2010	2010	2010	2010	2010	5
2009	2009	2009	2009	2009	2009	2009	2009	2009	2009	2009	2009	6
2008	2008	2008	2008	2008	2008	2008	2008	2008	2008	2008	2008	7
2007	2007	2007	2007	2007	2007	2007	2007	2007	2007	2007	2007	8
2006	2006	2006	2006	2006	2006	2006	2006	2006	2006	2006	2006	9
2005	2005	2005	2005	2005	2005	2005	2005	2005	2005	2005	2005	10
2004	2004	2004	2004	2004	2004	2004	2004	2004	2004	2004	2004	11
2003	2003	2003	2003	2003	2003	2003	2003	2003	2003	2003	2003	12
2002	2002	2002	2002	2002	2002	2002	2002	2002	2002	2002	2002	13
2001	2001	2001	2001	2001	2001	2001	2001	2001	2001	2001	2001	14
2000	2000	2000	2000	2000	2000	2000	2000	2000	2000	2000	2000	15
1999	1999	1999	1999	1999	1999	1999	1999	1999	1999	1999	1999	16
1998	1998	1998	1998	1998	1998	1998	1998	1998	1998	1998	1998	17
1997	1997	1997	1997	1997	1997	1997	1997	1997	1997	1997	1997	18

Note: This age chart is for SOFTBALL DIVISIONS ONLY, and only for 2016.

LITTLE LEAGUE® OPERATING POLICIES

OPERATING POLICIES

LOCAL LEAGUE ADMINISTRATION

Separately, each of the various elements which contribute to the operation of the program affords assistance to those who play Little League. Together they function in teamwork with Little League International, whose primary responsibility is service to more than one (1) million volunteers and 2.5 million participants.

Here is a brief outline of the functions of the component elements:

1. The Local League

The league is the basic unit of organization. It serves the home community and is the core of the volunteer aspect of Little League.

At this level, managers, coaches, umpires, league officers, auxiliary, and other personnel come into close association with the children. It is in the local league perspective that the public sees Little League.

Within the framework of rules and regulations of Little League, the local league is autonomous. It establishes its own administration, elects its board of directors, and maintains an organization best suited to meet the needs of Little League in the community.

2. The District and the District Administrator

The field organization, which provides a broad area of administrative service and counsel to local leagues, comprises thousands of competent and experienced volunteer leaders.

Since 1955, Little League has made it possible for leagues to elect a District Administrator as a step towards effecting better service to the league and closer liaison between the league and Little League International.

The District Administrator is responsible to the leagues in the district to acquaint them with information disseminated out of Little League International, assisting them in settling problems, reviewing with them proposed amendments, reporting to them on the business of the Congress, and interpreting adopted changes. The District Administrator is expected to conduct the election in the district, call meetings whenever necessary, assist in the organization and counseling of new leagues, review and investigate the organization; review and investigate problems referred by Little League International, and be well informed on policies, rules, regulations and other pertinent information. Since the District Administrator holds a position of trust and responsibility, that person must be experienced and familiar with all areas and all leagues in the district.

However, the District Administrator never has the authority to suspend or waive any rule or regulation, nor to forfeit any International Tournament game.

ROLE OF LEAGUE PRESIDENT

Apart from all other considerations, sound leadership, couched in knowledge, experience and common sense, is the greatest requirement and most exemplary qualification of the man or woman selected as president of a Little League.

While efficient organizational and administrative abilities are desirable credentials, the search for good leadership must transcend all other attributes in the adult who gives direction to the Little League movement in the local community. Dedication to the goals and purpose of Little League is inherent in the volunteer aspect of those who serve, but all who serve are not equally gifted with the qualities of leadership.

OPERATING POLICIES

Baseball and softball are the names of the games, but Little League is the name of an elite program and initiative that has given these sports their best dimensions. The stature and integrity of Little League are hard-won hallmarks, accompanied by men and women who have given outstanding leadership at many levels.

A fine tradition of unselfishness and dedicated effort has been passed on annually to thousands of incoming league presidents. Little League is a better and more vital program because of them. Each year as local leagues expand to embrace more participants, the mantle of leadership becomes more demanding and imposes more trust and responsibility upon the league president.

The president learns certain fundamental obligations which have been spelled out in rules and regulations. But the degree of the understanding of the motivations underlying Little League — and the extent of the president's personal leadership in the sensitive area of youth activity — are over-riding qualifications which best gauge a president equal to the responsibility.

The president has many responsibilities in the administration of the league. Each president is elected by, and is accountable to, the local league Board of Directors. Duties of a president are described within the limits of the league constitution which should give each president wide latitude in overseeing the affairs of all elements of the league.

As the chief administrator, the president selects and appoints managers, coaches, umpires and committees. All appointments are subject to the approval of the league's Board of Directors. They are responsible to the president for the conduct of league affairs, both on and off the field. Importantly, the president is the officer with whom Little League International maintains contact and who represents the league in the council of the District Organization.

The president should be the most informed officer of the league. Each president must know the regulations under which Little League operates and in authorizing the annual application for charter, binds all members of the league to faithfully observe the regulations. Little League reserves the right to require a league to remove any officer who does not carry out the terms of charter application. Serious violation can result in loss of the league's charter.

Beyond the requirements of league administration, the president should personify the best public image in reflection to the community at large. Each president should take an active role in gaining support and winning friends for the league.

The increase of youth activities in a recreation-minded nation challenges Little League to earn the respect and interest of the community. Little League is competitive with many other agencies in this regard. It is in this field that the league president and all other officers must give dignity and stature to Little League representation.

Over the years, Little League has worked out a successful formula for maintaining the autonomous character of local league operation. But it has also established a close-knit liaison with the local league by means of intercommunication between the president and all field levels up to and including Little League International.

It is imperative that the league president maintains updated contact information with Little League International to ensure that important communication is received and shared with appropriate league officers. To register for electronic notifications or verify your email address, visit LittleLeague.org/register.

OPERATING POLICIES

It is by means of this free exchange in service and counsel that Little League is a cohesive unit of more than 7,000 leagues, each with an open channel to Little League International. The local league president is one of a great family of league presidents whose aggressive interest in the total program has fashioned — and will continue to fashion — the design of Little League wherever it is played.

LEAGUE OFFICERS

Annually, the regular membership of each Little League is required to meet and elect a Board of Directors. Following the election, the Board of Directors will meet and elect its officers from within the membership of the board. The officers required are: President, Vice President, Secretary, Treasurer, Player Agent, Coaching Coordinator, and Safety Officer. If a league also operates a Intermediate (50-70) Division, Junior League, Senior League, and/or Big League, a Vice President or other personnel should be designated to supervise, as is also the case for those leagues operating Little League, Junior League, Senior League, or Big League Softball programs. All officers should be members of the league's Board of Directors.

League duties concerning player selection, the transfer of players from Minor Leagues and schedule supervision, should be properly vested in the league's player agent.

Briefly, the duties of league officers and Board of Directors can be summed up as follows:

Board of Directors - The management of the property and affairs of the local league shall be vested in the Board of Directors. The directors shall, upon election, immediately enter upon the performance of their duties and shall continue in office until their successors shall have been duly elected and qualified.

The board membership shall include the officers, including player agent, and a minimum of one manager and one volunteer umpire. (Only volunteer umpires may be elected to the board.) The number of managers and coaches including Minor League representation elected to the board shall not exceed a minority of the total board members. Every board member should have a copy of the Little League Rulebook with Operating Policies for reference to proper operating procedures and policies.

The Board of Directors shall have the power to appoint such standing and special committees as it shall determine by the constitution and to delegate such powers to them as the board shall deem advisable and which it may properly delegate.

The board may adopt such rules and regulations for the conduct of its meetings and the management of the league as it may deem proper.

The board shall have the power by a two-thirds vote of those present at any regular or special meeting to discipline, suspend or remove any director or officer or committee member of the league, subject to provisions of the constitution.

President - Presides at league meetings, and assumes full responsibility for the operation of the local league. The president receives all mail, supplies, and other communications from the Little League International. The president must see to it that league personnel is properly briefed on all phases of rules, regulations, and policies of Little League. The league president is the contact between the local organization and Little League International.

Vice President - Presides in the absence of the president; works with other officers and committee members; is ex-officio member of all committees and carries out such duties and assignments as may be delegated by the president.

OPERATING POLICIES

Secretary - Maintains a register of members and directors; records the minutes of meetings; is responsible for sending out notice of meetings, issues membership cards and maintains a record of league's activities.

Treasurer - Signs checks co-signed by another officer or director; dispenses league funds as approved by the Board of Directors; reports on the status of league funds; keeps local league books and financial records; prepares budgets and assumes the responsibility for all local league finances.

Player Agent - Conducts annual tryouts, and is in charge of player selection, assists president in checking birth records and eligibility of players; serves as a member of the Board of Directors of the local league and generally supervises and coordinates the transfer of players to or from the Minor Leagues according to provisions of the regulations of Little League.

Safety Officer - Coordinates all safety activities; ensures safety in player training; ensures safe playing conditions; coordinates reporting and prevention of injuries; solicits suggestions for making conditions safer; reports suggestions to Little League International through the league president and prepares the ASAP plan for submission to Little League International.

Umpire-in-Chief (U.I.C.) - Serves as coordinator of and advises the league President on the league umpire program; responsible for recommending umpires to the league President for appointment to the league umpire roster; recruiting and retaining volunteer umpires; establishing a league umpire training program consistent with Little League® guidelines; coordinating and assisting with conducting umpire clinics at league and district level; communicating rule changes to league umpires; scheduling league umpires for regular season games; evaluating league umpires using established guidelines to maintain program integrity; further continual improvement, and prepare league umpires for advancement to tournament levels; communicating with and providing updates to the District Umpire Consultant on the league umpire program, and attending Umpire Training programs at the District, State, Region, and/or Headquarters level.

League Information Officer - Sets up and manages league's official website; sets up online registration and ensures the league rosters are uploaded to Little League; assigns online administrative rights to other local volunteers; encourages creation of team web sites to managers, coaches, and parents; ensures that league news and scores are updated online on a regular basis; collects, posts, and distributes important information on league activities including direct dissemination of fundraising and sponsor activities to Little League, the district, the public, league members, and the media; serves as primary contact person for Little League and ACTIVE Team Sports regarding optimizing use of the Internet for league administration and for distributing information to league members and to Little League International. Provides player, coach and manager records to Little League International in electronic format.

Coaching Coordinator - Represents coaches/managers in league; presents a coach/manager training budget to the board; gains the support and funds necessary to implement a league-wide training program; orders and distributes training materials to players, coaches and managers; coordinates mini-clinics as necessary; serves as the contact person for Little League and its manager-coach education. Receives and distributes coaching information from Little League International and distributes to all coaches and managers.

Sponsor Fundraising Manager - Solicits and secures local sponsorships to support league operations; collects and reviews sponsorship and fundraising opportunities; organizes and implements approved league fundraising activities; coordinates participation in fundraising activities; and maintains records of monies secured through sponsorship and fundraising initiatives.

Concession Manager - Maintains the operation of concession facilities; organizes the purchase of concession products; responsible for the management of the concession sales at league events; schedules volunteers to work the concession booth during league events; collects and reviews concession related offers including coupons, discounts, and bulk-purchasing opportunities; and organizes, tallies and keeps records of concession sales and purchases.

Marketing/Public Relations Manager – Oversees new player recruitment efforts; develops and maintains a league marketing plan focused on player recruitment and retention; oversees efforts to market new divisions of play and initiatives offered by the league; works with local media to promote the interests of Little League, and coordinates efforts to make the local Little League visible in the community year round.

PROCESS TO OBTAIN WAIVERS OF RULES AND REGULATIONS

When a league applies for its annual charter with Little League, it pledges to abide by all the rules and regulations of Little League. However, under special circumstances, it may become necessary to apply for a temporary waiver of a rule or regulation.

It is very important to remember that a league must not take any action contrary to Little League rules and regulations until receiving expressed, written permission through the Charter Committee waiver system. A league wishing to apply for a waiver of a rule or regulation must do so via the following method:

1. The local league Board of Directors votes whether or not to request the waiver.
2. If the local league Board of Directors votes to request the waiver, the president writes a letter, detailing the request. Supporting documents should be attached, and forwarded to the District Administrator.
3. The District Administrator includes his/her written opinion, and forwards all documents to the Regional Director by June 1 of the current year.
4. The Regional Director will present the situation to the Charter Committee for action.
5. The Charter Committee will inform the Regional Director of its decision, and the Regional Director will inform the District Administrator.

NOTE 1: Any request for a waiver that does not follow the above steps may be delayed.

NOTE 2: If a waiver request involves more than one league, all leagues involved must submit appropriate documentation.

NOTE 3: All waiver requests to the Charter Committee must be submitted in writing by the league president before the start of the league's regular season or June 1, whichever occurs first. Requests must be submitted to the regional office through the District Administrator.

LOCAL LEAGUE DRAFT METHODS

Methods for Existing Leagues

Of course, the Managers must keep in mind that they must not select more than eight players in a given age group. The team roster may be comprised of players of league age 9, 10, 11, and 12 unless modified by the local league according to options established by Little League. The local league may opt to allow only 10, 11, and 12, or 11- and 12-year-olds, to try out for the major division.

Secrecy: Players shall never be told the position in which they were drafted.

Bonus Picks: Each manager requiring eight or more players prior to the draft to complete the roster will be allowed one bonus pick at the completion of round four. If more than one manager is allowed bonus picks under this section, the order of rotation will be identical to that being followed in the draft.

NOTE: All other draft methods for local league Major Divisions, other than the three outlined below, must be approved by the Charter Committee prior to the draft.

Plan A - Conventional Draft Plan

When a thorough tryout program has been completed, the last-place team of the preceding season gets the first choice in every round of the draft, the next to last place team gets the second selection in every round and the remaining teams select in the reverse order of standing.

For the purpose of explanation, let us assume that there are four teams in the league.

First Round:
> Fourth place manager selects the first player
> Third place manager selects the second player
> Second place manager selects the third player
> First place manager selects the fourth player

Second Round:
> Fourth place manager selects the fifth player
> Third place manager selects the sixth player
> Second place manager selects the seventh player
> First place manager selects the eighth player, etc., until the rosters are completed.

Plan B - Redraft

This draft is actually in two separate parts. The first part includes those players who:

A. are returning from a Major team in the same division, AND;

B. have registered for the current season.

This first draft of returning players must be completed before the second part of the draft, and all returning players who qualify under both conditions above must be drafted. Managers are not permitted to waive a draft choice.

The second part of the draft includes all players who are eligible for selection and have attended the required number of tryout sessions.

The draft rotation follows the reverse order of finish from the previous season, with the last place team's manager receiving the first pick, then the second-to-last place team, and so on, or the managers draw numbers to determine who will select the first player. For instance,

… in a four-team league, the manager of the last place team from the previous season makes the following player selections: 1st choice, 8th, 9th, 16th, 17th, 24th, 25th, etc.; The manager of the team that finished in third place makes the 2nd choice, 7th, 10th, 18th, 23rd, etc.; The manager of the team that finished second in the previous season makes the 3rd choice, 6th, 11th, 14th, 19th, 22nd; The manager of the team that finished in first place gets 4th choice, 5th, 12th, 13th, 20th, 21st, etc., until selections are completed.

NOTE 1: Because there are no players returning to a particular team, and because coaches cannot be named until the draft is completed, Options 2 and 4 (see "Options On Sons, Daughters And Siblings") do NOT apply when using this draft selection plan.

NOTE 2: When the second part of this draft method begins, the draft order starts with the team that is due to draft next after the completion of the first round.

Alternate Method for Plan B: Instead of having two separate drafts (one for returning players, and one for new players), a league may elect to conduct a regular draft wherein, if a number of returning Major League players has not been drafted by the time that same number of draft picks remain, those returning players must be the only players eligible from that point forward in the draft. (**Example:** With nine picks left in the draft, there are nine players who were Major League players in the previous season still not drafted for the current year. Those nine players become the only nine eligible players, and must be drafted.)

Plan C - Blind Draft Method

Step 1: Decide how many Major teams your league will operate for the season. Take the number of eligible 12-year-olds that signed up that opted for Major level play and divide by 8 (the legal number of 12-year-olds Little League allows).

Step 2: Each manager is assigned a team name (i.e., Rockies, Padres, etc.) and allowed to place their child/children on the roster. No 10-year-olds should be placed on any roster until all other eligible 12- and 11-year-olds are given a roster spot.

Step 3: All eligible 12-year-old names are placed in a non-transparent container; a single name is selected at random and placed on the next team's roster. Each name is drawn and placed on the next team roster until all 12-year-olds have been selected. If no roster positions remain, the 12-year-old draft is stopped.

NOTE: According to Regulation V - Selection of Players, all candidates who are league age twelve (12) must be drafted to a Little League Major Division, Intermediate (50-70) Division (baseball), and/or a Junior League team(s) in accordance with Regulation IV(a).

Step 4: All eligible 11-year-olds that would like to be considered for play at the Major level are placed in the non-transparent container. Each name is drawn out and placed on the next team roster until either all 11-year-old names have been selected, or the team roster is full.

Step 5: All eligible 10-year-olds that would like to be considered for play at the Major level are placed in the non-transparent container. Each name is drawn out and placed on the next team roster until either all 10-year-old names have been selected, or the team roster is full.

Step 6: All eligible 9-year-olds that would like to be considered for play at the Major level are placed in the non-transparent container. Each name is drawn out and placed on the next team roster until either all 9-year-old names have been selected, or the team roster is full.

OPERATING POLICIES

Methods for Local Leagues in their First Year of Operation

Plan A - Serpentine Draft Plan

The managers draw numbers to determine who will select the first player. In a new four-team league, the manager who draws number one makes the following player selections: 1st choice, 8th, 9th, 16th, 17th, 24th, 25th, etc.; The manager who draws number two makes the 2nd choice, 7th, 10th, 18th, 23rd, etc.; The manager who draws number three, 3rd choice, 6th, 11th, 14th, 19th, 22nd; The manager who draws number four, 4th choice, 5th, 12th, 13th, 20th, 21st, etc., until selections are complete.

Plan B - Team Draft Plan

Another way of balancing the teams in the first year is to use a plan developed with success in some communities. Under this plan, the manager and coaches of all the teams select the best players during the tryouts for the regular league. Normally, they select at least 60 players (four-team league) in the age pattern desired (**Example:** 32 twelve-year-olds, 20 eleven-year olds and eight nine or ten-year-olds.)

Managers and coaches should attempt to divide the players into four teams of equal strength, with the player agent coordinating the activity. When they play several practice games to double-check their judgment, and make any switches of players between teams which seem desirable, the teams are numbered and the managers draw the numbers out of a hat to determine which team each will manage the next season. In this plan, an equitable understanding must be established to permit a manager to acquire a son or daughter for that manager's team by a player trade if this seems desirable.

Plan C - Blind Draft Plan

Step 1: Decide how many Major teams your league will operate for the season. Take the number of eligible 12-year-olds that signed up that opted for Major level play and divide by 8 (the legal number of 12-year-olds Little League allows).

Step 2: Each manager is assigned a team name (i.e., Rockies, Padres, etc.) and allowed to place their child/children on the roster. No 10-year-olds should be placed on any roster until all other eligible 12- and 11-year-olds are given a roster spot.

Step 3. All eligible 12-year-old names are placed in a nontransparent container; a single name is selected at random and placed on the next team's roster. Each name is drawn and placed on the next team roster until all 12-year olds have been selected. If no roster positions remain, the 12-year-old draft is stopped.

> **NOTE:** According to Regulation V - Selection of Players, all candidates who are league age twelve (12) must be drafted to a Little League Major Division, Intermediate (50-70) Division (baseball), and/or a Junior League team(s) in accordance with Regulation IV(a).

Step 4: All eligible 11-year-olds that would like to be considered for play at the Major level are placed in the non-transparent container. Each name is drawn out and placed on the next team roster until either all 11-year-old names have been selected, or the team roster is full.

Step 5: All eligible 10-year-olds that would like to be considered for play at the Major level are placed in the non-transparent container. Each name is drawn out and placed on the next team roster until either all 10-year-old names have been selected, or the team roster is full.

OPERATING POLICIES

Step 6: All eligible 9-year-olds that would like to be considered for play at the Major level are placed in the non-transparent container. Each name is drawn out and placed on the next team roster until either all 9-year-old names have been selected, or the team roster is full.

OPTIONS ON SONS, DAUGHTERS AND SIBLINGS

An option is an agreement between a manager and the player agent covering a special condition. All options must be in writing (except No. 1) and be submitted to the player agent 48 hours prior to the draft. The options are as follows:

1. **Brothers/Sisters in the Draft**
   When there are two or more siblings in the draft, and the first brother or sister is drafted by a manager, that manager automatically has an option to draft the other brother or sister on the next turn. If the manager does not exercise the option, the second sibling is then available to be drafted by any team.

2. **Brothers/Sisters of Players Currently on a Team**
   If desired, a manager shall submit an option in writing on a draftee if the player candidate's brother or sister is a member of that manager's team. If such an option is submitted, the manager MUST draft the sibling within the first three draft selections.

3. **Sons/Daughters of Managers**
   If a manager has sons and/or daughters eligible under Regulation II for the draft, and wishes to draft them, he/she must submit the option in writing. If so stated, the parent/manager is required to exercise the option at or before the close of the specific draft round, depending on the League Age of sons and/or daughters. Parent/manager option takes priority over any other option.
   NOTE: These provisions also apply for managers having eligible brothers or sisters in the draft.

4. **Sons/Daughters of Coaches**
   A NEW coach shall not be appointed nor approved until after the draft to avoid "Red Shirting" of players through selective coaching appointments.
   A returning coach, through the manager, may exercise an option in writing to the player agent provided:

   (A) The coach has served as a manager or coach in the league (at any level) for the past two years AND,
   (B) The coach is returning to the same Major League team as last year.

   IMPORTANT: In order for a manager to exercise this option, the coach must qualify under BOTH conditions above.

5. **Draft Rounds**
   If an option is submitted in writing for the son and/or daughter of a manager or coach, such candidate must be drafted in or before the following round:

BASEBALL

Draft Round	Little League	Intermediate	Junior	Senior	Big
5	9-10	11	12	14, 13	16, 15
4	11	12	13	15	17
3	12	13	14	16	18

OPERATING POLICIES

SOFTBALL

Draft Round	Little League	Junior	Senior	Big
5	9-10	12	14, 13	16, 15, 14
4	11	13	15	17
3	12	14	16	18

6. **Special Considerations Which Apply**
   (A) If the manager so chooses, the option on son or daughter may be waived.
   (B) In the event the parent becomes a manager in another league, that parent may not claim the son or daughter.
   (C) Players are eligible only in the league whose boundaries include the parent/manager's home residence (as defined by Little League).
   (D) When a vacancy occurs during the playing season, the player selected to fill the vacancy becomes a permanent member of that team, governed by the same regulations as all members of the team selected in the draft.
   (E) All players, including sons/daughters of managers and coaches at the Minor League level, are subject to the draft.
   (F) Parents of Major League players who become managers or coaches after their children have been selected to a Major team may not automatically claim their sons or daughters, but may trade for them at the proper time, subject to requirements for trading in the next section.

(**NOTE:** THE LITTLE LEAGUE DEFINITION OF RESIDENCE IS LOCATED IN THE "LITTLE LEAGUE RESIDENCY AND SCHOOL ATTENDANCE REQUIREMENTS" SECTION OF THIS RULEBOOKS.)

Alternate Method of Operation - The Regular Season

To aid leagues that are having a difficult time getting enough players for their regular season teams the following option is available:

A pool of players from existing regular season teams can be created with players that are willing to participate in extra games during the regular season when teams face a shortage of rostered players for a regular season game.

Guidelines:

1. The league's player agent will create and run the pool. The league's player agent will use the pool to assign players to teams that are short of players on a rotating basis.
2. Managers and/or coaches will not have the right to randomly pick and choose players from the pool.
3. Players used from the pool will not be allowed to pitch, except during the player's own regular season scheduled game.
4. Pool players that are called and show up at the game site must play at least nine consecutive defensive outs and bat once.

For details on age alignments for Intermediate (50-70) Division/Junior/Senior/Big League, see Regulation IV of the rulebooks.

OPERATING POLICIES

LOCAL LEAGUE MAINTENANCE OF ROSTERS

Duration of Title

Each player acquired shall, for the duration of their major Little League career, be the property of the team and league or division making the acquisition, unless subsequently traded or released. **NOTE:** When local league elects to utilize "common pool draft method" players shall remain property of the league or division making the acquisition. (**Exception:** If the league's Board of Directors opts to use the Plan B or Plan C draft method for existing leagues, all returning Major Division players must be drafted first, but are not required to be placed on the same team on which they participated previously.)

Regulation II(d) allows the Board of Directors to continue as a player any child whose residence changes after becoming a member of the league. (See the restrictions in the regulation.) However, the best interests of the child should be taken into consideration by the Board in exercising this right.

(**NOTE:** THE LITTLE LEAGUE DEFINITION OF RESIDENCE IS LOCATED IN THE "LITTLE LEAGUE RESIDENCY AND SCHOOL ATTENDANCE REQUIREMENTS" SECTION OF THIS RULEBOOK.)

Trading

Following the draft, managers may, if they desire, trade players until 14 days after the first scheduled game. ALL TRADES SHALL BE MADE THROUGH AND WITH THE APPROVAL OF THE PLAYER AGENT. The following restrictions also apply:

1. Minor League players may not be traded for Major Division players.

2. All trades must be player for player only. (**Example:** Two players from Team A could not be traded for one player on Team B.)

3. Trades involving a player for draft choices are not permitted. (**Example:** A manager cannot trade his/her right to pick the third player overall for an existing player on another team. However, once the draft is complete, a trade may be consummated, providing it meets all other criteria for trading.)

The player agent(s) must monitor any attempts by managers and parents to manipulate the system and thus create an imbalance in the league. ALL TRADES MUST BE FOR JUSTIFIABLE REASONS AND BE APPROVED BY THE LOCAL BOARD.

Replacements

When a player is lost to a team during the playing season for any of the following reasons:

1. He/she moves to another city or state too distant to commute for practice and play;

2. He/she is injured and will not be able to return to play within a reasonable period of time (local league board decision);

3. He/she has for personal reasons decided to terminate his/her association with the team;

4. Any other justifiable reason, reviewed and approved by the Board of Directors;

The manager of the team losing a player shall promptly advise the player agent. The player agent shall advise the president and the board. If loss of player is approved, the president will send a letter of release to the player and the parents stating player is released from the Major League team and the league for a justifiable reason. This action creates a legal opening for a replacement on the team roster.

OPERATING POLICIES

The manager shall review the available player list with the player agent and shall select a replacement. The replacement becomes a permanent member of the team.

NOTE: Failure by the manager to advise the player agent of a player's continued absence should result in disciplinary action against the manager.

Expansion

Option One: When a league expands by four teams or more teams in one season, it is highly desirable that all of the players be placed in the player pool and the selecting start from "scratch." Many leagues have permitted the established teams to remain intact while giving the new team or teams an opportunity to fill their rosters from new players before the "old" teams select their replacements. When the "old" teams are permitted to retain a nucleus of experienced players, the new teams frequently lose a majority of games by lopsided scores and in too many cases go through a season without winning a single game. It often takes a new team two or three years to come up to league strength in this way, and thus creates an imbalance, an unhappy competitive situation and decreases possibilities for constructive experiences for the participants.

Option Two: If a league has a strong foundation, this expansion plan may seem adequate and less drastic. It may be better than starting from scratch.

When a league expands from four to five or more teams, it would be more beneficial to all concerned if each manager would give up, in a one team expansion, one 12-year-old, and one 11-year-old, and expanding into two teams to give up two 12, and two 11-year-olds. These players will then be placed in a common pool for selection by the new teams. This would give each new team a nucleus of older experienced players. Once this nucleus of eight players is established, the remainder of the teams would be filled through regular bidding or draft.

Option Three: This plan provides the most favorable competitive balance between existing teams at the Major League level over Options One and Two when a local league expands it's Major League to provide additional opportunity for more candidates to participate at the Major League level. Plan Three incorporates many basic features of a plan used successfully in professional baseball. This plan simply has every existing team placing players in a player pool from which the new expansion teams will draft players in a preliminary draft.

The player pool is formed by the following procedure:
1. The team with the fewest returning players will place one player into the pool and in doing so, will establish the key to the number of players all other teams can retain.

   For example, let's assume a division expanding from five teams to six:
   Major Team A has four returning players — contributes one player to expansion pool;
   Major Team B has five players returning — contributes two players to expansion pool;
   Major Team C has five returning players — contributes two players to expansion pool;
   Major Team D has six players returning — contributes three players to expansion pool;
   Major Team E has six returning players — contributes three players to expansion pool;

2. In one-team expansion using this example, the expansion team manager chooses three players in a preliminary draft. All players remaining in the Major League expansion player pool then return to their original teams. (If the expansion is by two teams, each chooses three players, alternating picks.)

OPERATING POLICIES

3. The regular draft of Minor League players will then begin with the expansion team(s) drafting first in each round. The established teams then draft in reverse order of the finish in last year's schedule.
4. Any trading of players, which may be a necessity, will follow immediately after the draft has been completed. Trading of players can continue until the 14th day after the start of the playing season.

Team Reduction

If the number of teams is to be reduced at the Major League level, the Board of Directors decides which team is to be deleted from the division. All current Major League players affected must be reassigned to a Major League team by one of these two methods:

A. Through a preliminary draft (reverse order of finish) prior to the regular player draft involving new candidates. Once the preliminary draft is complete, the regular player draft starts over in the reverse order of finish, without regard to the last team to pick; or,

B. Through a regular draft wherein, if a number of returning Major League players has not been drafted by the time that same number of draft picks remain, those returning players must be the only players eligible from that point forward in the draft. (**Example:** The number of teams is reduced, putting six Major League players back into the draft. At the draft, with three selections left to be made, there are three players from the six returnees who have not yet been drafted. Those three players become the only three eligible players, and must be drafted.)

Divisional Play

When a league charters more than 10 teams in their Major League or when required by action of the Charter Committee, it is necessary to form two divisions (usually an American and National Division). This is accomplished by one of these four methods:

1. Divide all candidates within the division by odd and even birthdates. For example, candidates with odd birthdates are assigned to the American Division and even birthdates to the National Division. This method could result in an imbalance of candidates and talent during a particular year, and could require members of the same family to participate in separate divisions.

2. Use the first letter of the last name (surname or family name) to separate candidates between the two divisions. Under this method, the letters A-L would be assigned to one division and M-Z to the other. Like the first method, this could result in an imbalance of candidates and talent. However, it generally results in members of the same family remaining in the same division.

3. Using a geographical alignment, the players in each division are separated by a boundary line within that of the league itself. Like the first three methods, this could result in an imbalance of candidates and talent.

4. All teams in both divisions draft from all eligible candidates using the "Common Pool Draft Method." Teams select players alternately between the divisions. This always results in a balance of candidates, and offers a better chance for equal talent distribution between the two divisions.

   NOTE: Once a candidate is league age 9 years old or is enrolled for the first time

OPERATING POLICIES

after the candidate attains the league age of 9 and is assigned and/or drafted into a specific division (Example - American/National), the candidate cannot transfer to the opposite division(s) during their entire Little League career. This means that a candidate assigned and/or drafted to a minor or major league team in the American Division cannot transfer to a National Division team. If the player moves between divisions, they will be deemed ineligible for tournament play. If a league decides to redraft in any form or trade players, this note still applies.

Under any method, players already assigned to Major League teams can be retained by their teams, if the League decides to do so, by application of Regulation II(d) and/or IV(h). Forms for requesting waivers under either of these regulations must be filed annually.

Interleague Play can be requested. However, each division must field its own Tournament Team.

Forms for Divisional Play are available from the Regional Office. Whatever method is used must be approved annually in writing from the Charter Committee before implementation. When leagues receive Charter Committee approval to either operate in divisional format or to operate more than one league under a single management, there can be no transfer of Major division players between divisions or leagues without written approval of the Charter Committee in Williamsport.

DIVIDING A LEAGUE

It may become necessary to divide the league — thus creating two chartered leagues. Such a division can be accomplished easily and requires no extra fields for play. Under any method, a single Board of Directors can operate both charters, if recommended by the District Administrator and approved by the Charter Committee.

This realignment can be accomplished by one of five methods:

1. Reduce boundaries to include a smaller population. This is the least desirable method, unless some accommodation is made for the population no longer in the league boundaries.

2. Divide the league's service area geographically to provide for two charter areas. This is the most desirable method, particularly if the "new" league is afforded playing fields within its new boundaries.

3. Divide all candidates by odd and even birthdates. For example, candidates with odd birthdates are assigned to the American League and even birthdates to the National League. This method could result in an imbalance of candidates and talent during a particular year and could require members of the same family to participate in separate leagues.

4. Use the first letter of the last name (surname or family name) to separate candidates between the two leagues. For example, candidates with last names beginning with A-L would be assigned to the American League and those with last names beginning with M-Z would be assigned to the National League. Like the previous method, this could result in an imbalance of candidates and talent. However, it generally results in members of the same family remaining in the same league.

5. All teams in both leagues draft from all eligible candidates using the "Common Pool Draft Method." Teams select players alternately between the leagues. This generally results in a balance of candidates, and offers a better chance for equal talent distribution between the two leagues.

   NOTE: Once a candidate is league age 9 years old or is enrolled for the first time after the candidate attains the age of league age 9 and is assigned and/or drafted into a specific league (Example - American/National), the candidate cannot transfer to the opposite league(s) during their entire Little League career. This means that a candidate assigned and/or drafted to a minor or major league team in the American League cannot transfer to a National League team. If the player moves between leagues, they will be deemed ineligible for tournament play. If a league(s) decides to redraft in any form or trade players, this note still applies.

Under any method, players already assigned to Major League teams can be retained by their teams, if the League decides to do so, by application of Regulation II(d) and/or IV(h). Forms for requesting waivers under either of these regulations must be filed annually.

Interleague Play can be requested. However, each league/division must field its own Tournament Team(s).

Forms for Dividing a League are available from the Regional Office. Whatever method is used must be approved in writing from the Charter Committee before implementation.

NOTE 1: A league wishing to apply for a waiver of Regulation II(g), or any rule or regulation, must do so via the method prescribed in the "Little League Policies and Principles" chapter of this book, in the "Waivers of Rules and Regulations" section.

NOTE 2: When leagues have received Charter Committee approval to operate multiple leagues under a single management, there can be no transfer of Major division players between leagues without written approval of the Charter Committee in Williamsport.

LOCAL LEAGUE ELECTION PROCEDURES

These recommended procedures conform to the Sample Constitution. If followed, they will result in fewer accusations of "election rigging" and, possibly, fewer chances of lawsuits.

1. The first step should actually be taken at least a month before the election:
2. Establish a Nominating Committee, which should consist of at least three board members and any number of regular members. The Nominating Committee's purpose is to ensure that there will be enough persons interested in being on the Board of Directors to fill all the possible positions. Its purpose is NOT to limit the potential number of nominees. It should also attempt to ensure that there are enough persons interested in individual positions as officers on the board.
3. Proper written notice stating date, place and time shall be given to all regular members in good standing ten (10) days in advance of the date the election is to be held.
4. All regular members must have paid their membership dues and have in their possession their membership I.D. Cards plus they must be active and be in good standing to be eligible to vote and/or become a nominee for election to the Board of Directors.

OPERATING POLICIES

5. Absentee ballots may be obtained IN PERSON from the Secretary. The ballots should have a number of blank lines equal to the maximum number of persons who could serve on the Board of Directors that year. The absentee voter then fills in the number of names desired IN ORDER OF PREFERENCE. The ballot should then be returned IN PERSON to the Secretary IN A SEALED ENVELOPE to be delivered to the Election Chairman at the meeting, still in the sealed envelope. (**NOTE:** Because Robert's Rules of Order no longer recommends it, proxy voting is to be discouraged in local Little League elections.)

6. When the election portion of the annual meeting takes place, the first order of business is to determine if a quorum is present. Quorum for many leagues is one-third of the total registered regular members, or a number of percentage acceptable to the local league regular membership at a meeting in advance of the annual meeting.

7. Once quorum is established, it is proper to determine how many members are to be elected to the board. The local constitution establishes a number that should be elected but this number can be increased or decreased depending on need by a two-thirds majority of the membership present.

8. After the number of Directors to be elected has been determined, the nominating committee will report and present the established required number of candidates who have been screened and have accepted to serve if elected.

9. After the nominating committee's report is accepted, the nominations shall be opened to the floor and any regular member may nominate another regular member as a candidate for election to the Board of Directors.

10. After the membership present has completed their efforts to nominate additional members, the nomination procedure will be closed by affirmation of the membership.

11. Every regular member will receive one ballot and will list names of eligible candidates in the number to be elected determined previously in the meeting.

12. The appointed Election Chairman, the clerks and tellers will gather and count the ballots. The total number of ballots shall be no more than the number of members present, except if the league has a provision for absentee ballots and which have been properly obtained and returned to the Secretary of the league in a sealed envelope prior to the election.

13. The persons in the number specified to be elected who have the highest number of votes by a majority vote (51 percent or more) shall become the new Board of Directors. The only exception is the number of managers and coaches elected to the board must be a minority. (Regulation I (b))

14. Following the election, the board shall meet as a body and elect the officers of the board from within the membership of the board.

15. The Secretary of the board, as the first official responsibility, shall notify Little League International, the Regional Director and the District Administrator of the election and the identity of the officers so proper communications may commence with the new Board of Directors on or after October 1st, or whenever the fiscal cycle begins for the local league.

OPERATING POLICIES

THE OFFICIAL SHOULDER PATCH

The Little League Official Shoulder Patch is the only recognized identification which sets a Little Leaguer apart from all other children who play baseball and softball. The patch symbolizes the affiliation with the Little League program and a reminder of the mission of promoting sportsmanship, discipline, teamwork and physical well-being for the millions of Little Leaguers throughout the World. The Official Shoulder Patch affixed to the uniform prevents confusion in public identification, especially in news photos of accidents, etc. It is also important in the latter vein as insurance protection.

Use of the Official Patch is mandatory for all divisions of Little League for both regular season and tournament play.

Patches worn 3" below left shoulder seam on raglan sleeve;

1" below seam on set-in sleeve; over left breast on sleeveless style.

Patches are worn 3" below the left shoulder seam on raglan sleeves, 1" below the seam on set-in sleeves, and over the left breast on sleeveless jerseys. The Umpire patch is worn 4" below the left shoulder seam on set-in sleeves. The jacket patch is worn over the left breast 6" below the shoulder seam.

The Tee Ball Baseball patch, Minor League Baseball patch, Little League Baseball patch, Intermediate (50-70) Division patch, Junior League Baseball patch, Senior Baseball League patch, Big League Baseball patch, Tee Ball Softball patch, Minor League Softball patch, Little League Softball patch, Junior League Softball patch, Senior League Softball patch, Big League Softball patch, Challenger patch, and Umpire patches can only be ordered through Little League International (LittleLeagueStore.net or call 800-874-2852), by visiting any Regional Office, or through LittleLeagueUniforms.com as part of a uniform jersey purchase. **Simulation or reproduction of the Patch in any form is a violation of trademark rights. Abuses should be reported immediately to Little League International.**

LITTLE LEAGUE POLICIES AND PRINCIPLES

Principles of Conduct

The vitality and growth of any major youth program is dependent upon its integrity and its individual entity. To the extent that the time and energies of its members are diverted to other similar activities, the more limited will be its prospects for continuing success. Failure to maintain an identifiable organization, responsibility for which remains separate and distinct from others, inevitably will result in a loss of public enthusiasm and, ultimately in a process of declining interest and support.

Little League traces its current status as an outstanding youth organization to the unwavering devotion of the many thousands of persons who have unselfishly given their utmost support to the development of leagues in communities throughout the world.

If Little League is to maintain its present stature and develop its fullest potential, the adult participants, both new and old, must recognize their responsibility in observing certain general principles:

OPERATING POLICIES

Code

1. No officer or board member of a Little League and no District Administrator or other representative of a group of Little Leagues shall, at the same time, hold office or be a member of the Board of any other youth baseball/softball league or function as an official or representative of such a program.

2. No corporate or business entity should raise funds in the name of the league or District without active league participation and decision making.

3. Cooperative solicitation of funds is discouraged. If fundraising with other community organizations, receipts from any general community solicitation should be distributed equitably among participating organizations according to a formula established at the outset and publicly disclosed at the time of the solicitation. In no event should any solicitation be made in the name of Little League in a manner which may create the impression in the minds of the public that the funds received will be devoted to Little League purposes in greater amount than is the actual fact. All funds due to local Little League from any cooperative solicitation shall promptly be turned over to the officers of such leagues without condition or limitation.

4. The loan, sale or any commercial use of Little League records, including lists of players, coaches, umpires or volunteers and/or their addresses by any officer or director of a Little League or by a District Administrator is considered highly inappropriate, is contrary to Little League policy and is strictly prohibited.

5. Little League has, on many occasions, expressed support and commitment to the principle of equal employment opportunity. It is our policy to recruit, hire, train, and promote individuals, as well as to administer any and all personnel actions, without regard to race, color, religion, age, sex, national origin or ancestry, marital status, status as a disabled or Vietnam Era Veteran, or status as a qualified handicapped individual, in accordance with applicable law. This statement applies to volunteers as well as employees.

In this regard, we have developed a Sexual Harassment Policy for league and District Administrator operation. Consequently, any incident or situation that you believe involves discrimination or harassment of a sexual nature or otherwise should be immediately investigated for corrective action. If necessary, in accordance with the Sexual Harassment Policy, it should be brought to the immediate attention through proper channels to your Regional Director who will contact the Little League International Director of Human Resources and the Senior Vice President of Operations and Program Development. Investigation and any corrective action that Little League International determines is appropriate, up to and including dismissal is done so at the organizations discretion.

Little League will not tolerate any unlawful discrimination or harassment and such conduct is prohibited. In this regard, the following Sexual Harassment Policy is for your implementation.

SEXUAL HARASSMENT POLICY

A. **Policy:** It is the policy of Little League International that all of the parties involved in the operation of chartered Little Leagues will provide a League and District Administrator operational environment which is free of all forms of discrimination including incidents of sexual harassment. No individual shall be subjected to verbal or physical sexual behavior. Sexual harassment will be treated as misconduct, and may result in the application of appropriate corrective action up to and including dismissal.

B. **Definition:** Sexual harassment is unwelcome, unsolicited behavior of a sexual nature which creates a hostile environment and/or interferes with an individual's ability to do their duties. Examples of sexual harassment could include but are not limited to, the following:
   1. Unwelcome behavior.
   2. Repeatedly asking a person for a date.
   3. Making suggestive or provocative comments of a sexual nature and/or displaying sexual visuals.
   4. Suggestive looks or leering.
   5. Creating an intimidating, hostile or offensive operational environment.
   6. Making acceptance or rejection of sexual advance
   7. Retaliating against any person reporting instances of sexual harassment.

C. **Report Procedures:**
   1. Any person who believes they have been sexually harassed shall contact their immediate superior or the official in charge of the Organization, except as noted in C-3.
   2. If a complaint of sexual harassment is made directly to a superior, the superior shall contact the official in charge of the Organization before taking action.
   3. If the allegation of sexual harassment is made against the person's immediate superior, the complainant shall contact the Organization Head above the alleged harasser or the official in charge of the Organization, or depending on the level of the complaint, the Regional Director.
   4. If the complaint of sexual harassment is handled informally, the superior will document their actions and forward, through channels, to the official in charge of the Organization.
   5. If a full investigation is requested or required, the complainant shall contact the official in charge of the Organization, and through channels the Regional Director, Little League International Director of Human Resources and the Senior Vice President of Operations of Little League International.
   6. Any subsequent complaints of a similar nature against an individual, including those involving a different person, shall require a full investigation.

D. **Responsibilities** - Organization Heads and Official Parties shall:
   1. Monitor the League and District Administrator operational environment to ensure that it is free of sexual harassment.
   2. Ensure incidents of sexual harassment are processed in accordance with this policy.
   3. Take immediate action to guard against any adverse impact or reprisals against any person who uses this procedure.

OPERATING POLICIES

4. Ensure that parties under their position do not engage in any type of sexual harassment.
5. Ensure that confidentiality of reports of sexual harassment is maintained.
6. Consult the official in charge of the Organization for guidance in all sexual harassment matters, and that official, if necessary, will consult for guidance through channels, the Regional Director, Little League International Director of Human Resources and the Senior Vice President of Operations Officer of Little League International.

To these general principles of conduct, we trust all other youth baseball and softball programs will subscribe in the conduct of their own activities.

CONFLICT OF INTEREST POLICY

It is considered critical that Members of the Board, Officers of Little League Baseball, Incorporated, Committee Members, Employees, District Administrators, Assistant District Administrators and all Field Personnel shall not engage in any activity which gives rise to, or could give rise to, an appearance or claim of self-dealing, divided loyalty or conflict of interest by reason of such person's position with Little League International.

In the event such person has reason to believe his or her activities or anticipated activities could give rise to any such claim, he or she shall have a duty to disclose such activities or anticipated activities to the Board of Directors.

In the event any such person may either directly or indirectly be a party to or be in any manner financially interested in any contract or agreement with Little League International for any matter, cause or thing, such contract or agreement shall be made in violation of this Policy and the same shall be null and void.

In addition, any such person violating this Policy will be subject to Article VII of the By-Laws of Little League International, entitled "Disciplining Members, Directors, Officers, and Field Personnel." Article XII provides for disciplinary action including but not restricted to removal or suspension, for any act, conduct or involvement contrary to the rules, regulations and policies of the corporation or which might tend to bring the Corporation into disrepute, or for any failure to perform properly the duties and responsibilities assigned to each person.

LITTLE LEAGUE CHILD PROTECTION PROGRAM

The entire Little League family, from the Little League International staff to the volunteers, knows that the greatest treasure we have is our children. As adults, we want to ensure that these young people are able to grow up happy, healthy and, above all, safe. Whether they are our children, or the children of others, each of us has a responsibility to protect them. They are our future, and an endless source of joy.

Unfortunately, there are those among us who would seek to do harm to these children, to rob them of their right to feel safe and grow up in a free and healthy environment. These are child abusers, and although it is not an easy or pleasant topic for any of us to think about, the fact remains that child abuse happens. Like many national youth organizations, Little League seeks to attract the most qualified and enthusiastic volunteers to assist our programs. At the same time, we must be aware that this could make us a target for child abusers, since statistics show that the largest number of sexually abused children range in

OPERATING POLICIES

age from 8 to 11 years. Clearly, dealing with child abuse is a major concern for everyone involved in Little League.

Since Little League could not exist without the time and effort that volunteers and parents donate, it is important to communicate directly with the volunteers. For that reason, this statement on the Little League Child Protection Program should be freely copied and distributed to all adults in the local league.

Defining child abuse is the first step in battling it. Child abuse can take several different forms, and it is important for us to make clear right at the start what the prevention goal of the Little League Child Protection Program is.

Definition of Child Sexual Abuse

Big Brothers/Big Sisters of America defines child sexual abuse as "the exploitation of a child by an older child, teen or adult for the personal gratification of the abusive individual." This form of abuse could involve a range of sexual activities, from touching to non-touching offenses, and may also include acts that are considered non-sexual, but are done for the gratification of the abuser. This might include talking to a child in a sexually explicit way, voyeurism, or exposure of genitalia to a victim and/or victim's exposure of his or her genitalia.

A crucial step in stopping child abuse before it happens is knowing who might be a child abuser, and where child abuse might happen. For better or worse, the answer to each question is simple. Where can it happen? Anywhere. Who could be a child abuser? Anyone. However, we needn't feel that this makes our task impossible.

The National Center for Missing and Exploited Children, a leading national child protection advocacy group, defines child abuse as "the physical or emotional injury of a child (17 years old or younger) by a person who is responsible for the child's welfare." Although Little League recognizes emotional abuse as a serious offense that should never be tolerated within the organization, the primary objective of this program is more specific: the protection of Little Leaguers from child sexual abuse, as well as the protection of all adults in the organization from being placed in difficult or uncomfortable situations with the children in their care.

Myths and Stereotypes

Child abuse knows no social, economic or geographic boundaries, but there are a number of statistics at our disposal to help us identify warning signals. What we need to do is separate these facts from the stereotypes that have surrounded child abuse for many years. Let's take a look at some of the fiction and fact, as compiled by Big Brothers/Big Sisters of America.

"Sex abusers are dirty old men." Not true. While sex abusers cut across socioeconomic levels, educational levels and race, the average age of a sex offender has been established at 32.

"Strangers are responsible for most of the sexual abuse." Not true again. Fact: 80 to 85 percent of all sexual abuse cases in the US are committed by an individual familiar to the victim. Less than 20 percent of all abusers are strangers.

"Most sex abusers suffer from some form of serious mental illness or psychosis." Not true. The actual figure is more like 10 percent, almost exactly the same as the figure found in the general population of the United States.

"Most sex abusers are homosexuals." Also not true. Most are heterosexual.

"Children usually lie about sexual abuse, anyway." Not true. In fact, children rarely lie about being sexually abused. If they say it, don't ignore it.

"It only happens to girls." Again, not true. While females do comprise the largest number of sexual abuse victims, it is now believed that the number for male victims is much higher than reported.

And this last item on our list points to one of the greatest obstacles in identifying sexual abuse cases: Sexual abuse is shrouded in secrecy. This is because often abusers scare children into silence by saying things like: "This must be our secret-if you tell, something awful will happen."

Child victims are made to feel as though they've brought the abuse upon themselves; they're made to feel guilty.

For these reasons, sexual abuse victims seldom disclose the victimization. Consider this: Big Brothers/ Big Sisters of America contend that for every child abuse case reported ten more go unreported.

Clearly, there's a need within our organization for education on the subject of child sexual abuse. Children need to understand that it's never their fault, and both children and adults need to know what they can do to keep it from happening.

Education/Prevention of Child Abuse

Education is the most important tool for both our children and our adults. It empowers them to recognize potentially compromising situations, and it places a barrier between abusers and their victims. Here are a few education and prevention suggestions for our Little League volunteers and children.

Meet with them. Since Little League operates with a number of volunteers, our membership changes from year to year. Thus, it is important to hold regular meetings in which both volunteers and parents can talk about child abuse, and ask questions.

Make our position clear. Little League has a clearly defined policy for dealing with child abuse. Make adults and kids aware that Little League will not tolerate child abuse in any forms.

Stress the role of adults. Children should be encouraged to take an active role in protecting themselves, but ultimately the responsibility for ensuring their safety rests with us, the grown-ups. We are better able to identify potentially uncomfortable situations, for ourselves as well as for them. The welfare of our Little Leaguers is the highest priority in any situation.

Encourage the "Buddy system." It's an old maxim, but it's true: There is safety in numbers. Encourage our kids to move about in groups of two or more children of similar age, whether an adult is present or not. This includes travel, leaving the field, or using the rest room areas. It's far more difficult to victimize a child if they're not alone.

Provide additional information. There are a number of organizations that will gladly assist our efforts to protect our young people, several of which are listed below. Feel free to give these names, numbers and addresses to parents and volunteers, as well as kids.

National Center for Missing and Exploited Children
2101 Wilson Boulevard
Arlington, VA 22201-3052
800-843-5678
us.missingkids.com

OPERATING POLICIES

National Children's Advocacy Center
Visit nationalcac.org/locator to find a center near you.

Nonprofit Risk Management Center
1001 Connecticut Avenue, NW, Suite 900
Washington, DC 20036
202-785-3891
nonprofitrisk.org

General Guidelines

In addition, the basic safety procedures that Little League follows as a general rule can also be applied specifically to the identification and prevention of child abuse situations. Adhered to properly, these guidelines can enable children and adults to better protect themselves.

Rides — Children dropped off too early or picked up late are targets. Little League parents and volunteers should be encouraged to pick up and drop off on time. And children should be warned about strangers; about not riding with them, about telling someone if they're approached by them.

Access — Controlling access to areas where children are present, such as the dugout or locker rooms-protects them from harm by outsiders. It's not easy to control the access of large outdoor facilities, but visitors could be directed to a central point within the facility. Individuals should not be allowed to wander through the area without the knowledge of the Little League volunteers.

Lighting — Child sexual abuse is more likely to happen in the dark. The lighting of fields, parking lots and any and all indoor facilities where Little League functions are held should be bright enough so that participants can identify individuals as they approach, and observers can recognize abnormal situations.

Travel — When traveling with the team, make sure that children are sharing rooms with Little Leaguers of the same age. Girl's rooms should not be adjacent to boy's rooms, and rooms should not have adjoining access, either between children or children and adults.

Shower and Toilet Facilities — Most Little Leaguers are capable of using toilet facilities on their own, so there should be no need for an adult to accompany a child into restroom areas. There can sometimes be special circumstances under which a child requires assistance to toilet facilities, for instance within the Tee Ball and Challenger divisions, but there should still be adequate privacy for that child. Again, we can utilize the "buddy system" here.

Rooting Out Child Abuse — A Five-Step Screening Process

Once we know what child abuse is, and where to look for it, we are better able to prevent potential child abusers from entering the ranks of Little League. Another aspect of this prevention is screening all applicants who wish to be managers, coaches, Board of Directors and any other persons, volunteers and/or hired workers who provide regular services to the league and/or have repetitive access to, or contact with, players or teams.

The term "volunteer" in this context refers to every person in the organization coming in contact with the kids: program workers, coaches, bus and car-pool drivers, maintenance workers, etc. The goal is to find caring, competent individuals who can provide a safe, positive climate for Little Leaguers.

OPERATING POLICIES

Little League requires a five-step process for selecting individuals to fill volunteer positions:

1. **Application** - All local leagues are required to use the Little League Official Volunteer Application for all Managers, Coaches, Board of Directors and any other persons, volunteers and/or hired workers who provide regular service to the league and/or have repetitive access to, or contact with players or teams. The Little League Official Volunteer Application is available online at LittleLeague.org. The applicant must also submit a government issued photo ID, usually a driver's license, in order for the league to verify that the information on his/her volunteer application is correct, i.e. spelling of name, address, date of birth, etc.

2. **Background Check** - A background check in compliance with Regulation I(c) 8 and 9 must be conducted on every individual that is required to complete a volunteer application prior to the applicant assuming his/her duties for the current season. The individual is required to consent to a background check on the volunteer application. The local league must conduct a nationwide search that contains the applicable government sex offender registry data. Information regarding free background check services is available at LittleLeague.org. Just click the "Learn More" tab and look under Risk Management.

3. **Interview** - The applicant should be made fully aware of the position of Little League regarding child abuse. No person who is a known child-sex offender shall be allowed to participate in any manner in the Little League program.

4. **Reference Checks** - This is important to determine if any information from the references differs from that garnered from the volunteer application and/or during the course of the review.

5. **Exclusion of Certain Individuals** - No local league shall permit any person to participate in any manner, whose background check reveals a conviction or guilty plea for any crime involving or against a minor. A local league may prohibit any individual from participating as a volunteer or hired worker, if the league deems the individual unfit or inappropriate to work or volunteer. The local league must conduct a nationwide search that contains the applicable government sex offender registry data. (**NOTE**: The United States Department of Justice National Sex Offender Public Registry is free and available at nsopr.gov.

In addition, Little League strongly encourages all leagues to also utilize the national criminal records search available through the Little League website. This additional criminal records check may provide additional important information regarding the criminal records of individuals whose crimes do not require that they be listed on a sex offender registry. If no sex offender registries exist in a province or country outside the United States the local league must conduct a more extensive search of a country, province or city-wide criminal background check through the appropriate governmental agency unless prohibited by law. Failure to comply with this regulation may result in the suspension or revocation of tournament privileges and/or the local league's charter by action of the Charter or Tournament Committee in Williamsport. If a local league becomes aware of information, by any means whatsoever, that an individual, including, but not limited to, volunteers, players and hired workers, has been convicted of, pled guilty, pled no contest, or admitted to any crime involving or against a minor, the local league must contact the applicable governmental agency to confirm the accuracy of the information. Upon confirmation of a conviction for, or guilty plea to, a crime against or involving a minor, the local league shall not permit the individual to participate in any manner.

OPERATING POLICIES

Additionally, the league president should inform the parents of all children who have had contact through the league with the excluded individual of any Public Record information that is the basis of the league's decision to exclude the individual. Public Records are documents received from a governmental body/agency that are available to the general public.

Volunteers are important to the operation of the local leagues. However, to protect the children involved in the local leagues, it is necessary to require the volunteers to complete a volunteer application and consent to a background check. In order to protect the privacy of volunteers, the following procedure has been established:

1. The local league president shall retain the volunteer application and any attached documents on file for the year of service.

2. The local league president shall only share any personal non-public record information contained in the volunteer application or attached documents with other league officers in order to make personnel decisions.

3. The local league president should maintain the record of a volunteer for at least two (2) years after the volunteer is no longer in the league. When it comes time to dispose of these records, they should be shredded as they contain sensitive information. All actions concerning these records must comply with any applicable laws.

4. Leagues should also maintain records in the case that the league has taken action or made a decision based upon the information contained in the records. The records should be maintained in a locked and secure area, such as the president's home and not in a club house or similar facility.

Enforcement/Reporting Of Child Abuse

No matter how much education and prevention we put in place to stop child abuse, it can still happen. In the unfortunate instance that a case of child sexual abuse is suspected and/or reported, specific steps should be in place to deal with the situation. Let's take a look at these.

Reporting — Although child abuse reporting laws vary from state to state, there is some consistency to them and their general intent is to encourage reporting suspected child abuse to child protective services, including law enforcement agencies. If an individual suspects a case of abuse within their league, they should go through their league president and District Administrator, who will forward them to the proper law enforcement agency. Information regarding reporting child abuse can be found at LittleLeague.org. Go to the "Learn More" section and look under Risk Management.

Investigating — An individual and alternate with significant professional background should be chosen by the league from the community to receive and act on abuse allegations. These individuals will act in a confidential manner, and serve as the league's liaison with the local law enforcement community. Little League volunteers should not attempt to investigate suspected abuse on their own.

Suspending/Terminating — When an allegation of abuse is made against a Little League volunteer, it is the duty of the organization to protect the children from any possible further abuse by keeping the alleged abuser away from children in the program. If the allegations are substantiated, the next step is clear: Assuring that the individual will not

OPERATING POLICIES

have any further contact with the children in the league. The Nonprofit Risk Management Center urges Little League organizations to develop policies on suspension and termination of volunteers with a lawyer who can advise about their effects on the rights of the alleged abuser.

Immunity from liability — According to Boys & Girls Clubs of America, "Concern is often expressed over the potential for criminal or civil liability if a report of abuse is subsequently found to be unsubstantiated." However, we want adults and Little Leaguers to understand that they shouldn't be afraid to come forward in these cases, even if it isn't required and even if there is a possibility of being wrong. All states provide immunity from liability to those who report suspected child abuse in "good faith." At the same time, there are also rules in place to protect adults who prove to have been inappropriately accused.

CHILD ABUSE - A FIVE-STEP REVIEW

Let's recap the steps you can take to protect your Little Leaguers:

1. Know what it is, and know where to look. Defining child abuse, and separating the truth from the myths, better enables us all to spot potentially dangerous situations.

2. Educate the Little League parents, volunteers and children. They need to be supplied with the information necessary to protect everyone. Let the children know that it's never their fault.

3. Follow safety procedures. Employing basic rules, such as the "buddy system," can lessen child abuse from happening in the first place.

4. Screen applicants carefully. An effective five-step screening process can keep potential child abusers out of our Little League programs, and keep our kids safe.

5. Don't be afraid to speak out. Both Little League children and adults need to feel safe to come forward. If an individual honestly feels something is wrong, the laws are in place to protect them.

QUESTIONS AND ANSWERS ABOUT THE CHILD PROTECTION PROGRAM

1. What do we, as a league, have to do to comply so that we can be chartered for the next season?

    Since 2003, the local league has been required to have all board members, managers, coaches, and other volunteers or hired workers who provide regular service to the league or/and who have repetitive access to or contact with players or teams fill out the Little League Official Volunteer Application. Additionally the league has been and is required to conduct a background check on each of these individuals. Since 2007, the local league has been required to conduct a nationwide search that contains the applicable government sex offender registry data as opposed to conducting statewide sex offense registry search. Little League Baseball and Softball will require each league to sign an agreement on the charter application that they will comply with Regulation I (b) and I(c) 8 & 9. The leagues are also required to sign a statement on the tournament enrollment form verifying that the process under the regulation has been completed and implemented. Failure to sign the agreement on the charter application will result in the league not being chartered and failure to fulfill the requirement of the regulations

OPERATING POLICIES

will result in the league's status being referred to the Charter/Tournament committee for action to revoke the league's charter and all privileges.

2. What type of background check is required by the new regulations?
   Effective in 2007, the local league must annually conduct a nationwide search that contains the applicable government sex offender registry data. In addition Little League strongly encourages all leagues to also utilize the national criminal records search available through the Little League website. This additional criminal records check may provide additional important information regarding the criminal records of individuals whose crimes do not require that they be listed on a sex offender registry. More information can be obtained by going to LittleLeague.org/childprotectionprogram. The first 125 checks through First Advantage are paid for by Little League International and are free to each chartered Little League. If additional checks are necessary, they will only cost the league a nominal fee per background check conducted.

3. What type of offenses are we screening for when we conduct a background check?
   Local leagues are conducting a search of the nationwide sex offender registry for anyone who has committed sexual offenses involving minors. An individual who has been convicted or plead guilty to charges involving or against a minor, no matter when the offense occurred, must not be permitted to work or volunteer.

4. Who in the local league should be responsible to process the background check information?
   Little League Baseball and Softball recommends the Board of Directors appoint the local league president and two other individuals to handle the background checks. These individuals may be from the board or individuals outside the board. For instance, the Board of Directors may appoint individuals who have significant professional background in this area, such as law enforcement officers or individuals with a legal background.

5. What if an individual has previously had a background check?
   Each league must conduct its own background check on the appropriate individuals annually.

6. What will result in termination of a volunteer under these regulations?
   Any background check that reveals a conviction or guilty plea for any crime involving or against a minor must result in immediate termination from the league. Additionally, volunteers who refuse to submit a fully completed Little League Volunteer Application, including their Social Security Number and a government issued photo ID, must be immediately terminated or eliminated from consideration for any position. This includes individuals with many years of service to your league unless the league has used the First Advantage Background Screening tool (available on the Little League website) in previous seasons. Those returning individuals can use the current Little League "Returning" Volunteer Application which does not require the Social Security Number or Date of Birth as those items are already included and redacted in the First Advantage program for returning volunteers.

7. What if offenses involving or against minors are pending prior to or after appointment to a position in the local league?
   We suggest the individual not be appointed or should be suspended from his/her current position pending the outcome of the charges.

OPERATING POLICIES

8. What if there are convictions or other offenses NOT involving or against minors?

   Even though convictions or other offenses may not be against a minor, the local league Board of Directors still may deem these individuals as inappropriate and/or unfit and may prohibit him/her from working as a hired worker or volunteer within the league.

9. Who is to be made aware of the information found on the background check?

   The local league president shall only share personal information contained in the volunteer application, background check or other information obtained through the screening process with other members of the Board of Directors in order to make personnel decisions. If the information obtained through the background check is public record and causes an individual to not be appointed or to be terminated, Little League Baseball and Softball recommends this information be shared with the parents/guardians of the children who have had contact with the individual previously.

10. Where should these records be maintained and for how long?

    The local league president shall retain each volunteer application, background check information, and any other documents obtained on file and maintain the record of a volunteer for at least 2 years after the volunteer is no longer in the league. When it comes time to dispose of these records, they should be destroyed as they contain sensitive information. All actions concerning these records must comply with any applicable laws. Leagues should also maintain records in the case that the league has taken action or made a decision based upon the information contained in the records. The records should be maintained in a locked and secure area, such as the league president's home and not a club house or similar facility.

11. What is the timetable for completing the screening of each individual?

    The league must complete the annual screening process prior to the individual assuming his/her duties for the current season. This would include the individual submitting a completed volunteer application and the league completing an appropriate background check. The applicant must also submit a government issued photo ID, usually a driver's license, in order for the league to verify that the information on his/her volunteer application is correct, i.e., spelling of name, address, date of birth, etc.

12. What resources are available through Little League Baseball and Softball to assist this process?

    The current Little League Official Volunteer Application is available at LittleLeague.org/VolApp. In addition to meeting the minimum requirement of checking the United States Department of Justice National Sex Offender Registry, (nsopr.gov) Little League strongly encourages all leagues to also utilize the national criminal records search available through the Little League website. The first 125 checks conducted through First Advantage are paid for by Little League International and are free to each chartered little league. If additional checks are needed, they will only cost the league a nominal fee per background check conducted.

13. What will it cost my league to implement this initiative ?

    There is no fee required for the Department of Justice Sex Offender Public Registry website, which checks sex offender registries in all fifty states. In addition, Little League strongly encourages all leagues to also utilize the national criminal records search

OPERATING POLICIES

available through the Little League website. This additional criminal records check may provide additional important information regarding the criminal records of individuals whose crimes do not require that they be listed on a sex offender registry. More information can be obtained by going to LittleLeague.org/childprotectionprogram. The first 125 checks conducted through First Advantage are paid for by Little League International and are free to each chartered Little League. If additional checks are needed, they will only cost the league a nominal fee per background check conducted.

14. When should local leagues begin to conduct background checks on volunteers and hired workers?

   In accordance with Little League Regulation I(c) 8 & 9, local leagues must conduct background checks on all volunteers and hired workers prior to the applicant assuming his or her duties for the season. Background checks must be completed on all individuals who are required to complete the "Little League Official Volunteer Application" and who provide a regular service to the league and/or have repetitive access to, or contact with, players and teams. This includes, but is not limited to, managers, coaches, Board of Director members, and other persons or hired workers.

15. Does this initiative also apply to those individuals that assist the manager and coaches at practices or games?

   Yes. Any individual who provides regular service to the league or/and has repetitive access to or contact with players or teams must fill out the Volunteer Application with a Social Security Number, provide a copy of a government issued photo ID, and go through the background check process.

16. Who is going to coach the team if a screened manager or coach is no longer able to fulfill his/her duties?

   Any permanent replacement cannot assume their duties until the volunteer application and background check has been completed. The league may temporarily assign a board member or another screened individual to fill the vacancy until the proper process and appointment has been made.

17. Should our league wait until the entire screening process has been completed to submit our Charter Application and Insurance Enrollment Form?

   No. The appropriate league officers must sign the statement on the form agreeing to adhere to the new regulations requiring the use of the new volunteer application and background screening process as outlined in Regulations I(b) and I(c) 8 & 9. Once this section is completed the balance of the charter application can be completed and submitted to Little League Baseball and Softball.

18. As the league president or an official of the local league, how do I explain the need for this initiative?

   These requirements were implemented in 2002 by Little League and your local league to:
   1. protect our children and maintain Little League as a hostile environment for those who would seek to do them harm.
   2. protect individuals and leagues from possible loss of personal or league assets because of litigation.

OPERATING POLICIES

3. take advantage of current technology and laws that have made background check information accessible to your local league. This is an example of the revised mandatory Little League Volunteer Application. A version that can be filled out electronically and printed from your computer is available at LittleLeague.org.

STANDARDS FOR LIGHTING

Required Minimum Standards

These minimum standards are required for all lighting installations after the date of adoption by Little League. The effective date is July 1, 1992, unless otherwise noted within these standards. Any modification in existing lighting systems after this date must be done so as to result in a lighting system in compliance with current standards. To be in compliance, a system must meet all required minimum standards.

General

1.1 - Lighting Performance Recommendation

Achieving proper light levels on the field is important for participant playability and safety. Systems should be designed to not drop below specified light levels. The quantity of equipment needed is determined by the efficiency of the lighting system and maintenance practices, particularly relamping. Leagues should evaluate the energy efficiency of the system and consider the warranty, maintenance program and light level guarantee provided by the manufacturer. There are two acceptable methods of achieving the specified light levels.

A. **Preferred Technology**

By utilizing a series of power adjustments, a lighting system is able to provide "constant light levels" and greatly extend the life of the lamps. In addition, this generation of lighting has high performance optic characteristics that enable reductions in the quantities of luminaires needed to meet design targets, lowering installation and operating costs. Light levels are typically guaranteed for up to 25 years with this technology.

B. **Prior Technology**

Computer designs are done using two sets of values. One predicts "initial light levels" when lamps are new. The other predicts "maintained light levels" after the lamps have passed through a depreciation in light output. It is important to have the lighting designer use a maintenance factor adequate to account for this depreciation in light output throughout the life of the lamp. A value no greater than .70 shall be applied to initial light levels to predict these maintained values. Quality manufacturers are willing to provide guarantees of lighting performance.

C. **Performance Requirements**

Playing surfaces shall be lit to an average constant or target light level and uniformity as specified in the chart below. Lighting calculations shall be developed and field measurements taken on the grid spacing with the minimum number of grid points specified on page 13 of these standards with the light meter held horizontally 36 inches above the field surface. Measured average illumination level shall be +/- 10% of predicted mean in accordance with IESNA RP-6-01, and measured at the first 100 hours of operation. Uniformity of the lighting shall be such that the highest measure of quantity of light on the field is not greater than the lowest measurement per the ratio listed in the table below. On the entire field area, the changes in the quantity of

OPERATING POLICIES

horizontal footcandles should not occur at a greater rate than 10 percent per 10 feet, except for the outside perimeter readings which may change at a greater rate.

To review the Lighting Standards in their entirety, please visit LittleLeague.org/LightingStandards.

COMMUNICATIONS AND LEAGUE PROMOTIONS

Successful communications in any organization helps cultivate and maintain the best image by not only encouraging better knowledge and understanding of the organization's goals, benefits and operation, but also to effectively keep your players, parents, volunteers, and community informed

In Little League, making sure that the program is known in the community will help earn the respect and support that is essential to successful league operations. To establish the league as an effective force and working agency of the people in the community requires an active avenue of communication, projected to those who serve as well as to reach all levels of community interest. That can come through working with the local news media, updating your own website and social media accounts, and keeping your parents and volunteers informed.

Communicating with Your League

Nearly all correspondence from Little League International, literature, handbooks, newsletters, and a variety of other communications is channeled to the league by way of the league president.

It is essential that president makes this information generally available to league personnel, parents, and in some instances to the public through news media or the league's online outlets.

People who are active in the local program — they range over many categories of volunteer service — should be kept up-to-date on the affairs of the league and the overall program. Their efficiency and contribution to the local program is impeded if they are not informed fully.

Local leagues have an open line of communication to Little League International at all times and are urged to make use of it whenever necessary. The president and staff of Little League International welcome comment from local leagues as a means of providing mutually beneficial communication, as well as the regional staffs.

Communicating with the Media

Little League is the biggest name in youth sports, and the general public and news media will want to know what's going on locally. One of the best ways to be an ambassador for your local league and Little League International is through communicating with the media and your community.

Identifying a person in your league to handle your public relations efforts is a great way to ensure that your league's news and events get to the local news media. Develop a media list of the best contacts at the various news outlets that cover your community, and be sure to send them media alerts prior to events and press releases. Getting the word out through the media about what you're accomplishing can help your league grow. You're encouraged to develop a positive, working relationship with the media. If a member of a news outlet contacts you about a sensitive situation, please contact your District Administrator or the

OPERATING POLICIES

appropriate Little League Regional Office. Sample media releases and templates can be found at LittleLeagueToolkit.org.

News outlets are encouraged and permitted to cover local Little League events (write stories, take photos, and shoot video) regular season games, and tournament action. You're encouraged to help the media as much as you can with their coverage, while ensuring that at no times the media interfere with your game operations. Any time a member of the media wishes to conduct an interview with a Little Leaguer, the player's parent(s) and/or manager or coach must be present throughout the interview. Only working news photographers and videographers with proper news organization credentials are permitted on the field of play, subject to league approval (as noted in Rule 3.15) in any level of Little League Baseball and Softball. Such personnel should never be permitted in dugouts, nor anywhere on fair territory.

Remember, the words "Little League" should never be used as merely a descriptive term for all youthful athletic programs. Whenever they appear in print, the words "Little League" should always be capitalized or placed in quotes so as to maintain the trademark significance. A public relations director for a local league may wish to inform members of the media that "Little League" and "Little League Baseball" are listed in the Associated Press Stylebook and Libel Manual, and should never be used in reference to non-Little League activities. And, a news outlet can only use photos and video of your Little League activities for editorial purposes. Any promotional or paid usage must be submitted to Little League International for approval.

Communicating Through Online Media

Having a website and keeping it updated with information, important dates, contact information, game schedules and scores, and updates from Little League International is just one way to use online communications.

Another important online tool is social media. Creating a Facebook page or Twitter account for your district can help you connect with a broader audience. Keep your social media posts light and fun, with photos from your leagues, stories from the news, game schedules and results, and posts from Little League's social media. When you have urgent messages you need to communicate or events to promote, use social media as a tool to spread the word.

Remember, once it's posted on any website, that statement or image is public. Be careful when you're posting and make sure that you're reflecting your league in the most positive light and that you have permission to use the photo. If your community members start posting or tweeting about a specific issue, encourage them to contact the league via email or attend the next public meeting. Getting into a social media discussion that could become heated should be avoided.

Obtaining Approval to Use Members' Images

Leagues are encouraged to have parents or guardians sign a model release each season. A generic sample model release can be found here: LittleLeague.org/ModRel. This release should give the league permission to photograph, video, or utilize the image or likeness of the player in initiatives that support the growth and promotion of the league and its activities through any advertisements or social media sites. Such use should only grant permission to the league not to any other entity.

OPERATING POLICIES

If a league or district chooses to enter into an agreement with a photographer or videographer for a game, tournament, or other league event, Little League International recommends that a formal agreement be arranged between the League and the photographer/videographer. It is recommended that model releases be secured from participants before such an agreement is procured.

Game Broadcasting and Streaming

Little League International in South Williamsport, Pa., is the only body that can authorize or disallow the live streaming, webcasting, televising, or radio broadcasting of any game(s). A contract (provided by Little League International) must originate with the local District Administrator, tournament director, or local Little League president. (See Regulation XV)

No telecast, broadcast, webcast (recorded or live) of any Little League Baseball or Softball game (in any division) can take place unless the proper contract is completed and approved. This applies to all productions, even if they are unsupported by advertising, sponsorship or subscriptions.

To download a contract for games below the Regional level, visit LittleLeague.org/GameContracts.

For the Regional and World Series tournament levels, all contacts must be originated by the Little League International Communications Department in South Williamsport. Contact Chris Downs, Director of Publicity, 570-326-1921, Ext. 2238; cdowns@LittleLeague.org.

For local leagues, districts, and media personnel, Little League International has guidelines regarding how Little Leaguers should appear in newspapers, on television, in magazines, etc. To download a PDF file of the document, visit LittleLeague.org/LittleLeagueAppearance.

Non-Editorial Media Request

If any business or entity contacts your league about participating in a promotion, commercial, documentary, or anything outside of editorial coverage of your events or games, please note that you must seek approval from Little League International prior to participating in any paid, promotional activity, that identifies your league or shows any Little League logos, patches, or other marks.

WEBSITES

Local League or District Websites

Local leagues and Districts are permitted to host websites that assist with communicating information about their activities in the local community. The local league name, affiliation with Little League, registration, facilities locations, board members and other information for parents and volunteers should be clearly stated on the website.

Any league or district that wishes to host a website, which includes Little League Trademarks in any fashion must submit their LEAGUE URL (Universal Resource Locator) into the Little League Data Center annually. The URL should be a combination of a league or district's name in conjunction with the words "Little League" or "LL." An example of how a URL should appear: HometownLittleLeague.org or PA12LittleLeague.org.

Use of the Little League Trademarks, logos and links to LittleLeague.org are permitted on websites operated by local leagues or districts, however, permission must be granted in advance by contacting marketing@LittleLeague.org. Under no circumstances may a league,

OPERATING POLICIES

district, or person register a website using the words Little League in a website address for any other purpose other than to represent their local league or district. If teams within local leagues also host websites, they are required to follow these guidelines and the guidelines for use of Little League Trademarks. Team URLs are not required to be submitted to Little League International. It is strongly encouraged that local league board members visit the websites of their associated teams to ensure appropriate content is being provided.

Leagues are also encouraged to secure model releases as part of the player and volunteer registration process. This allows leagues to host images or video of players participating in league activities.

Little League reserves the right to review any league or district website that uses Little League Trademarks and logos. If content is deemed inappropriate, the league will be required to remove the content.

Change for 2016: Local leagues or districts are no longer required to maintain an eteamz.com website. Leagues or Districts may continue to use at their discretion, if desired.

Additional information on use of websites, online registration and other technology can be found on LittleLeagueToolkit.org.

LITTLE LEAGUE TRADEMARKS

Little League Baseball, Incorporated, more commonly referred to as "Little League", is a federally-chartered corporation to which Congress has granted the exclusive right and owner of the following trademarks, service marks and other designations: LITTLE LEAGUE, LITTLE LEAGUER, LITTLE LEAGUE BASEBALL, BIG LEAGUE LITTLE LEAGUE BASEBALL, SENIOR LEAGUE LITTLE LEAGUE BASEBALL, LITTLE LEAGUE SOFTBALL, LITTLE LEAGUE CHALLENGER DIVISION, LL, LLB, and the Little League Emblems or logos (e.g. keystone patch, Character, Courage and Loyalty logo), among others. Collectively these are referred to as the Little League Trademarks, which identify its products and services in the United States and other countries including Mexico, Canada, Japan, Australia, among others.

Local League Use of the Words "Little League"

Local leagues receive permission per the annual charter agreement process to use Little League Trademarks in connection with authorized local league activities as described in THE OFFICIAL REGULATIONS, or in the OFFICIAL RULES of the 2016 Little League® Rulebook.

This permission, which is effective only while a league remains chartered, includes the right to use Little League Trademarks as part of the local league name, and to use that trademark and the Little League Emblems or logos on stationery, uniforms, in press releases issued by the local league, in programs, and at the local league facilities on scoreboards, and other signs. All such uses of Little League Trademarks must include the local league name such as the city, town or other similar reference.

Limitations of Using the Words "Little League"

Chartered leagues may not use the Little League Trademarks in connection with any other activity or program, or as a part of a composite name covering unrelated programs. The Little League Trademarks may not, for example, appear on stationery, bulletins, advertisements, social media posts or press releases of other sports organizations, commercial

OPERATING POLICIES

enterprises, or businesses. For example, the local league should not grant permission to a local business to advertise its association with the local league whereby the local business directly profits from the use of the name.

Further, the Little League Trademarks may not be used separately or in connection with the name of any other program or activity for the purpose of soliciting funds to be used for activities other than Little League activities.

Soliciting Funds Using the Words "Little League"

The use of the Little League Trademarks by any person, organization, business entity or league not chartered by Little League or in an unauthorized fashion is an infringement of Little League Trademark rights.

It is the policy of Little League International not to endorse any company, commercial product, or service with the exception of those items of approved playing equipment and other materials and entities associated with Little League International. Any use of the Little League Trademarks, unless expressly granted by Little League International, which falsely tends to imply such an endorsement is an infringement.

Restricted Use of "Little League" By Third Parties

Under no circumstances may local leagues, District Administrators, or other field personnel permit the Little League Trademarks to be used on or in connection with any business products or services. The local league does not have the right to assign the use of Little League Trademarks to any third party entity.

Further, the Little League Trademarks are representative of specific baseball and softball programs chartered with Little League International and should not be used as merely a descriptive term for all youth athletic programs. Whenever they appear online or in print, the Little League Trademarks should always be capitalized and refer only to the activities of Little League.

Exploitation of the Little League program, a league, a team, or individual players, for the benefit, financially or otherwise, of an individual or a business will not be condoned. Leagues which permit any type of exploitation run the risk of losing their charter.

Little League International encourages all leagues and its members to use our partners of Little League International, especially licensed partners, to produce any special goods, products and/or fundraising requests that could benefit the local league. Such partners are familiar with the policy regarding Little League Trademark usage. There may be a situation, however, in which a league or district cannot use a licensed partner to perform the special need. Little League International requires a single-use agreement be completed to fulfill the league's needs.

A single-use agreement may permit a league or district to use a supplier outside of our licensed partner. A league or district can request the usage of said Little League trademarks in various capacities, however, the understanding is that Little League Trademarks are only dispersed to any other party with the consent of Little League International. It is also understood that the outside supplier may not utilize the marks for financial gain. For more information on obtaining a single-use agreement, please email licensing@LittleLeague.org. Forms can also be found on LittleLeague.org/licensing.

OPERATING POLICIES

Guidelines for Use of "Little League" in Fundraising and Local League Sponsorship

Donors and sponsors of teams at any level of the Little League program should be motivated by the single objective of making a worthwhile community contribution. A local supporter should aim to assist youth and help make their community a better place in which to live. Sponsorships should be positioned as donations to the local league. Local leagues must recognize that they have a responsibility to the local community to see to it that funds collected in the name of the league are used for league purposes and not for any other purpose, however laudable it may be. Further, great care must be taken to assure that such funds are not diverted to line the pockets of some enterprising operator, business, or individual.

Sponsorship of leagues and teams is an important way for local Little Leagues to raise funds for operations. It must be understood, however, that sponsorship donation does not give the sponsoring entity any rights in the operation of the league or any team, nor does it give the local league sponsor the right to use Little League trademarks in any way. For example, such prohibited use includes giving a local business entity the right promote the local league in the business entity's advertising or public relations. The local league must conduct its own recognition efforts for any and all promotion of activities related to the local league operations.

No advertisement (lettering on uniforms, fence signs, program ads, website etc.) for sponsors may include direct references to alcohol, tobacco products or adult content. Leagues should carefully choose sponsors, avoiding those which may, according to local community standards, be offensive. Additional standards for sponsorship may be set by the local Little League.

Little League International reserves the right to prohibit any local Little League from accepting a sponsorship, advertisement or donation if it deems that the sponsor, advertiser or donor violates the provisions of the following statement: Little League does not limit participation in its activities on the basis of disability, race, creed, color, national origin, gender, sexual preference, or religious preference.

General Fundraising Guidance

District Administrators are urged to establish communication with their leagues in order to (a) give the leagues the benefits of their experience with proposed fundraising efforts, and (b) to pass on to them the experience of other leagues in similar ventures. Guidance should be provided on fundraising plans and efforts to gather funds from within the boundaries of the local league.

Upon occasion it has come to the attention of Little League International that leagues have been victimized by participating in fundraising plans proposed by outsiders as an easy means to obtain necessary funds. These schemes have been designed to exploit the warm feelings that local businessmen and residents in the community have for Little League. They run a wide gamut but essentially they involve the designation of the operator as an agent of the local league, authorizing him to contact businesses or members of the public in behalf of the local league. It involves the sale of goods, of advertising space, of magazines, photographs or consists simply of a solicitation of funds on a straight contribution basis.

A number of leagues participating in such operations have reported receiving a disproportionately small part of the total moneys collected. It also opens the door to abuses

OPERATING POLICIES

in the use of the Little League Trademarks and can be in violation of the terms of the league's charter. The Little League charter extends the privilege of using Little League Trademarks, however it does not grant the right of the league to extend the use thereof to another person, organization or business entity as noted above.

Without authority of any kind, some unscrupulous operators are prone to represent themselves as agents of Little League because of the magic of the name to solicit payment in the name of Little League and obtain checks made out to the local Little League. The local league has little control over such situations, and such abuses come to their attention or Little League International after the damage has been done.

The endorsing and cashing, in this manner, of checks made out to Little League may well constitute fraud or forgery. However, prosecution is difficult unless sup¬porting evidence (names, addresses, amounts, etc.) is gathered. Equally important, delay in uncovering these schemes may preclude effective steps to prevent many people from being bilked.

Make this a subject for league meetings. Request your volunteers notify you of any proposed money-raising plan involving outsiders. Examine the proposal, the need for a signed agreement or contract, and make certain there is no possibility that funds will be collected from within the boundaries of neighboring leagues. Then, contact Little League International with full details of the plan.

CROWDFUNDING

This policy is in regard to the use of any form of crowdfunding service or website-based platform for the financial benefit or gain of any level of Little League (i.e., local, district, state, provincial).

Crowdfunding can be defined as, the use of small amounts of capital from a large number of individuals to finance a project, business venture, or to fundraise for a specific cause or charity. Through the use of personal networking, social media platforms, and other internet based resources, funds can be raised to support these different campaigns or efforts from a grassroots level, such as a local Little League.

Per the Little League Operating Policies, charitable funding and contributions can be collected through web-based crowdfunding platforms, so long as standard Little League policies are followed when utilizing this means of charitable fundraising. Current policies state that in no manner should there be any solicitation by a third party or individual in the name of or on behalf of a local league; solicitation of funds is to be done by the league or district itself.

In addition, the use of any Little League registered logos and trademarks must be used in connection with the local league name, and should not be misrepresented or altered in any way, without first contacting Little League International. It's also important to keep in mind as with any league or district fundraiser that any promotion of the effort must be done by the league or district itself and not any outside entity such as local businesses or individual donors. Donations that are collected through this method should not be for any personal or business gain, but strictly to assist youth and to strengthen the community program.

While this may potentially be a way for a league or district to fundraise, it may not always be the most cost effective method of generating funding. When looking into different options related to crowdfunding, please be sure to investigate all the potential drawbacks that may impact the league or district's ability to collect the funds associated with

OPERATING POLICIES

a crowdfunding campaign. Because of the ease of creation of one of these crowdfunding campaigns, local leagues and districts should also closely monitor for individuals fraudulently misrepresenting themselves as a fundraising entity.

Crowdfunding may be a current means to raise funds but may not be the best solution for your league or district. A simple donation option on the league or district website may be a better means to collect donations.

NOTE: For more information regarding use of Little League trademarks in relation to local league fundraising and the solicitation of donations, please consult the Little League Policies and Principles section of the Official Playing Rules of Little League and LittleLeague.org for additional guidance

INDEX

Term - Rule	Page

A

Accident
  Prevents runner from proceeding - 5.10(c)(1) .. 83

Appeal
  Batting out of turn - 6.07 (a-b) 87–88
  Definition - 2.00 61
  Runner out on - 7.10 97
  Runner out when - 7.08(d, j, k) 95–96
  Status of runners - 7.12 99–100

B

Ball
  Alive/Dead - 5.02 82
  Batter touched by pitched - 6.08(b) 89
  Dead, runners advance - 5.09 82
  Dead, "Time" called - 5.10 83
  Defacing - 8.02(a)(3) 103
  Definition of a - 2.00 61
  Discolor/Damage - 3.02 69
  Penalty for an illegal pitch - 8.05 103
  Put in play - 4.03 74
  Putting in play - 5.11 84
  Specifications - 1.09 57
  Status of - 3.12 72

Base Coach
  Accidental/Intentional interference - 5.08 82
  Assisting runner - 7.09(h) 97
  Definition - 2.00 61
  Draws a throw - 7.09(i) 97
  Restrictions - 4.05 75

Batter
  Batting out of turn - 6.07 87
  Becomes a runner - 6.09 90
  Entitled to first base - 6.08 89
  Interference by - 7.09 96
  Interference, runner attempting to score. *See* Interference: When runner attempting to score - 7.08(g)
  Penalty for offensive team interfering - 7.11 99
  Substitute - 3.08(a)(2) 71
  Taking a position in the batter's box - 6.02(c) . 85
  Touched by a pitched ball - 5.09(a) 82
  When out - 6.05 85
  When out for illegal action - 6.06 87

Batter's Box
  Dimensions - 1.04 53

C

Casts
  Restrictions - 1.11(k) 59

Child Protection Program 168
  A Five-Step Program 174
  Definition of Child Sexual Abuse 169
  Education/Prevention 170
  Enforcement/Reporting 173
  General Guidelines 171
  Myths and Stereotype 169

  Q & A about the Child Protection Program 174
  Rooting Out Child Abuse 171

Communications and League Promotions 179
  Game Broadcasting and Streaming 181
  Online Media 180
  Non-Editorial Media Request 181
  Use Members' Images 180
  With The Media 179
  Your League 179

Conflict of Interest Policy 168

Crowdfunding 185

D

Defacing Ball. *See* Ball: Defacing - 8.02(a)(3)
Discoloring Ball. *See* Ball: Discolor/Damage - 3.02
Dividing a League 162

Double Headers
  Restrictions - 3.11 72
  Restrictions - 4.13 79

Draft Methods
  Existing Leagues 154
  First Year Operations 156

Draft Options
  Alternative Method of Operations 158
  Sons, Daughters, and Siblings 157

E

Election Procedure 163

Equipment
  Athletic supporter - 1.17 60
  Ball. *See* Ball: Specifications - 1.09
  Bases - 1.06 54
  Bats - 1.10 57
  Benches - 1.08 57
  Catcher's - 1.17 60
  Gloves - 1.12-1.15 59
  Helmets - 1.16-1.17 59–60
  Home base - 1.05 54
  Metal spikes - 1.11(h-i) 58
  Metal spikes, umpires - 9.06 108
  Not meeting specifications - 4.19(a) 80
  Observance of all rules governing - 3.01(a) 69
  Pitcher's plate, dimensions - 1.07 54
  Pitcher's plate, height - 1.04 53
  Throat guard, catcher - 1.17 60
  Throat guard, umpire - 9.01(a) 105
  Uniforms - 1.11 58
  Used for communication - 3.17 72

F

Fair Ball
  Batter becomes a runner - 6.09(a) 90
  Bounces or deflected out of play - 7.05(f) 93
  Definition - 2.00 63
  Goes out of playing field in flight - 7.05(a) 92
  Out of play - 6.09(e-g) 90–91

INDEX

Term - Rule	Page

Passes/touched by a fielder - 6.09(c) 90
Touched by a thrown glove - 7.05(c) 93
Touched with detached uniform - 7.05(b) 93
Touches a batter - 6.05(f) 86
Touches an umpire or a runner - 6.08(d) 90
Touches a runner or an umpire - 5.09(f) 83
Fielder
    Definition - 2.00 63
    Falls into dead ball area - 5.10(f) 83
    Falls into dead ball area - 7.04(b) 92
Fielder's Choice
    Definition - 2.00 63
Forfeited Game
    Definition - 2.00 63
    For actions by a team - 4.15 79
    Recording of - 4.18 80

G
Ground Rules
    Announced by umpire-in-chief - 9.03(c)(4) ... 106
    Established by - 3.13 72

I
Illegally Batted Ball
    Batter is out when. *See* Batter: When out for
        illegal action - 6.06
    Definition - 2.00 64
    With runners on base - 5.09(d) 82
Illegal Pitch
    Ball becomes dead - 5.09(c) 82
    Caused by catcher - 4.03(a) 74
    Definition - 2.00 64
    Penalty - 8.01 102
    When occurs - 8.05 103
Infield Fly
    Batter is out when - 6.05(d) 86
    Definition - 2.00 65
    Fielder intentionally drops - 6.05(k) A.R. 86
    Runner touched by - 7.08(f) Excep., Note 1 ....
        95–96
Intentionally Dropped Ball
    Batter out when - 6.05(k) 86
Interference
    Batter with catcher - 6.06(c) 87
    Batter with course of ball - 6.05(g) 86
    By a base coach with a thrown ball - 5.08 82
    By a batter or runner - 7.09 96
    By a preceding runner - 6.05(l) 86
    By authorized persons on playing field - 3.15 .. 72
    Definition - 2.00 65
    Fielder fielding batted/thrown ball - 7.11 99
    Fielder with batter - 6.08(c) 90
    Fielder with batter - 7.04(c) 92
    Outside of three-foot lane - 6.05(j) 86
    Plate umpire with catcher - 5.09(b) 82
    Runner with a thrown/batted ball - 7.08(b) 95

Thrown/batted ball by spectator - 3.16 72
When runner attempting to score - 7.08(g) 96

J
Jewelry
    Restrictions - 1.11(j) 58

L
League
    League Administration 149
    League Officers 151
    League President 149
Lights
    Resuming tie games due to failure - 4.12 78
    "Time" called due to failure - 5.10(b) 83
    Turned on - 4.14 79
Lighting Standards 178
    General 178
    Required Minimum 178

M
Mandatory Play
    For purposes of an at-bat - 2.00 61
    Requirements - Regulation IV(i) 36
    Substitutes - 3.03 Note 1 70
Maintenance of Rosters
    Divisional Play 161
    Duration of Title 159
    Expansions 160
    Replacements 159
    Team Reduction 161
    Trading 159
Missed Base
    Liability to be put out - 7.04 Note 92
    Runner fails to touch home base - 7.08(k) 96
    Runner out on appeal - 7.10(b) 97

O
Obstruction
    Definition - 2.00 66
    Play being/not being made on runner - 7.06 93
Overrunning First Base
    Batter-runner returns immediately - 7.08(c) 95
    Runner failing to return immediately - 7.08(j) . 96
    Runner out on appeal - 7.10(c) 98

P
Pitcher
    In resumption of game - 4.11(e) Note 78
    In resumption of game - 4.12 Note 78
    Legal positions - 8.01 101
    May not re-enter game as - 3.03(c) Note 69
    Preparatory pitches - 8.03(a) 103
    Shall pitch to first batter - 3.05(a) 71
    Taking a signal - 8.01(e) 101
    Throws ball out of play - 7.05(h) 93
    Visits by manager or coach - 8.06 104

INDEX

Term - Rule	Page

    Warming up - 3.09 71
Player's Position
    Substitutes take the place of replaced - 4.04 74
Playing Field
    Condition of - 3.10 72
    Dimensions - 1.04 53
Policies and Principles 165
    Principle of Conduct 165
    Code 166
Protesting Game
    Process - 4.19 80

R

Resuming Play
    After dead ball - 5.11 84
Runner
    Base touching requirements - 7.02 92
    Entitled to a base - 7.01 92
    Fails to touch home base - 7.08(k) 96
    Fair ball touches - 5.09(f) 83
    Including batter-runner may advance - 7.05 92
    Leaves base prior to ball being released - 7.13 .. 99
    Obstructed. *See* Obstruction: Play being/not
        being made on runner - 7.06
    Other than batter may advance - 7.04 92
    Out for base coach interfering. *See* Base Coach:
        Accidental/Intentional interference - 5.08
    Out on appeal. *See* Appeal: Runner out on - 7.10
    Retouching a base - 7.08(d) 95
    Running outside of baseline - 7.08(a)(1) 94
    Status of. *See* Appeal: Status of runners - 7.12
    Two occupying a base - 7.03 92

S

Sexual Harassment Policy 166
Scoring
    Batter becomes a runner - 5.06 82
    Fair ball goes out of playing field - 7.05(a) 92
    Regulation game - 4.11 77
    Status of runners. *See* Appeal: Status of runners
        - 7.12
    Team - 4.09 76
    While ball is dead - 5.02 82
    Winning run when bases full - 4.09(b) 76
Shoulder Patch 165
Spectators
    Actions of - 4.19 Note 1 81
    Entering the field - 3.18 73
    Interference. *See* Interference: Definition - 2.00
    Interferes with thrown/batted ball. *See* Interference:
        Thrown/batted ball by spectator - 3.16
    Mingling with - 3.09 71
Strike
    Definition - 2.00 67
Strike Zone
    Ball touches batter when in - 6.08(b) 89

    Definition - 2.00 67
Substitutions
    Accident incapacitates a runner - 5.10(c)(1) 83
    Bench cleared by umpire - 4.08 Penalty 76
    Manager notifies Umpire-in-Chief - 3.06 71
    Pitcher shall pitch to first batter - 3.05 71
    Position in batting order - 4.04 74
    Runner for another team member - 3.04 71
    Starters re-entering the game - 3.03 69
    Umpire-in Chief announces - 3.07 71
    Unannounced - 3.08 71
    When tie games are halted - 4.12 78
Suspended Game
    Definition - 2.00 67
    Umpire-in-Chief sole judge - 3.10(b) 72

T

Ten Run Rule
    When in effect - 4.10(e) 77
Tie Games
    Halted - 4.12 78
    Regulation game - 4.11(e) 77
Tournament
    Admission charge 118
    District Administrators 127
    Expenses 130
    Financial responsibility 127
    Games under lights 118
    Ineligible pitcher 119
    Ineligible player 119
    Insurance 116
    Mandatory Play 123
    Must play to advance 120
    Officials 127
    Physical conditions 128
    Player eligibility 113
    Playing equipment 116
    Playing rules 121
    Protests 118
    Radio 130
    Replacement of player, manager or coach 116
    Responsibility and Chain of Command 109
    Schedules 117
    Selection of fields 117
    Selection of tournament teams 110
    Starting time of games 118
    Substitutions 124
    Team practice 117
    Television 130
    Tournament Director 128
Trademarks 182
    Limitations 182
    General Fundraising Guidance 184
    Guidelines 184

INDEX

Term - Rule	Page

Restricted 183
Soliciting Funds 183
Use of the Words "Little League" 182

U
Unsportsmanlike Conduct
    Disqualified by Game Coord. - 9.03(d)(4) 106
    Disqualified by umpire - 9.01(d) 105

W
Waivers
    Waivers of Rules and Regulations 153
Websites 181

Take the Field in Style!

The easiest Little League® uniform ordering option, period.

1. design it
2. order it
3. PLAY BALL!

Order your team uniforms in minutes

Free shipping to the United States

Little League® Official Keystone Patch included

OFFICIAL UNIFORM OF THE
**LITTLE LEAGUE®
WORLD SERIES**

Place your order online at
LittleLeagueUniforms.com

© 2015 Little League Baseball, Incorporated. All Rights Reserved.

"I thought the course was AWESOME!"*

"I felt the course was poignant and would recommend parents to take the course."*

"Course was thought-provoking, and I do take what I learned to the ball field."*

"After reviewing this course, I recommended to the board of directors that this course be made mandatory for all parents."*

Baseball Hall of Fame Manager **TONY LA RUSSA**

stars in the

Little League® Second-Goal Parent® Quick Course

Use this free resource that guides parents in helping their children get the most out of their Little League Baseball and Softball experience. Get started today at **http://www.littleleague.org/pca.htm**

*What our online course users have been saying

**BETTER ATHLETES
BETTER PEOPLE**

www.PositiveCoach.org | PositiveCoachingAlliance | @PositiveCoachUS

LITTLE LEAGUE® UNIVERSITY
WILL TRANSFORM THE WAY
LITTLE LEAGUE VOLUNTEERS, ADMINISTRATORS, COACHES, AND PARENTS EXPERIENCE AND LEARN ABOUT THE LITTLE LEAGUE PROGRAM.

With the launch of the free website, LittleLeagueU.org, Little League will connect with visitors through engaging training videos and informative how-to articles, designed to educate users on the best practices for operating and enjoying a successful local Little League experience in your community.

This easy-to-navigate portal will feature customized instruction, an assortment of practice plans, and interactive quizzes for everyone involved in Little League, including District Administrators, League Presidents and local board members, umpires, coaches, and parents.

ENROLL TODAY
FREE EDUCATIONAL **RESOURCES**

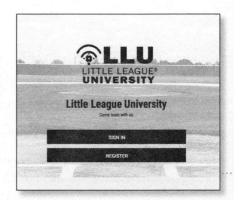

MANAGERS AND COACHES

- Age-appropriate skills and drills
- Practice plans
- Player fundamentals
- Direction on how to create a positive, fun experience for players and parents
- Best practices for coaching and managing games

DISTRICT STAFF

- Educational and operational tools
- Assembling a District staff
- How to effectively service and manage your district
- Agenda calendar and presentations
- Tips and operating tactics

LOCAL LEAGUE ADMINISTRATORS

- Marketing and promotion
- Board member training
- Description of league responsibilities
- Annual organization calendar
- Tips and operating tactics

UMPIRES

- "Basic 6," home plate and base mechanics
- Positioning instruction for two-, three-, four-umpire crews
- Situational case studies
- Umpire-In-Chief recruitment, training, and evaluation
- Best practices for pre-and post-game conferences

PARENTS

- The monthly *Parent Connection* newsletters
- Explanation and education on Little League rules, regulations, and divisions of play
- Volunteering in your local league
- Best practices for supporting your children, your local league; and enjoying the Little League experience